FOOTPRINTS

FOOTPRINTS

The 12 Men Who Walked on the Moon Reflect on their Flights, Their Lives, and the Future

Douglas MacKinnon and Joseph Baldanza

Illustrated with paintings by Alan Bean

ACROPOLIS BOOKS LTD.

WASHINGTON, D.C.

ACROPOLIS BOOKS, LTD.
Alphons J. Hackl, Publisher
Colortone Building, 2400 17th St., N.W.
Washington, D.C. 20009

Attention: Schools and Corporations
ACROPOLIS books are available at quantity
discounts with bulk purchase for educational,
business, or sales promotional use. For
information, please write to: SPECIAL SALES
DEPARTMENT, ACROPOLIS BOOKS, LTD., 2400
17th St., N.W., WASHINGTON, D.C. 20009

**Are there Acropolis books you want but
cannot find in your local stores?**
You can get any Acropolis book title in print.
Simply send title and retail price. Be sure to
add postage and handling: $2.25 for orders up
to $15.00; $3.00 for orders from $15.01 to
$30.00; $3.75 for orders from $30.01 to $100.00;
$4.50 for orders over $100.00. District of
Columbia residents add applicable sales tax.
Enclose check or money order only, no cash
please, to:
  ACROPOLIS BOOKS LTD.
  2400 17th St., N.W.
  WASHINGTON, D.C. 20009

**Library of Congress
Cataloging-in-Publication Data**
MacKinnon, Douglas, 1955–
   Footprints : the 12 men who walked on the
moon reflect on their flights, their lives, and
the future / Douglas MacKinnon & Joseph
Baldanza.
      p.   cm.
   Includes index.
   ISBN 0–87491–922–3 : $15.95
1. Astronauts—United States—Interviews. 2.
Project Apollo.
I. Baldanza, Joseph, 1950–   . II. Title.
TL789.85.A1M33   1989
629.45′0092′2—dc19
[B]   89–354
                                              CIP

Art Direction, cover design, and book design by Kathleen K. Cunningham

Dedication

To Anne—J.B.

To my mother Marie, my grandparents Michael and Anna MacKinnon, and George McNeil, and to my uncle Tom MacKinnon. Thank you one and all for shining the light during the dark times—from Doug MacKinnon

Acknowledgments

The writing of any book requires a great deal of outside assistance. *FOOTPRINTS* was no exception. With that in mind, the authors would like to gratefully acknowledge the time, talent, and patience of the following people: Cathy Mahar for her early advice. Howard Golden at NASA for his guiding hand. Steve and Judy Martyak for taking in two weary and hungry travelers. Anne Roussell for many, many things—not the least of which were reading and re-reading the manuscript, and being there for Joe. Bob Kane for his generous gift of time. Kip Lange, Trish DiMartino, Jean Thoms, Debbie Sudduth, and Margery Hannon for their expert typing and re-typing of a sometimes messy manuscript. Gerry Lange for his legal advice and friendship. Jack Clancy and Bruce Burke for their help in cleaning up a poor recording. Lia Baldanza for her early and much needed help. Richard S. Lewis for his experience and willingness to share that experience with two authors in search of information. Paul Foster, Frank Kelly, Kathleen Connolly, Don McLaughlin, Nancy Theis, and the rest of the gang at the White House for listening to Doug complain for six straight months. Judy Looker for assistance. Mike Collins for his example and sound advice. And finally, Dan Wallace, Kathleen Hughes, and everyone at Acropolis Books for their time and talent.

To those we have overlooked, our deepest apologies.

Doug MacKinnon
Joe Baldanza
April, 1989

Table of Contents

Foreword

Footprints ... impressions of ribbed spaceboots stamped into the moondust by the only human beings ever to have set foot on another world. Twelve modern explorers reflect on their adventures and tell what became of them when they returned.

Foreword

Oceans as yet undared my vessel dares;
Minerva lends the breeze, Apollo steers,
And the Muses nine point out to me the Bears.

      The Divine Comedy—Dante

Twelve men have walked on the moon: Neil Armstrong, Edwin Aldrin, Charles Conrad, Alan Bean, Alan Shepard, Edgar Mitchell, David Scott, James Irwin, John Young, Charles Duke, Eugene Cernan, and Harrison Schmitt. All are Americans, all are still living, and all are heroes in the truest sense of the word.

They occupy a very special place in history along with such figures as Columbus, Magellan, and Charles Lindberg. Out of a population of almost five billion men, women, and children on the planet earth, they are unique. They are the *only* human beings ever to have set foot on another world.

What was it like, as they waited behind gold-plated visors, to be catapulted into the heavens for a sojourn to the Moon—and what became of them when they returned to earth, when they returned to their families and friends? In *Footprints*, they reflect on their experiences, and how going to the Moon affected their lives, as well as their outlook on the rest of the world.

In all that has been reported and written about the epic achievement of landing men on the moon, a fascinating aspect of that enterprise remains obscure. Tom Wolfe called it the "most extraordinary and mysterious drama of the 20th century"—the individual, personal adventures of the astronauts, the men who made the landings and became the first explorers to visit another world.

These men are important and compelling figures of history. Their exploits were the concrete manifestation of the impulses in all of us. They were our collective eyes and minds on the most ambitious expedition ever undertaken. It is only natural that the rest of us should want—even expect—to hear what they have to say about it all and how it affected their lives.

We've entitled the book *Footprints* for the most basic of reasons: it is a word that conjures up the image of those ribbed spaceboot impressions stamped into the moondust with each astronaut's step. It is an image that has grown to become one of the most powerful symbols of the Space Age. They are quintessential trademarks, like the prehistoric tracks of our ancestors discovered in East Africa, that show a human presence and express the timeless, irrepressible urge in our species to move onward.

So, too, do the footprints left on the lunar surface by these twelve human beings forever proclaim Man's insatiable desire to explore, to go beyond the next horizon, and then the next. Ten million years from now, these same footprints will still bear lasting testament to the first tenative steps of humankind into the most mysterious and unforgiving environment of all: space—and the countless suns, planets, moons, asteroids, and comets contained there-in.

In any writing project about the Apollo Moon landing missions, even one involving the astronauts and ostensibly focused on them, there is a great temptation to spend too much time on the technology and machines involved. There is a basic interest, of course, in the hardware and techniques that made the moonwalks possible. But, in our estimation, this is secondary to the main story.

People are, and always will be, interested in the human side of any adventure. When President John F. Kennedy committed the nation to the goal of reaching the Moon, he was emphatic about "landing a *Man* on the Moon and returning him safely to earth," not a machine, not a TV camera, not a robot, a man. We would send one of our own on the quarter-million mile journey through space to make contact with our nearest celestial neighbor, and then return him safely to our waiting arms. It's been twenty years since the lunar module "Eagle," with Neil Armstrong and Buzz Aldrin at the controls, swooped down from space to make the first manned landing on the Sea of Tranquility. During the next three and one-half years that followed that historic landing, ten more men would make five more landings on that barren world.

Then, it was over! Finished! We haven't been back since. And we have no real plans to go back.

Looking again at that exciting time, what do these men have to say about it now? What stands out in their minds as most memorable about their journeys? What did they bring back with them besides a few hundred pounds of moon rocks and their own physically undamaged hides?

What inner calling was inside them that eventually brought them to Cape Canaveral to be hurled atop a tower of fire from the relative safety of earth into the dangerous void of space. Was it a call to duty, a matter of patriotism, or was it self-fulfillment—the next logical step in their careers as aviators? Were they looking for fame and fortune or were they more interested in the technical challenges of flying higher, faster, and farther? Were they captivated by the romance of spaceflight, the chance to play an important part in turning science fiction into science fact?

What went through their minds? What kind of inspirations did they get out there among the myriad suns? What was their real purpose? Were they excited? Fearful? Hopeful? All of the above? Did they believe things could ever be the same once they returned to earth? Or were they instead hopeful that things never would be the same?

When the Command Modules splashed down safely in the ocean, the media and the public considered the missions over, finished; on to another story. But in reality, for some of these men, the story was just beginning. The toughest part of the journey still lay ahead of them. This last phase confronted them with the difficulty of picking up their lives as Earthmen: the "Return to Earth" as Buzz Aldrin called it. Were they unprepared to resume a more "normal" life after their incredible encounter with the Cosmos?

How did having the "Right Stuff" in space collide with their earthbound well-being and peace of mind? Did NASA, despite the brilliant success in fulfilling John Kennedy's dream, ultimately fail these twelve men in not looking after the best interests of the moonwalkers when their missions were completed? Were they psychologically prepared for what awaited them back on earth? And was it NASA's job to prepare them? These are questions only the moonwalkers can really answer.

At a press conference following the flight of Apollo 17 Gene Cernan, who on that final mission became the last man to step off the moon, was asked how he would relate the significance of the moon missions to the public at large, to people who might not have a direct interest in the specific scientific findings. Cernan responded in this way: "I have a pet theory that you go out and you share those human personal feelings, the human personal aspects, emotions, the things you saw, the things you felt, the history that you lived while you prepared, while you were there, and while you're back with as many people as you can."

We hope this volume helps to make a contribution, at least in a small way, to that effort.

Douglas MacKinnon
Arlington, Virginia

Joseph Baldanza
Waltham, Massachusetts

April, 1989

Chapter 1

ALAN SHEPARD
Commander, Apollo 14

Present at the Creation

On the morning of May 5, 1961, as the rest of the world was rising to the gray routine of just another day, Lt. Commander Alan B. Shepard, United States Navy, met the predawn darkness in a bright silver spacesuit. He stepped out of the special van that brought him to the launch pad into the reflected glare of the spotlights aimed on the Redstone booster. Inside his sealed helmet he could hear the muffled sound of applause coming from the ground crew. He glanced up the white rocket for a glimpse of the tiny black cocoon he would soon climb into for the ride of his life.

The elevator deposited him in the "white room," a temporary shelter girdling the spacecraft during pre-launch preparations. He exchanged greetings with the technicians and strode to the hatch opening. John Glenn, his backup, helped shoehorn him into the cramped cabin, shook his hand, and backed away as the hatch cover was bolted on.

Alan Shepard was alone now in the capsule patriotically named *Freedom,* ready to become the first American to ride a rocket into space. The country was ready, too. A month before, the Russians, in an astonishing triumph, rocketed Yuri Gagarin around the world. Soon after that came the Bay of Pigs fiasco. The nation was being shaken out of the easy calm of the postwar Eisenhower era. A young, untested new president was at the helm now. The public was looking for a little reassurance.

Shepard made his preflight checks and waited for the final

countdown—and waited, and waited. An irritating series of minor problems kept pushing the launch time back. One hour. Two hours. Three hours. For almost four hours, Shepard waited while the rocket team worked. Positioned in a form-fitting couch, flat on his back facing skyward, his legs up and bent at the hips and knees, Shepard was starting to get uncomfortable. He was even forced to pee in his spacesuit; the rocket scientists hadn't figured on a lengthy delay, and since the flight was only going to last fifteen minutes, they didn't think it was necessary to provide him with a receptacle.

At T minus two minutes forty seconds, Shepard listened as the men in the control room discussed a high fuel pressure reading. This could mean a washout, a scrub, two more days of delay just to tinker with a valve that was probably all right in the first place. In his frustration, Shepard hopped on the line and spoke firmly to his fretting colleagues. "Alright," he said, "I'm cooler than you are. Why don't you fix your little problem and light this candle!"

That settled it. In a few minutes they lit the candle and *Freedom 7* was airborne. "You're on your way, Jose," radioed Deke Slayton, referring to Shepard's penchant for imitating Bill Dana's comic character Jose Jimenez.

"Everything's A-OK," Shepard called back. And the rest, as they say, is history. Al Shepard and his little craft were thrown 115 miles high. Unlike Gagarin, Shepard did not go into orbit. Instead, he followed a cannonball, or suborbital trajectory as they called it. He splashed into the Atlantic Ocean, intact, fifteen minutes later. He survived five minutes of weightlessness and proved out the control and life support systems of the Mercury spacecraft. It was one small step for the United States, and a giant leap for Alan Shepard—he was the first.

Five more Mercury flights followed. Then came the two-man Gemini series of ten flights. But, Alan Shepard had to watch it all from the sidelines. He wouldn't be able to ride a rocket again for ten years.

Alan B. Shepard, Jr. is an eighth generation New England yankee by birth. He was born in East Derry, New Hampshire, on November 18, 1923. He was an enterprising youngster and a good student. He excelled in mathematics and was described by a former teacher as also being "a good athlete, and a boy extremely well-liked." He went to a one-room country grade school and finished high school at the Pinkerton Academy in Derry, New Hampshire, in 1940. He went on to spend a year at the Admiral Farragut Academy in Toms River, New Jersey, before becoming a midshipman at the U.S. Naval Academy at Annapolis. He received his commission in 1944, looking to a career as a Naval Aviator. Before that, though, he owed the Navy two years at sea. He fulfilled that duty seeing wartime service on the destroyer *USS Cogswell.*

After the war, he began flight training, first in Texas at Corpus Christi, then in Pensacola, Florida. He earned his wings in 1947 and became a squadron fighter pilot. He later served several tours in the Mediterranean, flying fighters off of aircraft carriers.

In 1950 Shepard was accepted for training at the U.S. Navy Test Pilot School at Patuxent River, Maryland. After graduation, he participated in high altitude research of the atmosphere as well as aircraft flight testing. He also worked in the development of the new, angled carrier deck.

Between flight test assignments, he returned to fighter operations with a squadron on the West Coast. He finished at Patuxent as an instructor, leaving to attend the Naval War College in Rhode Island. He completed that course in 1957 and joined the staff of the Atlantic Fleet Commander as aircraft readiness officer.

The Russian Sputnik ushered in the Space Age at the end of 1957. Soon, the National Aeronautics and Space Administration was formed, replacing the old National Advisory Committee on Aeronautics. Plans were being made to put men in space, and the search was on for pilots. After deliberating on who would be the best candidates, President Eisenhower decreed that military test pilots would be the first astronauts. Invitations to volunteer for Project Mercury, the name given to the program, were sent out to 110 of the recommended best pilots. A disappointed Alan Shepard didn't get one. Never lacking self-confidence, he checked into it and found he was, indeed, on the list; his invitation had been misplaced.

The 110 were brought in for testing and examination, their number to be winnowed down to a select few. They were subjected to all manner of physical and mental trials. After the evaluations were completed, and the last cut was made, there were seven. And Alan Shepard, whose invitation was lost in the mail, was one of them.

The new Mercury astronauts—the "Original Seven" as they're called—were introduced to the public at a spirited press conference on April 8, 1959. They became instant heroes. "My feelings about being in this program are really quite simple," Shepard told *Life Magazine* a few months later. "Without being too Navy Blue and Gold, I'm here because it's a chance to serve the country. I'm here too, because it's a great personal challenger: I know it can be done, that it's important for it to be done, and I want to do it."

For the next two years, the seven prepared to fly into space. In classrooms they studied everything from astronomy to zoology.

In simulations and simulators, they practiced flight procedures. In factories, they worked with engineers to design and build the equipment. And, all the while, they were fiercely competing with each other for that first flight.

Alan Shepard received that satisfaction. Unhappily, before it was his turn again, he was grounded, the victim of Meniere's Syndrome, a nagging inner-ear disorder that's difficult to treat, and causes dizziness and hearing problems in its sufferers. He still wanted to fly, and believed some day he could fly again. So, he stayed with the program in a desk job, becoming Chief of the Astronaut Office in 1963. It was a powerful position that gave Shepard a lot of control in astronaut ground assignments, mission planning, and flight-crew selection. During that time, he also undertook a business career. He became quite wealthy from investments and various ventures, including two banks.

He eventually underwent surgery to correct his inner-ear problem. The operation was successful, and he was restored to flight status on May 7, 1968, nearly seven years to the day of his Mercury flight. The Apollo flights would be starting soon, and Shepard intended to be on one of them. He used his position in the Astronaut Office to full advantage and was able to land the Commander's seat on Apollo 13, replacing Gordon Cooper, who originally had the job.

As he got into the training regimen for the flight, Shepard felt he needed more time to prepare. So, he went to Jim Lovell, the Commander of Apollo 14, and asked him to trade missions: Lovell and his crew would fly Apollo 13, Shepard and his crew would handle Apollo 14. The exchange was agreed to and approved, to the great misfortune of Lovell and his crewmates. An oxygen tank exploded in the service module portion of the Apollo 13 vehicle as it was heading to the moon, wiping out all hope of making a landing.

Nine and a half months later, on January 31, 1971, Apollo 14, carrying Shepard, Ed Mitchell, and Stu Roosa, lifted away from Florida and headed for Fra Mauro, the place on the moon where Apollo 13 intended to go. Mitchell and Roosa were making their first flight. Counting Shepard's Mercury mission, total crew flight experience totaled fifteen minutes.

On February 5th, Shepard and Mitchell, despite a near abort situation, brought their lunar module "Antares" in for a successful touchdown at the Fra Mauro landing site. Roosa stayed aloft in the command module "Kitty Hawk." Shepard and Mitchell remained on the surface for a day and a half, spending just over nine hours outside the lander gathering samples and setting up scientific instruments. With typical elan, Shepard capped his stay on the moon by pulling out a #6 iron golf club head, fixing it to the handle of a prospecting tool, and hitting a few down the Fra Mauro fairways.

Leaving the moon, Antares performed a "direct ascent" rendezvous with Kitty Hawk, linking up with the command ship on the first orbit—a first for the Apollo series. The crew returned home on February 9th and entered an eighteen-day quarantine period. It was the last time an Apollo crew would be isolated for fear of biological contamination from the lunar surface.

Apollo 14 was the culmination of Alan Shepard's career as an astronaut. At 47, he became the oldest man to fly into space, and he had reached the moon. When asked before the flight why he stayed around so long when he could have been enjoying life at his mansion in Texas, he replied, ". . . I guess it's because it's about the only business I know. . . . It's something to which I enjoy making a contribution. . . . It's something I believe in. . . ."

Following Apollo 14, Shepard returned to Houston and his post as Chief of the Astronaut Office. In July, 1971, he was appointed by the president as a delegate to the 26th United Nations General Assembly, which lasted from September to December that same year. He stayed on at NASA until 1974, when he retired from both the space agency and the Navy, where he had attained the rank of rear admiral.

His long career has brought him many honors: two NASA Distinguished Service Medals, NASA's Exceptional Service Medal, The Navy Distinguished Service Medal, and Navy Distinguished Flying Cross, the Smithsonian Institute's Langley Medal, the Lambert Trophy, the Kincheloe Trophy, the Cabot Award, the Collier Trophy, and the Congressional Medal of Honor (space), among others.

Today, Alan Shepard continues his career as a businessman and financier. He and his wife Louise have two daughters, and live in Houston.

Adm. Shepard, you're one of the most prominent figures in the American manned space effort. You were there from the beginning. You were the first American in space, you were influential in management as Chief of the Astronaut Office, and you were the only Mercury Astronaut to go to the moon. From that vantage point, how do you see the space program today? Is it proceeding at a satisfactory pace and direction?

Well, that's a pretty all-encompassing question. I think that, certainly, I would say in some respects and in some capacities I think I'm in agreement with the way things are going. Certainly the Shuttle had its ups and downs; some of the downs are perhaps more imagined than real.

In what way?

Well, by that I mean that just the fact that you had the one accident, for example, doesn't really stop the momentum of the program. I think that in a program like that you certainly have to make improvements, and obviously, a lot of improvements *were* made during that time frame. So it really wasn't as if things were standing still for that two year-plus period. Although I suppose the media would have us believe that it did.

Was that situation comparable to the period after the launch pad fire in Apollo 1?

I think there are some analogies there, yes. Certainly, we made many improvements to the Apollo command-service module, the command module particularly. But certainly, these improvements probably prevented—well, let's say it this way: these improvements certainly made it a much more successful program than it could have been otherwise. And I think this is going to be the case with the Shuttle. The down time, as I said before, doesn't necessarily mean that progress is not being made and that improvements are not being made. I think it will be a better vehicle because of it. I guess the thing that I personally would like to see happen is that NASA get out from some of the responsibility of operating and flying four shuttle orbiter vehicles and let some other agencies come in and take over operations—the Defense Department, for example, or private enterprise. I think this has to occur eventually.

That's basically what the Reagan administration was advocating.

Well, there was lip service there, certainly. There hasn't been a lot of strong backing beyond that. And, I think that perhaps, from a practical point of view, that it's one of those things where you cannot just wave a magic wand and it will necessarily happen. I think there have to be some subsidies there during the changeover period. I think the Reagan administration, if you want to call attention to that fact, had fallen down in that respect. The idea is good, but you just can't wave a wand and have it happen overnight.

Deke Slayton, one of your fellow astronauts from the Mercury days, left NASA a few years ago to run a private company dedicated to the proposition of developing and providing commercial rocket launching services. Is he on to something there? Could he possibly become one of the first space tycoons?

Certainly, I think what Deke is doing is commendable. It's the sort of thing that has to happen eventually. Here again, it's in the transition stage, and what Slayton's company is doing now is taking over some of NASA's role with some of the sounding rockets that are being launched. I think that NASA is subsidizing it with launch facilities, and so on. I think that's the way things have to go. NASA is basically a research and development organization. They *ought* to be looking toward Mars, they *ought* to be looking toward lunar colonization, they *ought* to be looking toward space-station type activities, rather than just driving the Shuttle back and forth to orbit.

You've gained the reputation of being a pretty savvy and astute businessman over the years. Were you ever tempted to get into the private space business yourself? You certainly have the background for it.

Well, let me put it this way. I'm in the venture capital business here in Houston, and my partners and I are actively consulting with a couple of the major private companies with a view toward perhaps using some of our venture capital resources to help them.

At the time of your mission to the moon on Apollo 14, you expressed the confidence that the space program was "mature" and "Balanced". Apollo was successfully exploring the moon, there was talk of lunar bases and even going to Mars. Do you have that same confidence today? If not, what can we do to improve the situation as we look toward the 21st century?

At that time, of course, as I always have said over the years, the true value of money spent on the Space Program is in research and development, all the great spinoffs and fallout, everything we had from that. It's not a well understood theory, not a well understood function. It's not an exciting function. Nonetheless, it's still there and it's the backbone of what needs to be done. That brings me right back to where I was before, saying that the value, for example, of the R & D done on the Space Station is in the spinoffs. It enables people to take these products, services, and knowledge and make them applicable to everyday life. Technology has to continue to improve, not only space technology, but such areas as medical research. If we're going to compete with the rest of the world, we just have to keep building a better mousetrap every year.

You also said at that time that we probably could, and should, be spending more money on the space program. Can we do that now, at a time when the federal budget is so overextended?

If you talk in terms of absolute dollars and inflation, then I think we need to spend more in terms of absolute dollars. In terms of percentage of the GNP, or the percentage of the actual budget, I don't think we do ourselves any favors if we make large changes at this particular time. As I said before, it's hard to judge how much you should put into research and development, which is basically what we're talking about here, because you're not going to be able to predict with certainty how much bang you're going to get from your buck, and how much you're going to get back from this great mousetrap that you build in 1989. But, I think the level of spending percentage-wise really should not be decreased. If we could get the transition of more of the funds coming from private enterprise, then I don't see any need for any large increase in the amount of R & D dollars that NASA is allocated as a percentage of the national budget.

Are enough private dollars out there?

Oh yes, they're there. Investors can see some return in space, but they can't see it unless there are, as I've said, some subsidies involved. I think NASA and the new administration have got to pay some attention to that. It's nice, as we heard in the past, to say that this should be done. But, you have to give them a little incentive.

After the first couple of landings on the moon, public enthusiasm for man in space seemed to drop off to a considerable extent. You made the observation that, in part at least, this was due to a certain lack of understanding. Now, you've mentioned what you call the "true value" of the space effort, how it's in the R&D spinoffs and technical advancement, and how that isn't clearly understood by the general public. How can NASA, the government, or whoever increase that understanding, and awareness, and make it exciting again?

I don't think you can. I don't think it's a thing you can manufacture. The general public support of space has always been an emotional thing and always will be. It's just not something you can go out with Madison Avenue and create. It's a fact of life that the emotional response is there, and you really can't resort to subterfuge to create it.

Alan Shepard

What can they do to recapture the public imagination?

Well, sure, something exciting. Here again, one has to be careful. As I said before, it's going to go in cycles, it's not something you can keep at a fever pitch, or an even pitch, for any great length of time. It's going to be "Ho-hum, so they're flying another shuttle back to work, wish you luck." The managers in space research, NASA research, understand that. They're going to have to. It's just a fact of life. I mean, it's going to be exciting one year, and the next year it's going to be "Well, I'll wait 'till Mars comes along" or "I'll wait 'till they go looking for titanium on the moon." It's just a fact of life.

If you were still helping make decisions, what would your immediate goals be and what would you look to as long-range goals?

We have to provide orbiting laboratories, that is, the Space Station. It needs to be done on a cooperative basis with the European community. NASA can do this with relatively little effort. The knowledge is there, the materials are there, and I think that needs to be done. There are so many experiments that could be conducted in zero gravity, and the knowledge to be gained in manufacturing, and all those exciting vaccines, things of that sort. Also, an increase of the general knowledge about the planet Earth—the ozone problem, the greenhouse effect—all of these things that have been discussed politically but really haven't had a lot of research done on them on a world-wide basis. It has to be done on a global basis because ozone doesn't respect any political boundaries.

And the long-range plans?

Oh, I think interplanetary travel, no question about that.

You talked about cooperating with the European community. Are the Soviets included among that group? There has been a lot of talk about a U.S.-Soviet mission to Mars.

No, I don't think so. I don't think at this time that we can count on that. I think it's pleasing to note the thawing and improvement of relationships, but it's an area in which we should proceed fairly carefully. Certainly, it's good to consider these things, but right now Gorbachev's position is still precarious. I think we need to give him a little more time.

Are you fearful of any security breaches, or of putting ourselves in a vulnerable position in cooperating with other coun-

tries, that sensitive information and technology might end up in the hands of the wrong people?

We have to be careful about that, certainly. But I wouldn't use that as a reason not to get involved. You know, it's one thing to learn how to operate a black box, a sophisticated piece of equipment; it's another thing to learn how to design it and build it. It's part of what I was taking about earlier, about building a better mousetrap. You have to keep doing that every year because, sooner or later, somehow, other people are going to find out how you did it. And as long as it takes three, four, five years to create it—I mean, what's the generation time of a design of some highly technical machine or piece of equipment? It's about six to seven years. That's why our technology has to continue to improve, so we can build a better mousetrap in five or six years. You should be careful about how you share the information. But sooner or later, it's going to get out anyway.

And next year, the Soviets will be showing up with the stealth bomber.

We can't copyright things in this country in those areas.

It certainly looks like they've copied the Space Shuttle.

Oh, yes. Yes, I was a little surprised they went unmanned in that thing the first time.

Was that really a big surprise to you, that they were able to fly it and land it without a pilot?

I think the odds against them of being able to do that were pretty great. The odds were pretty great they would *not* be able to do it the first time.

In 1963 you became head of the Astronaut Office after being grounded with an inner ear problem. In that capacity, you had a hand in selecting new astronauts. Was it hard to see these new pilots coming in and flying while you had to watch from the sidelines?

It was difficult. Probably, the most difficult times had to be being down there at the Cape getting the guys ready, pat them on the shoulder, kick them in the fanny, then watch them go fly.

It must have been satisfying at the same time, though, preparing them, training them.

Alan Shepard

I suppose there was some satisfaction. But, obviously, my real objective was to fly again, and I had made a decision that I would stick around on that premise.

You waited ten years. You certainly showed a lot of tenacity.
Well, everything worked out fine, yes.

Your first flight, in Freedom 7 was on the Redstone, the least powerful of the manned launch vehicles: it developed something like 73 thousand pounds of thrust. Your second, and last flight, Apollo 14, was launched by the Saturn 5, the most powerful American rocket; it generated 7.5 million pounds of thrust. In fact, the escape tower atop the Apollo was more powerful than your original Redstone booster. Can you compare the two experiences? Can you give us some idea of the differences in the two rides, what you felt?
I guess I would make the comparison of the flights themselves, rather than the actual thrust involved. Like the fellow says, once you get thirty or forty feet off the ground, it doesn't really make any difference what kind of bird you're flying—you've got to make a good landing. But, I guess, certainly, my comment would be Wow! The difference of my personal experience in just ten years was staggering. If we said back in late '58, and in '59, when we started talking about it, that we could have made that kind of progress, it's very staggering to consider that in terms of thrust levels, capabilities, and so on. From a personal standpoint, there's no question about the fact that the first flight was very, very satisfying to me. We proved that a man could spend five minutes in weightlessness and not come back a blithering idiot, that he could fly the machine, he could communicate—all the things we knew we could do anyway. But, it was just a great amount of satisfaction to be able to do that. With respect to the lunar landing, it was totally different. Just the sense there, really, of being a part of a much larger program, to be one of the spokes in the wheel, so to speak. Nonetheless, you're personally satisfied, obviously, much like the case with the first man staying in there for that landing.

You mean getting through the problems with the abort program?
No, no, no. I mean just personally. I don't mean the physical problems. But oh yeah, we had a few cliffhangers.

In talking about the satisfaction of your first flight, you mentioned proving that a man could be launched into space, experience weightlessness, perform well, and not come back a "blithering idiot." That brings up a question about the doctors. Apparently, there was some friction, shall we call it, between the medics and the astronauts in those days—maybe to this day. Did you ever feel, deep down, that they were hoping something strange might happen to you, to vindicate some of their dire predictions about the effects of spaceflight on the human body?

Oh no, I don't think so. Basically, the problem was that you had a series of dedicated individuals, dedicated test pilots who were stacked up, one against the other. Still, everybody wanted a chance to fly. And, you had a medic looking over your shoulder in a position to say, 'Hey, this guy's got a wart on his left knee, so he can't fly.'

But, some of the doctors were predicting all sorts of weird, even horrible things would happen to men when they went into space; they would become disoriented, the weightlessness would cause physiological problems, that sort of thing. These same hand-wringers were reported to be a little disappointed that nothing really happened after all. In fact, almost all the astronauts found it to be a very pleasant experience.

Oh, I think that's taken out of context. Gee, I really don't feel that—it could be there were maybe some sour grapes on somebody's part, but that wasn't the prevalent attitude throughout the medical community.

Another early question was the suitability of women for spaceflight. Early in their program, the Soviets sent a woman up, a young parachutist. You must have received applications from women, a few at least, in those days.

It was just too early. Everybody had agreed that we needed to stay with the test pilots, certainly through the Apollo Program.

Even though male scientists like Harrison Schmitt, who had no piloting experience whatsoever, were chosen and trained to fly jets? Schmitt went on to fly Apollo 17.

You notice it was the last flight. Now that's nothing against Jack, I mean. He's a bright guy.

Might it have been awkward mixing men and women in the close quarters of an Apollo spacecraft?

I don't think that it probably would have been any more difficult than the social problems they have in the Shuttle today. I think it was based basically on the decision that we just didn't have any ladies that had been test pilots to the point where they had the experience. There was an educational factor, too, you know. Because, there's always the design and engineering considerations in having pilots who are also engineers helping with those parts of the project.

Original plans for Apollo 14 had your flight going to the Littrow Region, a formation in the central part of the northeast quadrant of the moon's visible side. Your flight was rerouted to the Fra Mauro area when Apollo 13 wasn't able to make it. Were you disappointed at all at not being able to go to your original target?

No, no. No problems with that. No, just point out the runway and let me land.

One of the things a lot of people really aren't familiar with is what the pilots in the lunar module are actually doing during the twelve or so minutes it takes to fly the LM from its starting position in orbit around the moon to a landing on the surface. Can you describe briefly what goes on in the cockpit during the landing phase of the mission? Is it all automatic, do you fly it down manually? How is it done?

The first part of the trip down is automatic; it's designed that way. The ground rules are such that that's really the way it *had* to be. Not that a man couldn't fly all the way down, but he's just not given enough information. It makes him a better pilot. The value of the man is in visual acuity, and in taking over in the event of a failure of the primary systems. So, in the first part of the descent, the commander is watching the primary navigation system and how it's doing, and the co-pilot is watching the secondary computer system and navigation system and how it's doing. During this time the spacecraft is flying almost horizontally, its legs pointing forward in the direction of the flight path. We're in the cockpit standing at the controls, in effect on our backs, looking up into space relative to the flight path. Obviously, you get to the point where you position the LM so that the landing gear are more or less pointing down. That maneuver is called "pitchover". At this point you can look out the window and see down to the surface. Now, you can use your visual acuity to select a good landing site, correct the designated landing spot in the automatic system—that's when the pilot makes use of his ability to come in and make the landing manually. We pretty much run it by the book, eyeballs out, watching every corner, watching every instrument you possibly could.

Was that kind of direct pilot control something that you, as pilots, insisted upon?

Well, I think you almost have to. I mean, as good as the navigation scheme was, when you have a Circular Error of Probability, a CEP of, you know, plus and minus half a mile or so, there's going to be a lot of boulders and craters in a half mile area—not tremendous ones, but ones that are large enough to be considered when trying for a smooth landing. It's just one of the things you put up with.

In the early days, it seemed that managers and scientists almost would have almost preferred to send you guys up as button pushers—breathing black boxes—and you really had to press to get pilot control, to have manual control override, that sort of thing. There was never any doubt, though, that you would have to have that capability in a lunar landing craft?

I think when you get something as large as the lunar module, you almost have to go that way. The automated landings that both the U.S. and the Soviets made were generally fairly successful because they had small, unmanned landers. Although they came in at some relatively unusual landing attitudes and angles, they were still able to get away with it because they were pretty small vehicles. But, when you put something big up there like a lunar module, you really have to count on a man's ability to handle the final few thousand feet, or few hundred feet, whatever it is.

You referred earlier to "a few cliffhangers" that you had during your descent to the moon. You had a faulty abort switch, your landing radar went out at one point—there were some tense moments. Ed Mitchell, your co-pilot, said that you both agreed that you were going to complete the landing, that everything was on the money—you were going in. Was that a decision you could make on your own at that point? Were you ready to override a ground control abort?

Next question.

Is that a no comment?

Next question.

Ed Mitchell, as you know, was dramatically changed by his trip to the moon. Did you experience anything like that? Were you affected at all by being out there in deep space?

I don't think Ed's been dramatically changed. I think that as a result of being recognized for his lunar accomplishments, he had the opportunity to participate in some areas with a credibility that he wouldn't have had otherwise. But, Ed's basically been pretty much the same, I think. I see him from time to time nowadays, and I don't find him that much different than he was before.

We're just referring to a certain change in attitude, or awareness that he's described. He's spoken about a shift from "Earth-centered awareness," as he calls it, to a deeper, universe-centered focus.

I'm not sure I'd use the same adjectives but, certainly, I think all of us have had those feelings. Standing on the moon, for example, or being in lunar orbit and looking back at the Earth, and realizing that it is, in fact, a very fragile place. It is, in fact, our home, and it's something that over the next fifty or a hundred generations we need to do something about. There's no question about that. I'm sure all of us have had the same kinds of feelings. I don't think I've changed all that much. Certainly, because of what I've done in my position in the program, perhaps I've had more credibility than some other folks in some areas. But let's just take business, which is my field. Sure, being famous is going to get you in the door to see the bank president, but it's not going to get you any more money than the next guy unless you've got a good proposal.

Apollo 14 had some important "firsts": you started from the lowest orbit to begin the landing maneuver—less than ten miles above the surface, and you made what is termed a "direct ascent rendezvous" to rejoin the command module, that is, you took off from the surface and met the command module during the first orbit. As a test pilot, were those particularly satisfying operations for you? Were they highlights of the mission?

Oh, I don't think that those necessarily were the highlights. I think the fact that we overcame, with the help of the ground of course, the software problem for the lunar descent, when we had a faulty abort switch; that, in fact, we were able to keep going during the landing radar problem; and the fact that we landed closer than anybody else did; and the fact that we brought back the oldest rocks. You know, for a crew they called the "three rookies," we thought we did a pretty good job.

You had fifteen minutes of spaceflight among you.

I hadn't flown in ten years, and Mitchell and Roosa had never flown. They called us the three rookies, so it was with some satisfaction that we came in closer, and brought back the oldest rocks, and accomplished those other things.

Did you feel any more pressure on yourself as the commander in that situation?

I don't think so.

You were quoted at one time as stating that space missions are really safer than routine test flying. Can you explain that?

Apollo 14 was probably in better shape than it would have been if we had not had an Apollo 13. As I've said before, the Apollo 1 fire made us improve the spacecraft. The flight of Discovery was probably one of the safest missions that will ever be flown. Sure, it's that little bit more attention, that sort of thing after you have some kind of problem. That's what I meant by that.

Back in 1959 when you and the others were named as the first group of astronauts, manned spaceflight was a blank slate; we had no real flight experience to build upon in the way you've just described in the Apollo and Shuttle programs. There was a lot of caution leading up to your first flight, America's first flight. No doubt most of it was warranted, considering the risks involved. But was the United States ready to go before the Soviets beat us to the punch by launching Gagarin in April of 1961? You had indicated around that time that the pilots were champing at the bit to start flying, that you all felt you were ready to go. Were the managers being overly cautious do you think?

I guess you're probably referring to the discussions we had with Von Braun about flying an extra unmanned Redstone. Certainly, from a piloting point of view, we felt that the anomaly that occurred during the flight of the chimpanzee Ham was understandable and correctable, and that we probably wouldn't have to fly an entire additional mission unmanned to prove that out. However, there was good, honest discussion about it, and the decision was made, and we all saluted smartly and did it. In retrospect, maybe even Wernher would have made a different decision had he known that the Soviets were going to fly that soon. I don't know.

Did you and the other astronauts get any indications from the NASA brass that maybe the Soviets were on the verge?

No. I never really talked to anybody about that. I don't know how much Gilruth knew, I don't know how much Webb knew, how many or what kind of secret briefings they had. If they had any, they weren't communicating it to us. That's probably because they didn't.

Alan Shepard

Did the Mercury astronauts lobby at all, as a group, to get things moving a little faster?

There were times when we realized that things couldn't be pushed—the spacecraft manufacturer check-out, and so on. But, I do think that for example, we would have liked to have flown that unmanned Redstone; to have flown it manned would've been neat. We would have liked to have flown another Mercury-Atlas mission after Cooper's flight, but we were overruled by both Webb and Kennedy on that particular issue.

That kind of frustration, now even felt by the public after the Soviet feat, was expressed almost poetically by you, lying on your back in your spacecraft on top of the Redstone Rocket, waiting through the delays to finally get going. The ground people were fretting over something or other and you finally radioed back to them and firmly told them to "Fix your little problem, and light this candle!" It was a galvanizing moment, one of the most electric in the history of the program.

Well, it must have been a stroke of genius.

By the way, how did you like your portrayal in the movie "The Right Stuff"?

Oh, I don't think the guy that played my role is anywhere near as good-looking, as articulate, or as anything else as I.

What about the movie itself?

Oh, it was okay. Of course, from an insider's point of view, I think that it did a disservice to a lot of folks. I think they kept Grissom on the hook for losing his capsule, which wasn't sure in real life. I think they were tough on Annie Glenn and her speech problem. I think they made Lyndon Johnson look like a clown. They made us look like we marched in and told Wernher that we weren't going to fly unless they put a window in. Those things didn't happen and they weren't true. So, there's a disservice done there from that standpoint.

Was there really that sense of raucous excitement, that bumptious atmosphere that was shown in the film? The NASA people were excited, the press was excited, the astronauts were raring to go, the whole country was excited.

Well, that's just as far as the public was concerned. Sure there was—there's a tremendous amount of emotional involvement with it. But, if you get a test pilot to conduct his life that way, he's not going to last very long. He's got to be very, very objective. You've got to work hard, you've got to understand yourself. It's a very methodical, analytical type of process. You know what they say: 'There are old pilots, and there are bold pilots, but there are no old, bold pilots.'

But you, the pilots, must have had some adrenalin pumping during that time. There must have been the heady sense of newness and adventure for you.

Yes, but I've been doing that sort of thing since I graduated from test pilot school in 1950. I don't know if you have available all the things I flew, and it's not that important. The important thing is that we were on the frontiers then, flying new airplanes. I was in on the first trials of the angled carrier deck. The USS Antietam came out with the canted deck, and I was one of the four guys chosen to fly on that thing, in the latest jet that we were flying in those days. My point is that's the kind of life that's been going on for most of us since 1950. We were going head-on with an airplane you probably never heard of. Grumman built the Mach 2; it was a Grumman F11F-1, and they put a big engine in it and put all kinds of extra control surfaces on it. And, I was doing zoom climbs against Yeager with the 104—you know, 90,000 feet, Mach 2, and this was in the mid '50s. I mean, these are the kinds of things that have been going on for a long time.

The general perception is that "this kind of life," as you referred to it, is characterized by danger and pressure, the drive to always perform at the highest level. The pilots seem to thrive in that environment, but it must have been hard on your family. Was it stressful for them? How did you handle that?

In the earlier flights, we'd been test pilots doing kind of strange things anyway, so there was that level of awareness among the youngsters, the children, in those days. Perhaps it might have been a little easier for them because of that. Actually, I think we took more time with them in those days to try to tell them what it was all about, why we were doing it, and so on, to try to bring them into the picture a little more. But sure, there's a lot of stress involved there.

Do you ever think that maybe you should have stayed on a little longer, maybe fly the Space Shuttle?

Oh no. No, no, no. When your time comes—you know, when you're through—well, you step down gracefully and try something else.

Let's say someone, maybe even a young person, was able to come back in time from a few hundred years from now, and was able to talk to you and wanted to get your impression of what going to the moon was all about. What would you tell him? What was the significance, the meaning of project Apollo?

I think I would have to again be very nationalistic about it, and to tie in the aspect of the technology being the underlying benefit of all the space program. Even as exciting or dull as it has been off and on over the years, to me that's the true value of it. And, to me, that's one very important aspect of the success of this nation of ours.

On a broader, historical level, did you ever see yourself as following in the footsteps of the great explorers, people like Magellan, Captain Cook, Columbus?

Certainly, there's some of the same motivation there, and again I'm talking in general terms. Sure, obviously somebody's going to get the credit for doing it. There has to be a certain focus, a certain hero. You can't relate to 323 guys who came across the Atlantic. But, just speaking in general, I think men, man is anxious to find out about these things. If advancement is there, certainly that's part of it. I think man, in general, is curious about what goes on in the rest of the planetary system.

Chapter 2

BUZZ ALDRIN
Lunar Module Pilot, Apollo 11

The Twists and Turns
of Fate

Fifty-four days after returning from the moon Buzz Aldrin stepped up to the rostrum in the U.S. House of Representatives to address a joint session of Congress:

"Distinguished ladies and gentlemen, it is with a great sense of pride as an American and with humility as a human being that I say to you today what no men have been privileged to say before: 'We walked on the moon.' But the footprints at Tranquility Base belong to more than the crew of Apollo 11. They were put there by hundreds of thousands of people across this country, people in government, industry, and the universities, the teams and crews that preceeded us, all who strived throughout the years with Mercury, Gemini, and Apollo. Those footprints belong to the American people and you, their representatives, who accepted and supported the inevitable challenge of the moon. And, since we came in peace for all mankind those footprints belong also to all the people of the world. As the moon shines impartially on all those looking up from our spinning Earth so do we hope the benefits of space exploration will be spread equally with a harmonizing influence to all mankind.

"Scientific exploration implies investigating the unknown. The result can never be wholly anticipated. Charles Lindbergh once said, 'Scientific accomplishment is a path, not an end; a path leading to and disappearing in mystery.'

"Our steps in space have been a symbol of this country's way of life as we open our doors and windows to the world to view our successes and failures and as we share with all nations our discovery. The Saturn, Columbia, and Eagle, and the extravehicular mobility unit have proved to Neil, Mike, and me that this nation can produce equipment of the highest quality and dependability. This should give all of us hope and inspiration to overcome some of the more difficult problems here on Earth. The Apollo lesson is that national goals can be met where there is a strong enough will to do so.

"The first step on the moon was a step toward our sister planets and ultimately toward the stars. 'A small step for a man' was a statement of fact, 'a giant leap for mankind' is a hope for the future.

"What this country does with the lessons of Apollo applied to domestic problems, and what we do in further space exploration programs will determine just how giant a leap we have taken."

Edwin E. Aldrin, Jr stepped into the world on January 20, 1930, in Montclair, New Jersey, the second of three children and only son of Edwin and Marion Aldrin. His father was a colonel in the U.S. Army, and an accomplished aviator. The path of his career crossed those of such luminaries as Robert Goddard, Orville Wright, Charles Lindbergh, and Billy Mitchell. His mother was the daughter of an army chaplain prophetically named Moon. Young Edwin collected the nickname "Buzz" from his older sister who, not yet able to correctly pronounce the word "brother," called him little "buzzer" (Aldrin has now changed his name legally from Edwin to Buzz).

As a schoolboy, Buzz Aldrin was energetic, competitive, and smart, a math whiz with a keen analytical mind. He took up physical culture with characteristic dedication and became a fine football player, gymnast, and pole vaulter. Aldrin graduated from Montclair High School and joined the Long Gray Line at West Point. He graduated with honors in 1951, electing to take his commission in the Air Force. He reported for six months of basic flight school in Bartow, Florida, then went to Texas for fighter training, against the advice of his father who preferred to see his son fly multiengine planes. To the younger Aldrin, however, fighters had it all over multis "for individual accomplishment, exhilaration, and just plain drama."

Buzz won his wings in 1952 and was eventually sent to Korea assigned to an F-86 squadron. The drama, exhilaration, and accomplishment all came his way as he flew sixty-six combat missions and shot down two MIG-15s. Returning to the States he became an aerial gunnery instructor at Nellis Air Force Base in Nevada, then attended the Air Force Squadron Officers' School at Maxwell Field in Alabama. A stint at the newly established Air Force Academy came next, first as Aide to the Dean of Faculty, then as a flight instructor for air training officers. In 1956, now married and a father, Aldrin moved with his family to Germany where he joined and became a flight commander with a tactical fighter wing. After three years duty in Europe he returned to the U.S. to continue his education, planning first to get a Masters degree at MIT, then going on to test pilot school.

After a year and a half at MIT he made the decision to forego test pilot school and stay on for his doctorate. At the same time, he put his application in for the second group of astronauts being picked, asking for a waiver of the test pilot requirement. He was turned down, but strongly, and rightly suspected that in future selections the mandatory test pilot rule would be dropped and advanced academic credentials would become desirable. He pressed on with his studies, pursuing the ins and outs of manned orbital rendezvous, the stately dance in which two craft come together across space. He became a virtuoso choreographer. He picked up his degree then spent a short time working on Air Force space projects. During that period he reapplied to become an astronaut and was selected for the third group in October of 1963.

Aldrin plunged into his work at NASA with his usual thoroughness and zeal. He had strong opinions and a penchant for forthrightly and bluntly pressing them that struck some of his colleagues as brash and abrasive. He was highly regarded, though, for his seminal role in making rendezvous in space a reality. His contributions in that area, and in spacecraft guidance, were enormous. In a memo written midway through the Gemini Program Flight Director Christopher Kraft praised Aldrin's work, noting that it "would be difficult to find anyone who contributed more in the area of crew activity and definition of associated spacecraft guidance requirements than Major Aldrin." Referring to rendezvous, Kraft wrote that Aldrin "almost singlehandedly conceived and pressed through certain basic concepts ... without which the probability of mission success would unquestionably have been considerably reduced."

Aldrin intensely wanted a Gemini flight, but when he finally got a mission assignment it was as backup pilot on Gemini 10. Customarily, that would have made him eligible to fly on Gemini 13—if there were a Gemini 13. But Gemini 12 was the last flight planned for the series before Apollo got underway. He was at a dead end as far as Gemini was concerned. Then, tragedy intervened.

In February of 1966, Charles Bassett and Elliot See, the prime crew of Gemini 9, were killed in a plane crash. Their backups, Tom Stafford and Gene Cernan, became the new flight crew. Aldrin and his partner, Jim Lovell, moved up to become their backups. The Gemini 9 situation, in effect, shifted all the assigned crews of the remaining missions ahead one flight leaving Gemini 12, at that point, without a crew. The job was given to Aldrin and Lovell. And so, "by the twists and turns of fate," as he later reflected, Buzz Aldrin would get his coveted Gemini flight.

Lovell and Aldrin completed the Gemini program in fine style. On November 11, 1966, they rode Gemini 12 into orbit for a four day mission. The planned rendezvous with an Agena target vehicle provided Aldrin with an opportunity to field-test his own theories. His work on manned rendezvous had always focused on the pilot's capacity to be able to effect the maneuver without having to rely completely on an automated system of computers, radar, and ground control. So, when the radar lock on Gemini 12 failed, Aldrin picked up his sextant and some special charts he had designed and started his calculations. To his own great satisfaction, and the relief of the people on the ground, he deftly arranged a successful meeting with the Agena.

Aldrin continued his adroit performance outside the spacecraft. On the second day he left the cabin on a spacewalk that lasted more than two hours. Astronauts on previous flights had encountered considerable difficulty in trying to move around and work effectively during EVA without becoming exhausted in the process. Aldrin was determined to conquer the spacewalk barrier. He trained hard before the flight to work out ways around the problems that had stymied his predecessors, spending many hours rehearsing his movements under water in a large tank to simulate the way he would be floating in weightlessness. His diligence paid off. He worked his way smoothly through the two hours with hardly a hitch. It was the most successful spacewalk of the Gemini series.

After Gemini 12 all attention turned to Apollo. When the crew assignments for the first several flights were announced, Aldrin found himself named to the backup crew of the third flight, which would have been Apollo 9. Crew rotation on Apollo followed the Gemini pattern which meant that Aldrin would likely get a seat on the sixth flight, Apollo 12. But fate started to twist and turn again. It happened that the lunar module to be included on the second mission, Apollo 8, would not be ready in time for the planned launch date, so it was decided to move that flight and its crew back a notch into the Apollo 9 position. The original Apollo 9 crew, with their backups, were jumped ahead to man the second flight. The revamped Apollo 8 mission ended up taking Frank Borman, Jim Lovell, and William Anders on a celebrated Christmas trip around the moon at the close of 1968; it put Buzz Aldrin and his backup commander, Neil Armstrong, on Apollo 11. Michael Collins, who was forced off the Apollo 8 flight because of a medical problem, was awarded the third position.

On January 6th, 1969, chief astronaut Deke Slayton summoned the trio to his office. "You're it," he told them. Slayton only confirmed what the astronauts already knew: after two more missions—in just a matter of months—they would be sent to try the first lunar landing.

On the morning of July 16th, with six months of intensive training behind them, Armstrong, Aldrin, and Collins were at the threshold. They enjoyed the traditional preflight breakfast of steak and eggs, then went through the exacting ritual of donning their spacesuits. They were taken to the rocket and installed into the command module "Columbia". The countdown ticked away unimpeded. At T minus seven seconds the engines started with an explosive flash, surging to full power at T minus zero. The six million pound stack defiantly pushed itself off the launching platform and started its climb to space. Reaching orbit, the astronauts and ground team went through the necessary checks then relit the third stage motor to force the spacecraft out to the moon.

Four days later, on Sunday afternoon, in orbit around the moon, Aldrin and Armstrong transferred to the lunar module "Eagle" to get ready for the landing. "The Eagle has wings," Armstrong exclaimed as the LM broke free from the command module. At five minutes past four Armstrong ignited the descent engine to begin their twelve minute powered braking to the landing site, a spot ahead of them to the west in a lunar flatland called the Sea of Tranquility. Armstrong and Aldrin arced steadily downward in the LM while back on the ground Mission Control monitored their progress. "Eagle, you're looking great. ... You're go for landing," rooted CAPCOM Charlie Duke. The LM was just a few thousand feet from the surface when Aldrin saw a yellow warning light flash on. "Program alarm!" he cried. The LM's computer was signaling that it was being swamped with too much work, a possible abort situation. A jolt went through Mission Control. From his front row console Steve Bales, the guidance officer, made the momentous decision to keep going. He correctly sensed that what was happening with the computer would clear up, that it would be okay. Armstrong took over manual control at 500 feet. Seeing an uninviting boulder field rising to meet them, he kept the LM hovering and flew it farther downrange to safety. At 4:17 PM, with fuel running low, he gently eased Eagle down. To erupting cheers at Mission Control Armstrong sent his report: "The Eagle has landed."

The two astronauts remained inside the LM for the next several hours using the time to rest a bit, eat, and prepare for their historic moonwalk. Finding a free moment before his meal, Aldrin removed a Eucharistic wafer, some wine, and a small chalice from his personal kit. He took communion, and offered a silent prayer of thanksgiving.

It was past 10:30 PM before they opened the hatch. Armstrong went out first and cautiously stepped down the ladder. At 10:56 he took the first step onto the moon. Aldrin followed a few minutes later. For the next two hours Armstrong and Aldrin went about their planned tasks of collecting rock and soil samples and setting out scientific instruments. They also erected an American flag and received a very long distance phone call from President Nixon. Shortly after 1:00 AM both astronauts were safely back in the LM cabin. They lifted off the following afternoon just before two o'clock to rejoin Mike Collins for the trip home. Three days later, on July 24th, Columbia and her crew splashed down in the Pacific Ocean. The astronauts spent the next seventeen days in quarantine in the unlikely event they had been contaminated by microbes lurking in the moondust. National celebrations and a grueling world tour followed.

Aldrin stayed with NASA until July of 1971. Recognition of his achievements came in the form of many honors, including the Presidential Medal of Freedom, the Air Force Distinguished Service Medal, and Distinguished Flying Cross, the NASA Exceptional Service Medal, the Legion of Merit, the Harmon Trophy, the Collier Trophy, the National Geographic's Hubbard Medal, the Goddard Trophy, and many more.

On leaving the space program Aldrin resumed his military career as the new commandant of the Air Force Test Pilot School at Edwards Air Force Base in California. The pressures and demands of his astronaut career, particularly the post-flight hullabaloo of Apollo 11, had exacted a heavy toll, however. The result for Aldrin was depression and alcoholism. He sought help through psychotherapy, and subsequently made the decision to retire from the Air Force in March of 1972. In 1973 he wrote a book about his life and emotional struggle called *Return to Earth*.

Today, Aldrin describes his life as "filled with happiness". He continues his work in manned space travel, developing and advocating strategies for a sustained and evolutionary approach to space exploration. He has set his ideas down in a soon to be released book titled *Men From Earth*.

Buzz Aldrin is the father of three grown children. He married for the third time in February of 1988. He and his wife Lois live in southern California.

Who would you describe as your biggest influence in aviation?

I guess my father's activities just because I was close to him. At least, his involvement got me thinking about aviation. During World War II, because he was serving overseas with the Air Corps, I was following his aviation activities. Of course, knowing that Doolittle was a friend of the family's just brought me a little closer when he was involved with the Tokyo raid.

Did your father ever suggest to you, or persuade you, that you might have a future flying into space yourself? Did he encourage you along those lines, knowing Goddard's work?

Not particularly in the direction of space. There was more of a practical thing of getting into piloting positions in the Air Force. A seed was planted in attending a military school before entrance into the Air Force. The Air Force became a separate service at about the same time I entered West Point. There wasn't an Air Force Academy at that time. You could get into the Air Force by going to the Naval Academy or by going to West Point. They were taking twenty-five percent of each class into the Air Force. I elected to go to West Point. Actually, my father's preference was the Naval Academy. But, I felt that was somehow a diversion.

How do you mean?

You had to learn a lot of inappropriate things. We were not directly contributing. Maybe it's an oversimplified way of looking at it.

Your father's career was quite interesting. He knew and worked with some of the great aerospace pioneers—people like Orville Wright and Robert Goddard. Can you describe that relationship for us?

I wouldn't say it was a close working relationship. My father had Goddard as a professor of physics when he was going to Clark University as an undergraduate. And, in later years, he followed Goddard's rocket work and observed that he needed some funding support. My father realized that in those years, the mid-twenties, that he wasn't really the person who could bring that about. But, if he could get Lindbergh to understand what it was, Lindbergh could talk to Guggenheim, and Guggenheim had the money that could support the things that Goddard was doing. So, he played a role as catalyst in bringing those people together, which resulted in Lindbergh and Guggenheim acting in a way to fund Goddard's work.

Did your father know Lindbergh, too, then?
Oh, yeah. My father was an aide to Billy Mitchell in the Philippines in 1919 and '20 when he met my mother, who was a daughter of an army chaplain by the name of Faye Arnold Moon. He was the captain of chaplains.

That's a wonderful coincidence—your mother coming from a family named Moon.
My father came back and was stationed here, and then went back on an airplane and married Mother in the Philippines. Then, he came back the other way around the world on a boat.

Did you ever get a chance to meet any of those men yourself?
I met Doolittle. I don't think I ever met Lindbergh.

What was your father's relationship with Orville Wright?
I'm not sure how close that was, I don't really know. Dad was involved in the Signal Corps and the aviation branch of the engineering school in the early '20s. That was the engineering school at Cook Field that later became the Air Force Institute of Technology at Wright Field. In the early '20s, a lot of lieutenants and captains were processed through that school; my father was the commandant. They became the generals of World War II in the Air Corps.

He was actually one of the founders of that school, wasn't he?
That's right.

On Apollo 11, your partner, Neil Armstrong, described a lunar landing trajectory as "a strange and eerie sensation, not difficult, but somewhat complex and unforgiving." Did you find it that way? Did you find it was kind of eerie as it was happening?
Well, it didn't give me the impression really of a glide, of an airplane-type slowing down. It really wasn't that bad. It was an instrumented thing that you did in a simulator. In actual fact, I didn't have the luxury of sightseeing and looking out the window. My role was primarily one of looking at what was coming up on the changing computer displays and other instruments, and relaying that information to Neil, who was looking out the window. So, he could spare his vision to do that when he felt he didn't have to

look at instruments. I was enabling him to get a better pilot's perspective by giving him the verbal interpretation of what I was reading on the instruments. That cost me the ability to look out and put the maneuver into a perspective other than a simulator doing something, maneuvering from one heading to another or one attitude on an eight-ball. You don't always have the out-the-window impression of what the hell is going on.

This certainly wasn't a simulation. Did you have a rush of adrenaline as you finally started the engine up and powered in? What was the sensation like, that you were finally going down?

There was a significant building a crescendo that only reached its relief at the moment of actually coming down in an appropriate place with enough fuel, where it was soft enough so that you could stay, so you didn't have to lift off again.

You said that mostly you were watching the instruments. Did you see the boulder field that Armstrong saw which you had to fly over?

I really didn't see what he was doing at that point. If I did, it was a quick little glance out the window. I can't say that I really viewed what was there that needed to be avoided. With it there, I felt it was that much more imperative for me to let him look up to see what he was doing. So, I could supplement and enable him to do that by being more efficient and tell him what was happening inside the cockpit.

Once you were down, unknown to you and Armstrong, a fuel-line problem developed. There was a blockage in one of the fuel lines causing pressure to build up in one of the fuel tanks in the descent stage. Apparently, the liquid helium had frozen one of the fuel lines and there was a plug of frozen fuel choking it off. In a recent book called Chariots for Apollo, *it was reported that on the ground they were in a near panic because they saw this sudden rise in pressure in one of the descent stage fuel lines and didn't know what to do. Many of them wanted to get the two of you out of there, just leave the problem behind and not worry about a possible explosion. They talked about it as possibly being like a hand grenade going off and not knowing what it would do to the ascent stage. Some of the engineers wanted to burp the engine for a fraction of a second to blow the plug out. But, apparently it resolved itself. When did you find out about that, or did you ever?*

I am not sure that we ever really did. If it solved itself, they probably wouldn't have troubled us with it in-flight and it probably faded into a point where they thought it might be best just to leave it undiscussed. Then, it got to a point where it was too late to tell us about it. And if they had told us, we'd have probably said, 'Why the hell are you telling us about it now?'

It wouldn't have bothered you then, not knowing about something that potentially dangerous?
It certainly wasn't something that was in our scan to determine what was wrong, to be able to do something about. I guess, my sense is that the best knowledgeable intellects were working on the problem, and we probably wouldn't have added much more than just confusion.

What would you have thought about starting up the descent engine for just a fraction of a second to sort of blow it out as they were thinking about. Would you have had reservations about that?
Yes, because we pretty well wiped out that possibility by venting things right after touchdown. We immediately went through a procedure to plan for liftoff because I felt that was the best thing to do, the best thing anybody could do after landing was to immediately get ready to lift off. So, that's why that was put in the flight plan, that we prepared for the hour and a half checklist leading to liftoff just as if it was twenty hours later. It had been three days or more since we'd rehearsed that, and that could come at anytime if anything wrong developed. Unfortunately, you come up with something like that and the next crew says, "Well, Gee, we have to do something different. If this was painted blue, why we have to paint it green. If it was a good idea for them, why, obviously, we don't have to do it anymore."

Was there any concern among the Apollo 11 crew early on during the planning of Apollo 10 that they would get within 50,000 feet of the surface and NASA might decide to send them all the way?
No. We just never thought that NASA would do that. I think it would have been opening themselves to great criticism to have discussed that with the Apollo 10 crew, saying that if everything looked okay, we'll give you the go to land, but we just won't tell anyone else. That would have been a very poor way to plan a mission, I think.

But, around that time, wasn't there some worry in NASA, indications that maybe the Soviets were trying to put something together to get there ahead of us?

I don't think they were that worried. We were wrestling with the fact that apparently a G booster blew up on the 4th of July '69. It could have been a dual countdown; there seems to be some evidence supporting that there was a crew available for a dual countdown, and that was cancelled. The proton was cancelled after the G booster blew up. But, whether that could have resulted in an Earth-orbit rendezvous, a lunar-orbit rendez-vous, and a successful landing, I think that would have been stretching things quite a bit. By that time, there wasn't much we could have done, anyway.

Can you describe what it was that necessitated the Apollo 10 mission in the first place? Why go all the way to the moon, come within ten miles, and not land?

I guess I was in favor of suggesting a full dress rehearsal for as many things as you could possibly do. In the Gemini program, I tried to instill the opportunities and re-rendezvous, in a rehearsal mode the kind of rendezvous that would be required for all sorts of abort conditions, in Apollo. When we set about defining maneuver relatively, they rehearsed it. They essentially carried out the things that simulated approaching it for a period of time. So, when Apollo 10 came along, it was natural to take everything just as if they had just put themselves into an orbit-following ascent. That was an exercise in lunar orbit with separation and everything that, of course, Apollo 8 didn't do, and 9 was in Earth orbit. It just seemed that to go right to a full-blown landing mission was a little ambitious, perhaps overly ambitious.

When you finally climbed down to the surface, your first words were "Magnificent. Magnificent desolation." Can you recall your emotion at that time, at finally being out on the lunar surface? Can you describe that a bit?

Well, that certainly wasn't within the first couple of minutes of being out. By that time, I had already gone through a brief check of stability imbalance, holding on partially and not holding on. I had taken a moment or two to take a leak and then I started moving around for the next thing to do. And, there was a bit of conversation between Neil and I making that observation. Something being magnificent and at the same time . . . most things that are magnificent are not usually considered desolate. Things that are desolate are not usually considered magnificent, but the two words together certainly, in a sense, described what was there.

Once you emerged from the LM, what surprised you most about the lunar surface? What was totally unexpected?

I guess the powdery consistency that varied so much with depth. In other words, the same material on the surface, the same dust you could find right on the surface on the top eighth inch, was the same thing down several inches. But, in its undisturbed form, it was so much more densely packed the deeper you got. The net result was that you would be on a ten-foot supposedly plush pile of talcum powder, and you'd only sink in a quarter of an inch. That's kind of unusual. Usually, you'd think if you're on a mound of talcum powder that you'd sink in like it's snow, several feet. But, that's because air molecules are in it. I guess it surprised us about as much as it did the soil mechanics people, until they realized that the content was this fine glass powder. They had to believe very strongly that it was quite dense from bouncing radar signals off of it, and also from the Surveyor impacts, photographing those. So there was no question about our sinking in deep. But, the fact that it was powder and still had those same properties was a little unusual. We were so geared for the unexpected, but things went so smoothly, and it was easier than anticipated to move around. It's no big revelation, it's nothing you shout about and it doesn't make big news copy, but it's a pleasant realization that you're in a situation with no surprises.

Were you also surprised in the sense that it went so smoothly? Because Michael Collins was quoted after the flight as saying that going into the flight he thought it was a 50/50 chance that you were going to pull it off.

Well, I think that that's a reevaluation after what we might have agreed was about a 60 to 80 percent chance of a mission success, but a crew-safety factor of better than 95 percent. To pull it off, we sort of agreed that if we touched down, then couldn't even get outside the thing but lifted off, that was fulfilling reaching the moon and bringing somebody safely back to Earth. But, I figure that being able to have nothing happen to prevent you from proceeding with powered descent, then successfully touching on the ground qualifies, and if we'd accomplished that, that was mission success. We figured our chances of doing that were 60 to 80 percent and that's probably what Mike was referring to when he said 50 percent of pulling it off. I don't think he was referring to a 50 percent chance of coming back with Neil and Buzz as part of the crew.

Buzz Aldrin

He did say that he felt a little safer in the command module. He would be propelled back if you guys couldn't get off the surface. He realistically noted the fact that he couldn't land the command module to rescue you two if something went wrong.

Well, I wouldn't expect him to just stay there and watch us. We wouldn't have begrudged him the chance to get back.

Did you and Neil Armstrong ever ask for an extension to stay longer on the surface?

No, I don't think we had the opportunity. It wasn't particularly my desire to raise the issue.

Personally, would you have liked to have stayed out longer? Did you feel you could have done more?

Oh, I think so. I'm not sure how much longer we had the capacity for, which I think in our backpacks was a bit more limited than in later missions. I'm sure there were a lot more things to do that could have been done. But, then, we would have had to reorganize at the last minute and figure out what we were going to do for another thirty minutes.

If you had to do it over again, would you trade your two hours on the surface during the first mission for twenty-two hours on the last missions?

They had three periods of seven hours each. It amounted to about that much? Well, from this point, twenty years downstream, I don't think I'd want to put in all that twenty-two hours at the expense of being on the first mission.

That was important to you?

Yes; I can't say that in all the moments of the last twenty years, I've always felt that way. I think that's the way I feel now, and certainly would stick by that.

You had planned to conduct a communion ceremony and then were told by NASA that you had to do it in private. Were you disappointed by that?

Initially, I was. I think anybody with an idea that they think is appropriate has a degree of pride of authorship, and you would like people to know about it. I think if somebody, a Moslem, for example, landed there and asked the rest of the world to face east or face Mecca at that particular moment, we'd feel that's a little bit too parochial. So, in retrospect, I feel that it was handled appropriately because it was made known after the fact. I felt I didn't violate what

I think. Deke Slayton told me to do or not to do by saying that I wanted to take a moment and give thanks in my particular way, and let it go at that.

It was handled well?
I thought so. Whether Deke agreed exactly with that or not, he was probably saying to himself, 'Gee, what's he going to say next?'

Is it still your opinion that there was an implied slight against the military by having a civilian as the first astronaut to walk on the moon?
No, I don't think so. I really think that it's just the roll of the dice, the play of the cards, how people ended up matched the way they were, and changed because of this and that in the missions. The mission assignments changed somewhat, the crews rotated because of the LM not being available for the second Apollo flight. Then, that flight got put into a large orbit, then a circumlunar, and then a lunar orbit mission. With the way the crews were put together coming off of the Gemini program, it fell together that way, and I don't think anyone gave that much forethought as to what the significance might be of having as the commander a civilian, and a LM pilot a Navy or Air Force person. To try and engineer that would have been very difficult on Deke's part, it probably would have been frustrated, and it wouldn't have worked. Whereas, if they had just put a bunch of crews out there and let it happen however it happened, then that's the way it is. Okay, now that's how you get the crew there, and there's order of seniority and order of positions, and delineating what the roles are; it's a call of the game as to which predominates. The principles of workload distribution resulted in the right seat copilot guy in Gemini always being the one that had more experiments and did the EVAs, because the commander had the workload of doing the aborts during the launch and the additional workload of controlling the spacecraft during reentry. Certainly, on Apollo, the commander has more than enough keeping him busy, to prompt someone to consider minimizing the load that person had in terms of the lunar surface activities. That, of course, runs into conflict with seniority and historical rewards that come along with rank having its privileges, and all that. So, why not just call that one and decide which predominates. Rusty Schweickart made the EVA on Apollo 9, and there was no question as to whether he or McDivitt was going to do that, when it came time to do the EVA, in that supposition, it wasn't that surprising to me that one would choose to have the

commander exit first. It turned out that examining things further—the details and the contingencies, the way the hatch was located—if we'd had a contingency with one guy that was halfway out or one guy was out and the other guy was still in, then the guy who was out had to come back in again and at that point, you couldn't pressurize the LM. If the contingency you had was of that nature, you had the lift off that way. There was no way that the two guys could change positions. So, you might end up with a copilot occupying the pilot's position for an emergency liftoff, and you wouldn't want that to happen. That's kind of complex to explain, but that is a fact of life. If the decision had been made the other way for some other reason, right at the last minute, we might have reversed this decision once we'd thought about that particular contingency. But, I'm sure the decision was made arbitrarily before we got down to looking at "what if's."

There's always been a lot of debate in the media.

It's a natural thing for the media to want to try and make a controversy out of, and it smacks of coverup when you try and deny a coverup. You've got to establish that everything else exists that precluded covering up, to convince somebody that you're not covering up something. So, it's an awkward position but it's an understandable one when you have media trying to get a little bit more excitement, differences of opinion, and controversy.

It was an overall NASA decision then, and you and Armstrong both had a hand in it? Or was it more Neil as the commander having the prerogative to decide who went out first?

No. Well, as I describe it in *Return to Earth*, I could see that our training was not crystallizing because no one would touch the hot potato of saying for sure this was the way the lunar surface activities were going to be. So, I went and talked to Neil about it. I said we needed to settle this situation one way or the other. I don't know *what* I would have said my preference would have been at that point. But, his observation was that he recognized the significance of that event and wasn't going to arbitrarily rule himself out of some historical position. I didn't think that was very satisfactory so I went to George Low and told him that I felt we needed a high-level decision on it and hoped that, if it were made soon, that it would not be subject to reversal later. Otherwise, our training would suffer. He assured me that we would have a decision shortly, and we did.

You mentioned contingencies and moving around in there. At one point Armstrong swung around and his backpack broke the engine arming switch, didn't it?

No, it was my backpack that hit the engine arm circuit breaker, because that was on the right side of the cockpit. It was on my side. It was my backpack. The broken circuit breaker is in my safe deposit box.

No kidding? You still have it?

It looks like any other broken circuit breaker.

It was reported that Armstrong was ready to stick a ballpoint pen into it to complete the circuit.

We had several pens, and what was needed, since where it was broken off it was clear from what the ground saw with their telemetry, and what I could see, that it had not been pushed in. So, we needed to be convinced that if we did push it in, that it would stay in and if it didn't push in at all, and stay in, that we had another way around it. The ground studied the problem for quite a while, and we advanced to the point in the checklist of pushing it in, and it stayed in, so we didn't worry about it. We didn't sweat the problem of having to pull it back out again because we couldn't think why we'd want to do that.

You brought up a good point about the contamination question and your isolation. Did you feel that all that was worthwhile, especially since there really wasn't an "air tight" quarantine?

It was kind of silly to make a big issue out of it, but, hell, I didn't have any more information to make a smarter decision to argue with them, to say, 'Oh, no, there isn't any chance that that could happen.' It's up to somebody to make a value judgment and it turned out that we were insulated for a week to ten days after we got back, and it was not that unbearable. It was relatively comfortable, and we did have some insulation from the outside world while things calmed down a bit.

Once they opened up the command module to throw in your special quarantine suits, didn't that defeat the whole purpose?

Well, yes, I know that all these little things that make it not all that wise. You wipe off the garment, put a rock on it, and drop it in the ocean; it's going to propagate all sorts of germs down on the bottom of the ocean, then all of a sudden everybody's going to be exposed.

Buzz Aldrin

They made a big deal out of this, but at the same time as, as soon as you were down, they opened the hatch. Who knows what might have drifted out or washed out if seawater splashed in?

I guess we paid as much attention as we reasonably could without compromising safety and scientific results.

Why didn't they just bring the entire capsule back onto the carrier?

That had certainly been thought of a number of times. After Gus's spacecraft sank, they looked at the strength of the cabled. I think they did plan at one time to do that. Then, they found out that the command module floated upside down, which they really hadn't anticipated. They found out that the swinging back and forth was a little hazardous for bringing the crew on board within the spacecraft. It would take a lot longer to do, and they'd be bobbing around, getting sick and all that. So, that decision was made before we came along, and nobody asked us our opinion on it.

Did you and Mike Collins have a bet with Neil Armstrong that, once you hit the water's surface, you wouldn't tip over?

Not that I recall. I wouldn't be too surprised if it's one of those things that gets manufactured after the fact. Who supposedly had a bet?

It was you and Mike Collins against Neil, Neil saying that the spacecraft would tip over, and you and Mike working together to make sure it didn't. You had to release the parachutes at exactly the right instant, unhook the parachutes so they didn't drag it over when you hit the water.

In retrospect, since we did screw it up, we probably could have rehearsed that a few more times and realized that we were going to have to do that in the face of being jolted considerably. But, we weren't the only ones.

Your flight was a magnificent achievement; no aspect of it really was unremarkable. But, does anything particular stick out in your mind, more than anything else about the flight that you remember? Is there one thing that stays with you about the flight?

The good thing is that it was a marvel we were able to, step-by-step, overcome little setbacks and advance so progressively, mission after mission; to be able to do that and really only have one major setback in Apollo 13, in the Saturn V, and so on. I'm getting this appreciation because I'm looking through the rather hastily put together Soviet plans to try and do something like that, I guess we just had the advantage of things coming along in sufficient time to be able to conveniently make a few changes here and there. And they didn't have that good fortune. Everything tended to slip, because I'm convinced that they were trying to upstage us as much as they possibly could. It was just that either we didn't have difficulties or they did, that slowed down the progression of their big booster and some of their preliminary accomplishments in the development of Soyuz.

On your own flight, what stands out that you think *about more than anything else?*

It's like when I think about being in combat in Korea. There were two episodes; one of them was essentially a piece of cake, but I shot out of range, and I wish I could do it again. The other, the second one, was a very hairy situation and I felt I'd like to do that one again. I could've gotten a lot more out of it, I could've been a lot more effective. In Apollo 11 I sure would, in a sense, like to do that one again. In retrospect, I think I would be a lot more relaxed, aware, observe and, maybe, with some of the pressures off. To be able just to savor and absorb more the second time you do something. I think different people have different abilities to be at their peak observational capacity in new situations. I don't think all humans are alike in that way. People who end up being really outstanding test pilots are able to come into a new situation with a new airplane and be very competent and outstanding observers the first time. I've felt that, in airplane flying, that has taken time to develop. I wouldn't put myself at the top of the list in the category of being a real sharp observer the first time you were given the chance to observe things. When I look back on things I think, 'Geez, I wish all of that could happen again. Even though it was pretty simple and straightforward, being on the first mission, it would be nice to just do it all again, then single things out and observe them again.' Again, right now, reflecting on that, for the future, I'm just a little fearful that we're liable to go to Mars and feel obsessed as soon as we reach Mars to go down to the surface immediately, plant the flags, and kick up dust. We've spent a long time on the surface of the Earth trying to get away, to get in orbit so we could look back on the planet from orbit and do things from orbit. In contemplating going to Mars, it seems as though as soon as we get into orbit we want to immediately go down and land, and I think that's not a very wise way to look at it. So, I'm trying to foster the other point of view of getting the maximum done in a gradual way before you give in to those temptations, because there certainly are going to be plenty of people cheering for those hasty moves.

What's the biggest adjustment you've had to make since Apollo 11?

Well, one of the things—I tried unsuccessfully, it turned out—was to resume my Air Force career after leaving NASA. Making the decision to finally leave the Air Force was one of the hardest things I've ever had to do. But, you know, I didn't realize, when I thought of it, the full significance of the title of the book I wrote back in 1973, *Return to Earth.* I've discovered exactly how descriptive that is. I have great problems when I go on a really neat trip, let's say, and I get really enthusiastic about what's going on and then I get home to all the tasks and problems there have to deal with them. The bills. Maybe the car doesn't work. All the things I have to deal with when I get back, plus all the things that I've accomplished on the trip, all that is "return to Earth," that's return to home. And, I had it in a bad way with Apollo. I had to come back and conclude that people look at me differently now and I have to live up to that and adjust to that. If I'm a sensitive person and a bit introverted, I set myself up for a difficult period of coping. Had I understood that, I would have preferred not to be on the first landing mission because I didn't really want to deal with all that stuff. But, by that time, I couldn't quite change my mind. I wanted to be there and at the same time, I wasn't quite sure I wanted to be there.

Around the tenth anniversary of the landing, I had my own readjustments of a personal nature that I went through and I think put me in a unique position to be able to judge what living with being on a pedestal means. At that time, I think it was in a newspaper, somebody designed a cartoon showing a number of robot-suited figures in varying sizes from the largest, with a number one, on down to number twelve. They were all identical and all drifting away from the moon except for one of the twelve encompassed in a cage, and that was number two. I looked at that and thought how cruel it was of the cartoonist to single out one person and say that he's in a cage. The guy had a lot of insight and showed that. I had built cages around myself for various reasons. But, I didn't think that was a particularly accurate portrayal and perspective of that particular time. I've had to come to grips with all that. I've adjusted to it in some ways and have risen above where I ever was before. That particular experience put me in a lot of turmoil.

How do you mean?

Having become a hero all of a sudden when you didn't really intend to do that. Some people *want* to do that because it has an impact on different people.

Doesn't that just go with the territory? The public always has a demanding curiosity about celebrities, they want to know certain things about them.

Well, in what regard? To see what philosophical changes have happened? You know, you get your psychic people, you get the mysterious, the bizarre. Did these guys catch anything while they were out there? How do they cope with fame? Do we have some more Elvis Presleys here? There are some things that are attractive to the public, but I'm not sure that we're *all* that interested in the attractiveness of being hung out for exhibit. Some people intend to go and make a name for themselves and become heroes and become desirable. They want to get their names on the front page. Some people, maybe, don't want to do that. I'm sure that being frustrated by various demands and having a sense of being used by your organization and by people who want this and that—and autograph seekers—it's not always the easiest thing to leave your privacy. If you want to do something, if you want to see someone after a meeting, you can't get away because fifty people want your autograph. You want to say, 'Forget it, you people! I'm here for something else.' Then, sometimes, you say, 'Well, these people gave me this, they put me here. I really want to sit and talk to them.' Depending on who you are and where you happen to be, you respond differently.

Doesn't each of you have a unique perspective that no one else has?

I don't really think that going out there and back creates that perspective. It's because you are now viewed as having done that by other people and *how they now view* you that gives you a different perspective. As a body, we reflect an experience and an investment. Because of that, we then respond and give thought to things maybe differently than other people do. I don't really know how to describe that.

You were in the third group of astronauts selected. How do you think your training and preparation for the Apollo missions compared to the early days of the original seven Mercury astronauts? Did NASA's standards become much more demanding?

I don't know who, when you say NASA, who in there would say it's up to me to do such and so. You're talking about people who are prima donnas. The Mercury people really controlled their own fate. I imagine most people think that we were the most examined, the most tested, the most qualified, the most documented people in the world, right? Wrong! There's not a single qualitative measure opposite anybody's name that testifies to the fact that Joe Blow can do anything better than Joe Schmo, because that would be competitive. It was NASA's desire not to be competitive, and that means we were never given tests to see how well you could do something.

You said that the original seven astronauts called their own shots. Was that cut down dramatically when the new fellows came in?

Well, they never asked me where the windows ought to go. It became clear that we needed to dock the LM something other than in front, and some people were going to dock it without seeing what you were docking with. So, they put a window in there, on the top side of the LM. But, it wasn't a very adequate window and it wasn't designed too well to do docking.

Some of the other astronauts got pretty playful on their flights. Did you ever think about "improvising" while you were on the surface?

Some people asked if I was the guy who hit the golf ball on the moon, you know, and I'll say, 'No, I don't do stupid things like that!' When I went, I was very concerned about doing the right thing while I was there and not making a spectacle out of it. That's the difference between being on the first mission and being on another one.

You mentioned earlier that you were never tested on a competitive basis with other astronauts. What were the implications of that policy?

One thing was that the people designing our training had no idea whether we observed the training that they gave us. That's not a very good way to run a railroad. I don't think that's the way the military would do it. And, I guarantee that's not the way the Soviets would do it. I don't think that's the way we ought to be doing it, but that's the way you do it when you don't want people prying into what's going on.

By people prying, do you mean the press?

Yes, somebody does something and then somebody wants to know what the answers are. The public domain—an investigative reporter—wants to come in and find out how much better John Glenn is than Alan Shepard. So, the system that existed was developed to minimize all that.

Weren't they worried also about a military connection with the program? Wouldn't they try not to administer tests that had military implications or that could be perceived that way by the media or the general public?

I don't know. You had aborted attempts at Air Force military command in the Space Program like Blue Gemini, the Manned Orbital Laboratory, and Dyna Soar, because somebody in the White House named Eisenhower wanted to have two different programs in NASA. Right or wrong, we have this desire to keep them separated, which almost means that the public can go in and crucify NASA if they do something military. Now, is that smart? I don't particularly think so. I think it's strictly what we *should* be doing.

Is NASA, in fact, doing a lot of military work? Two of the Space Shuttle missions were exclusively military and very hush-hush. Not much was known about them.

That's DOD (Department of Defense). It's not NASA's doing it. It's DOD. You can't say NASA is doing militaristic things. NASA is not doing militaristic things by definition. But, it can be misinterpreted by changing the words around, and pretty soon someone says, 'I didn't know NASA was doing military things—Oh, that's bad! Gee, we want space for peaceful purposes.'

Do you believe NASA misdirected its activities in terms of the Apollo program? There seems to have been no progression, no logical follow-through of the program.

I don't know. Maybe what you're getting at is that, if there's a craft to land a man on the moon then bring him back safely—you know, John Kennedy's challenge—that if we were going to do this, then it was also clear that this was a commitment for the nation to be preeminent in space, to be the leaders in this new era, and that it's not being the leader when you accomplish something and then let it go at that. But, people can interpret things differently, and the press, the public, and the administration found other things to do of more immediate interest. The funding dried up after we landed on the moon, so there wasn't anything NASA could do about furthering things because they weren't supported. They were left with a task force headed by the vice president to discuss what might follow, and they reached their conclusions in 1969, several months after our landing.

They recommended Mars, didn't they?

Among other things, they recommended a complete program of a permanent presence on the moon with nuclear rockets to and from the moon, nuclear transport for interplanetary purposes, and actually planning on early arrivals on Mars in 1982. Certainly, a modes arrival by 1986 or 1987. I think if that group had said, 'Hey, let's get to Mars by 1998,' they would have said, 'What in the world are you waiting for? Now, you talk about getting to Mars by 1998, and you talk about how are we going to afford it. How can we possibly get there? We're very technically competent now, but that's only ten years away. I don't know why we haven't done a lot of these things. It's a self-fulfilling prophesy, if you say you can't do something, you won't do it. That's the truth.

After your Apollo 11 flight, you went to work in NASA on Advanced Planning for future NASA missions. What kind of plans were you working on at that time?

That would have been in 1970. One of the things I was doing was representing the Astronaut Office in the Phase A or Phase AB definition of the Space Shuttle. That was the time when the thinking was that it still would be a fully reusable configuration two-stage, with a booster and an orbitor. I came into that process after it had been under way for a while, and there weren't any other flight crew representatives at the time. We were getting ready to evaluate proposals coming in from the major contractors. So, our group was on, I guess, what was called a source selection board of some sort. I think there was some less formal name for it because it was Phase B.

What do you mean by Phase A, Phase B, and so forth?

Phase A is the preliminary concept, Phase B is the preliminary systems definition. And, C and D usually gets to detailed drawings and developments leading to production. C and D are the ones with the firm commitment to build something. Phases A and B are prior to that.

Kind of like brainstorming?

Yes, but it's on a formal basis. Marshall Space Flight Center was designated as the lead center for the booster portion of this. It carried a launch trajectory so far up that was specified as an interface. The orbitor was managed by the Johnson Space Flight Center. I guess in those days it was probably still called the Manned Spacecraft Center. I was sort of feeling around to see where I fit in with this group, and I felt for sure that a lot of people would be wondering why, of this combination of vehicles, the only thing they seemed to be considering was a manned booster. Usually, the Astronaut Office is the one insisting on putting men on something so that you can guarantee its reliability and further the objectives of man in space. And, it's the flight control people that say, 'Well, we're not really sure we need men along in this thing.' So, it sort of surprised me that nobody was questioning the fact that all of these proposals of boosters had a cockpit with two guys in it.

In seeing the original designs, as you said, the entire booster itself would be flown back to be reused rather than having reusable strap-on solid boosters and an expendable liquid fuel tank the way the shuttle does now.

But, the mission that it would accomplish was a canned-type mission. In other words, it was the same for every flight, unless you had a major deviation, and lots of people were in lots of trouble if you had a major deviation. Normal mission was to fly up to a certain point, separate, turn around, and come back and land. It would be pretty much the same for every activity. There is not room for a lot of judgment and it certainly was subject to being done automatically.

That would have eliminated the need for the solid rockets that eventually took the place of that piloted booster.

Yes. There was no consideration for solid-rockets launch on this configuration. It was to be two stages; both of them would land on a runway and roll out, and then come back in like a giant airplane to be refueled and refurbished. So, I was being a devil's advocate, wondering why somebody does something, and did they really look at all the possibilities. The unusual was for me to perhaps raise a question or espouse the cause that maybe we ought to consider an unmanned booster. People said we have to have men in there to guarantee that we would be able to get the thing back safely, and we can't risk this expensive thing without having a man in it. My counter argument was, 'Well, if you have a problem, the concern you're devoting to the men in the booster is at the expense the guys that are in the orbitor who are in trouble. If you just worry about the guys in the orbitor and say to hell with the booster, you are more likely to be able to recover the guys in the orbitor.' Anyway, the net result was that the entire program was too expensive, and it was cancelled. They had to go back and redo the definition of the whole thing. When you asked the Marshall Space Flight Center why they put men in the booster, you realized that they were always jealous of Houston for having astronauts. They didn't have any astronauts in their vehicle, so they wanted men in their booster for their own ego. They wanted the importance of designing a vehicle that had a cockpit in it. But, just to be on the safe side, they had their contractors, Boeing, Martin, and Rockwell, do a study as to whether there ought to be a man in the booster or not, a manned versus an unmanned booster. Well, it doesn't take any idiot to realize that if you give a choice to an aerospace company to put a cockpit in it or not, for sure they are going to make a bigger profit by putting a cockpit in it. They were highly motivated to come up with putting a man in the booster, and it ended up being too expensive. But, just after it was cancelled, it was sincerely questioned by Dr. Guilruth in Houston. By that time, so much had been studied that it was too late to go back and review the redesign, or redefinition. It had to go back because it was so expensive and had been cut back to the budget allowed for it. That was when they came up with a partially reusable configuration of having a tank and the engine, the tank that almost goes into orbit being thrown away. Bring the engines back as part of the upper stage, have it burning from lift-off, and then use cheap, recoverable solid rockets. I wasn't around when that reconfiguration was designed.

Was Von Braun a prime mover on that version?
I don't recall what role he might have been playing in that. To my recollection, I think he had departed Marshall at that point.

As an experienced astronaut, were the solid-fuel rockets a fearful thing to you since they couldn't be turned off or controlled the way liquid fuel rockets can? Did you think that was a bad judgment?
One always has hindsight at this point.

There were people who insisted, von Braun among them, that American astronauts would never ride on solid rockets. Apparently, there was quite a debate.
I really hate to get used on one side or the other in that kind of discussion, since I wasn't around it all when it was defined. I can only express what would clearly be viewed as a biased, after-the-fact point of view.

These days you have been working with your cerveport space port (CERV) configuration. Is that still a viable option, do you think? Are you still working on that?
Well, I was trying to define the steps, the alternate steps that we could take when one tries to fulfill a CERV mission and use that

basic need to dictate the need for a configuration that could serve multiple purposes. In other words, whatever shell houses a return vehicle, if that same kind of shell in a light-weight version is grouped together to provide a permanent presence that can be maneuverable, then that can begin to do the things a space station is going to do through free flyers. Rather quickly, you see that you have taken on the whole establishment that already has decided of what it is going to look like, and how it's going to be. A number of the aerospace companies are proposing versions of the CERV that are expensive, high-tech with wings on them, that will make a lot of profit, or bare-bones shells that look like either Apollo or Gemini, with extremely limited utility for anything other than the CERV. They have vested interests in pursuing those designs rather than something that can be multipurpose. That's very frustrating when you see that nobody wants to work on or consider something that has multiple utilizations. Seeing that the station is not doing what I felt it ought to do, and their people fighting in the ISI, I finally, in frustration, decided to try and design the second-generation space station. I decided to try and figure what it is it has to do to accomplish depot missions to and from the moon, and depot missions to and from Mars, in an overall integrated plan. Then, when we understand how to carry out those outer orbit exploration missions, it will become a little clearer what's needed to support that flow of people, fuel, and cargo in low-Earth orbit. If I define a configuration for a lunar orbitor and L2 space depot perhaps the wisdom of that might dribble back down and be seen as useful before we proceed too far in solidifying the present spaceport. I am not trying to come up with an alternative design for the space stations directly, but if I'm defining what an L2 spaceport ought to be, I think I ought to know as much about it as someone who is designing a zero-gravity, space-materials processing research facility in low-Earth orbit. So, when they come to me and say, 'Oh, I don't think it ought to be that way,' I can say, then, 'What the hell do you know about? You know something about low-Earth Orbit. See, they are no longer experts in that depot field.

You seem to think that the space station as it is now being planned and configured, somehow falls short of its potential. Where do you see it lacking?

It's not providing mobility for outer-orbit activities, such as vehicle servicing, transportation to and from a delivery vehicle like a shuttle so that the delivery vehicle does not have to compromise its own payload capabilities and the station's altitude. If the station were built first as a depot, it could be put at a higher altitude with less drag or optimum altitude because once built, you would not have to take the shuttle all the way up to it. Instead, you would have a little OMV (Orbital Maneuvering Vehicle) that could come down and pick up the cargo from the Shuttle and take it back up to the station. It could replace the crew by taking the return crew down to the Shuttle, empty those guys out, pick up the new guys, and take them back again. By not bringing the Shuttle up another ten or twenty miles gains you another 10,000 pounds of cargo, or payload performance on the Shuttle. That's very remarkable, but you don't see anybody advertising that because it would point out the undesirable nature of what is being done, which is taking the Shuttle all the way to the station.

Would your concept cost any more money than they are spending now?

It puts things in a different perspective. A while back, we decided to maximize the return by developing commercial products. Somehow, the commercial use of the shuttle hasn't materialized to redo its cost and neither will, I believe, trying to advertise and get commercial customers on the space station. It's not going to be a pay-for-itself proposition because America Wallstreet does not invest in long term things the way foreigners do. I think these are things that we've just realized. So, what we're left with is a delayed, unenthusiastic facility that does not support interesting, appealing, adventuresome missions. Unfortunately, in order to build a facility that does do that, we either have to change and modify it, alter it, compromise it, or come up with a new program that will cost another ten to fifteen billion dollars. We have to start on that before we even put the present space station up. And, that's unacceptable. Who in the administration in 1993 is going to go before Congress and say, 'Mr. Appropriations Committee, we're within two years of putting up this Freedom Space Station and we're about ready, and I want to ask you for a new star. We want you to fund this thing called a space port. It's going to be in a different location and it is going to support activities to the moon.' They're going to say, 'Get out of here, what the hell do you think we paid you for earlier?' That's the dilemma that I think we are in.

Do you actually envision the Space Station Freedom being completed before the turn of the century?

Oh sure, we will, without a doubt, finish something, and hopefully it will be in the '95 to '96 time frame.

You don't see any problems or logistics in terms of shuttle launches and Defense Department needs and accommodations?

Yes, I do. I think we need an augmented payload delivery system. I think it needs to handle three categories of payload: cargo, propellants, and personnel. I don't see it coming in any other way than from shuttle-derived components in some way. I would imagine that it would be better off to do it in-line rather than side-mounted, the way the shuttle is side-mounted. Then that means putting the engines on the bottom of the external tank, aft of the cargo compartments, if you put two or three engines there, and put the cargo with some insertion engines on top of the external tank, I think the payload delivery is more efficient that way than just as a side-mounted facility, the wings, the airplane part of the shuttle building a cylinder on top of the three engines, RCS and the OMS. I have been led to believe by people that that's not too efficient a way to deliver a payload. You're forced to do it when it has wings on it, because to put wings like the shuttle on the top rocket that the first stage of which is going to go through max q. The stress you are going to get are because we can't put the shuttle the way it is, and a lot of times through the winds when they change. We've seen that. Imagine what it would be like if that shuttle was mounted on top of the ET, the stress you would have with wind shear if the engines were on the ET and the shuttle is at the top. We would never be able to launch. That's the way Hermes is going to go up. I don't think they've faced the problems yet.

You are not an advocate of the big, dumb booster philosophy?

Well, that's an oversimplification. I guess, in some ways, I probably am.

You advocate revitalizing Saturn technology. Not a gold-plated version, but just build these enormous engines and big fuel tanks to get a massive lift capability?

I think it's possible to maybe use some J2 engines that have already been built that are man-rated, or were man-rated for the Saturn. Upgrade that kind of technology without it being as sophisticated, perhaps, as a Shuttle main engine with the high turbines. I think there may be a place for those, and I think there may be a place for liquid strap-ons, liquid boosters instead of solid boosters. But, those are going to be developed, down the stream, and they're somehow going to have to compete. It was mentioned to me a while back by somebody that, if you look at a lot of the different refinements, it is doubtful we could afford to go both Shuttle-C or Shuttle-derived cargo vehicle and advanced solid rocket motors at the same time. One would probably have to be a bargaining chip for the other. I think we have to really look at the sequence of missions that can potentially get us somewhere in the next ten to fifteen years. Also, I'm just addressing myself to facets other than delivering cargo, which the Shuttle and other things can do. We're going to have to do that.

Do you believe we should establish a manned base on the moon and then work our way from there to Mars orbit?

I think they can be done almost simultaneously. I have a schedule drawn out that I think makes sense. It is optimistic, but it enables landings to take place on the moon around 2000, and fly-bys of the planet to take place about that time. Landings on Mars might not take place because I don't think they ought to take place really until they're able to stay. I don't think we ought to leave people at Mars in orbit around the surface until we're capable of leaving them there for a whole Mars cycle, two years. I think the degree of maturity that they get and they have, in terms of supplying landing craft contingency and whatever to supplement their activities in orbit, would enable them, then to venture down on and come back up again. You can do an awful lot from orbit that you can't do from the Earth, because of the time difference. You can control an awful lot of robots that are chiefly wandering around picking up things and looking at things and sending messages back to you. You can do a hell of a lot of productive things from orbit around Mars. What requires one to go down there and be there briefly and come back up again—I don't think we've thought that one out really well. But, certainly, it's going to be prestige and pride of achievement and accomplishment and the quest to be first to do something. And, I think that needs to be regulated in the future to prevent wasteful competition, or wasteful cooperation, advancing things too rapidly.

Would you have any advice to give to the first landing crew on Mars knowing what you do about being on the first lunar landing mission?

I think it's going to be difficult for the crew that has that opportunity and responsibility to keep an appropriate perspective. But, they're going to separated from the Earth, living with their own little, self-centered problems for a long period of time before they get the opportunity to go down on the surface; we're talking about months and months of just getting there, much more staying in orbit and maybe several teams of people being there before somebody ventures down. There probably will be a certain amount of impatience that will naturally come along with the opportunity to be first on Mars. It would be nice if that crew could talk their overall boss into giving them the opportunity to do it again if anything went wrong the first time, the way Paine supposedly gave us that option.

Was that really true?
That's what he said. And, I believe that we would have reminded him of it depending on what actually did cause us to abort the landing, and at what point. Obviously, if it was really bordering on pilot error and we had screwed up, and that caused us to abort at some point, I don't think we would have bothered to ask if he'd put us on the next crew going up there.

It was reported that Paine had made that promise to you.
I don't think that's something that ought to go unnoticed. I felt it was a noble enough gesture of generous concern for us not to take hasty actions. Whether it would have been carried out or not, at least it was worthy of note. Something to be held privately between us.

Are you and your Apollo 11 crewmates close? How would you describe your relationship today?
Yes, we get together whenever there's an event that both of us are attending. There isn't anything that I'm doing that I feel is important that I think requires checking it out with Neil or getting his opinion on it particularly. And, I think vice versa. Mike and I are both more into participating in some of the mechanics of the future. We're both also into writing down, of recording for history what we think about the past and the present, and the future. So, by being in Washington, Mike is more available when I'm there. And, I do that and probably will continue to do that. My son communicates with Mike from time to time. They saw each other over in Moscow before the Phobos launch, and they enjoy talking about things.

Are your other kids involved at all in that sort of activity, or are they pursuing different careers?
My oldest son is a flight attendant for Delta. I gave him an opportunity to get exposed a little bit to flying airplanes, but he didn't really take to it enthusiastically. My youngest son at least got through soloing airplanes up at the University of North Dakota, because they afforded that opportunity. But, he hasn't followed that through. Andy did get his masters degree with John Logsdon at George Washington in Soviet Studies and Space Policy. He got

his bachelors degree in international relations and Soviet Studies in particular, from the University of California at Santa Barbara. He's now working on a PhD in UCLA sponsored by Rand in Soviet language and policy economics involved in their space program activities. So, he's quite close to what's going on and wants to participate in the International Space University a year from this coming summer, which will be in Moscow. He has a neat opportunity to understand the pros and cons of SDI and the Soviet's response to what it is we do.

And your daughter?
She's expecting in April. She's going to make me a grandfather.

For the first time?
Yes. She's a top executive with the May Company, the department store, out in this area. She's been married for about two years, now.

You're a newlywed again. According to People *magazine, you actually gave your wife a piece of the moon. Did you really present her with a moon rock engagement ring?*
That's not correct, not at all. I sent them a letter correcting that, but they didn't print it. They misinterpreted several things that the press here locally had reported—correctly—that Lois and I had both relayed. Well, Lois more than I, because she thinks it was more facetious, maybe, or joking, or cute. It gets rather involved because it goes back to before 1976 when I thought that, approaching the 200th anniversary of the nation, that we ought to reflect on the accomplishments of that 200 years and perhaps choose that opportunity to have a celebration of Apollo and present those who reached the moon with a piece of it. Just as an event in 1976, since we weren't flying anything and hadn't been flying anything for quite a while, to celebrate the Bicentennial of the country. Well, the PR people at NASA didn't think that was too good an idea. I suggested to some other person that it would be a good idea and some reporter made an inquiry through NASA, and poor Joe Allen had to answer it, being the legislative representative to Congress. His response was a little naive, I thought, in saying that it was NASA's position that enough honor and recognition had gone to the top of the pyramid and that they felt that to further single out the crews by presenting them a piece of the moon wouldn't necessarily be appropriate. Of course, we knew that pieces had been given to heads of state around the world to governors—some of these governors left the State House and took their little moon rock with

them. So, it resides in their personal homes, now, instead of the State House. Anyway, it's one of those things that I've been trying to lobby for, that somebody would say, 'Hey, I think that's a good idea. Why don't we do that?' Bill Anders, Jim Lovell, and some other people have recently written letters to Fletcher but, somehow, nothing's been done about it. So, in keeping with that, before we got married, someone asked Lois, 'What's your engagement ring going to be?' 'Why,' she said, 'we're hoping to get a moon rock, but we don't have one yet.' Reporting that locally, it was correct, and I don't see where any of these people, having read the way the local reporters interpreted what Lois said, could have possibly gotten it wrong, unless they were just trying to come up with something flashy. I mean, it was totally a misstatement on their part.

None of the fellow astronauts ever received a moon rock of their own?
Nope, nope. Not yet. We might, one of these days.

It is surprising that no one was compelled to slip a lunar rock into their pocket and bring it back with them unbeknown to anyone else.
I wouldn't swear it hasn't been done. During the early flights, it was considered a piece of contaminated, forbidden stuff that could've had germs on it. That's why we were in isolation. It would have been really most inappropriate. As things relaxed a little, until the stamp episode, why, it might have been a cute thing to do. But, then, what do you do with something that you're not supposed to have without getting in trouble?

How do you see yourself now, twenty years after being on the first lunar landing mission?
I'm kind of sensitive to competitive comparisons, but I think I rate pretty damn high right now in doing things for the future of the people in an unselfish way. I mean, I get reimbursed for hardly a damn thing that I do in trying to make things better for everyone else and the space program. And, how much thanks do I get for doing that? Damn little. But, I get my compensation and satisfaction in other ways. What we're trying to do, now, is to be our own private citizens, accomplishing whatever it is we want to. If we want to be visible, fine. If we choose not to, we ought to be able to do that. I don't think someone like Neil Armstrong likes to be called a recluse, but one of the descriptions of Neil is that he doesn't like to come out in public.

Do you feel frustrated at all being a former astronaut now not being consulted or being able to participate with your experience the way you think you might be able to?

Yes, I do, and I have been. Hopefully, that will gradually sort itself out as we become more gray-haired sages. Perhaps, then, somebody will listen to us more. At the same time, I think I'm getting a lot smarter, sorting things out on my own, with and without the help of others. I think this next year is going to be key, because I think I've really put together some things that look very promising. It may not be exactly the way we ought to go . . . but maybe some study that gets done will help alleviate that, and with a change of watch in various parts of NASA, I think some of that frustration will sort itself out. It's so full of "not invented here", and observable to me examples of intentional blocking and unethical activities on the part of certain people for their own purposes. I mean, that's really petty, but I guess that's the way the world of business operates. Everybody is not out to make life easier for everybody else. This is in and out of NASA. It's frustrating to wonder why Rockwell or McDonnell-Douglas wouldn't jump with joy to make use of my services in the area of advanced planning. You know, just rubbing elbows for whatever peanuts they might think it's worth to them. Why would they *not* be interested? That's got to make somebody feel a little bit paranoid about being left out or something. But, people of recognition, whether inflated or otherwise, are kind of a threat to the establishment, whether we really are or not. That's consistent with my observation and I think it's an inappropriate use of my experience to allow that sort of thing to happen. There's a wealth of experience that exists; it's hard to manage. It's very hard to manage diverse points of view about something. Everybody's got a different point of view on it, but that doesn't mean we ought to walk away from those diverse points of view.

From the beginning, back in the Project Mercury days, and right up through Apollo, a substantial mythology has developed around your work—how you all were portrayed, how you were imagined to be.

You know, I don't see where any of us were like the image.

Chapter 3

PETE CONRAD
Commander, Apollo 12

Skylab's Mr. Goodwrench

The man in the white coat handed astronaut candidate Pete Conrad a blank sheet of paper.

"I want you to take a look at this and study it for a while," he instructed. "Then, describe for me what you see."

The impish Conrad couldn't resist. "It's upside down," he declared.

Pete Conrad didn't care too much for this kind of psychobabbling. Nor did he appreciate a lot of the other excesses of this psycho-physiological gauntlet he was being made to run. He was an experimental test pilot who wanted to be an astronaut, not some experimental animal—wasn't he? And, he wasn't afraid to make his dissatisfactions known either, or to hand it right back to his inquisitors. In the end, though, his little rebellions and protests might have worried the experts, maybe gave them pause. No, they finally decided, not this one. So, they sent Conrad on his way. Later on, he would learn that his white-robed judges had deemed him unfit for extended space travel. That was 1959. Then, again, it was *only* 1959. Eventually, they would need more than that first group of seven who were ultimately chosen. When that time came, he would try again.

Charles Conrad, Jr. was born into a well-to-do Philadelphia family on June 2, 1930. He acquired the nickname "Pete" from his mother who originally wanted to name him Peter. His father had been a military balloonist in World War I, and it was perhaps from him that Pete developed an early love for aviation and flying. He started building airplane cockpits in his room around the age of nine. "I would look up pictures of Lindbergh's plane, then scrounge around for things, to try to duplicate it. I'd use soap boxes, thumbtacks, and chairs . . . then sit inside for hours pretending to fly," he revealed to *Life Magazine*. He learned to fly for real when he was barely out of his teens.

Pete's early schooling was at Haverford School in Haverford, Pennsylvania, and the Darrow School in New Lebanon, New York. After Darrow, he was accepted at Princeton University where, not surprisingly, he studied aeronautical engineering. He received his Bachelor's Degree in 1953, got married, and joined the United States Navy to become a Naval Aviator. As an air cadet he won his wings and eventually trained to fly jet fighters. He then advanced to the Navy Test Pilot School at Patuxent River, Maryland. He completed training at Patuxent in 1959 and stayed on for two years as an instructor and performance engineer.

It was while he was at Patuxent that NASA started its search for astronauts for Project Mercury. "I wasn't smart enough to see the handwriting on the wall about space flight until sort of late in the game," Conrad admitted in an interview. "I can honestly say, from a pilot's point of view, I doubted if space flight would be as fulfilling to me as jockeying around in conventional aircraft." Apparently, he even told his wife he would "never be foolish enough" to try to get into the space program. Nevertheless, he ended up with the likes of Alan Shepard, John Glenn, Jim Lovell, Gordon Cooper, Wally Schirra, and about a hundred others who turned out for the competition to become America's first spacemen. He survived the tortures of the tryout and made it to the finals, but finished behind Shepard, Grissom, Glenn, Carpenter, Schirra, Cooper, and Slayton. He went back to the Navy and served as an instructor in a fighter squadron at Miramar, California, thinking there was no longer a future for him as an astronaut.

In May, 1961, Alan Shepard led the Mercury team aloft with his fifteen minute suborbital hop in Freedom 7. Two weeks later, amid political clamor at home and abroad, President Kennedy looked at his cards, upped the ante about 20 billion dollars, and bet we could put a man on the moon by the end of the decade. NASA had its marching orders and would need more recruits to fly the upcoming two-man Gemini series and, ultimately, the three-man Apollo moonship. So, the call went out again and Conrad decided to give it another shot. He made it. In September, 1962, NASA announced the selection of Conrad and eight others as their second class of astronauts.

Each astronaut, in addition to his classroom studies and regular training, was given a specialty assignment in research and development—spacesuit development, booster technology, recovery systems, and so forth. Conrad moved into the area of instrument panel design and déjà vu cockpit layout for the Gemini, Apollo, command module and lunar module vehicles.

While the new kids on the block became immersed in Gemini and Apollo, the Original Seven were flying Mercury to its conclusion. Gordon Cooper ended that era in May, 1963, with a successful day-long orbital flight in his Faith 7 capsule. Project Mercury proved we could put a man into space, that he could survive and function—for a day at least—in that hostile and weightless environment, and that we could bring him back undamaged. But, the moon was still very far away. Before Pete Conrad and his fifteen comrades could seriously think about making that giant leap, they had to work out the intermediate steps and problems of longer duration flights: rendezvous, docking, and EVA ("extra vehicular activity," or spacewalking). That was the purpose of project Gemini.

The Gemini spacecraft was big brother to the Mercury capsule. It resembled Mercury in basic shape, but had room for two men instead of one, and was designed for flight lasting up to two weeks. Additionally, it was fitted with a large equipment section behind it to carry the extra fuel, power, and oxygen needed to support the crew for extended periods, and make it possible for the pilots to maneuver the vehicle for rendezvous and docking.

The first manned Gemini flight, Gemini 3, was launched on March 23, 1965. Gus Grissom and John Young took the new machine on a three-orbit shakedown cruise and became the first crew to actually "fly" a spacecraft when they powered their ship into and out of several different orbits by firing rocket thrusters. Gemini 4 followed in June with Jim McDivitt and Ed White aboard. They stayed up for four days, and White took the first U.S. spacewalk, floating outside the cabin for twenty minutes. Next in line were Pete Conrad and Gordon Cooper, prime crew for Gemini 5.

Gemini 5 was the most ambitious spaceflight attempted up to that time. Conrad and Cooper were scheduled to remain in space for eight days—the amount of time it would take an Apollo crew to travel to and from the moon.

An important aspect of this mission was the first flight test of the latest development in high tech power generators. By judiciously mixing two parts liquid hydrogen with one part liquid oxygen in a contraption called a fuel cell, two very valuable byproducts became available: electricity and water. The nice thing about fuel cells is that they're much lighter than storage batteries, and they don't run down; they provide continuous power as long as the hydrogen and oxygen are fed into them. The third major element of the flight was to be a series of rendezvous exercises with a special radar pod that would be cast out of the equipment bay after the spacecraft reached orbit.

Conrad, Cooper, and the fuel cells were sent on their way on the morning of August 21, 1965. Once in orbit, they released the radar pod and began preparations for the chase. But, the gremlins were busy, and soon Conrad noticed a steep drop in oxygen pressure of the fuel cells. The rendezvous was abandoned as flight controllers pondered the problem. After considering termination of the flight, it was decided to keep them going for at least eighteen more orbits. On the second day, however, the fuel cells started to come back and the astronauts were able to continue the mission. During the rest of the flight they conducted some observational tests and medical experiments. But, for the most part, it was an eight-day endurance contest marked by lack of sleep and cramped discomfort in the tiny cabin. And, Pete Conrad, the guy they said was unsuited for this kind of thing, made it through just fine. "We've qualified man to go to the moon," exclaimed Dr. Charles Berry, the astronauts' chief physician.

Conrad made his second trip into space just a little over a year later, as commander of Gemini 11. The intervening flights had progressed through the principle goals set for the program; rendezvous, docking, a flight of two weeks duration, and a limited success with EVA. The last two flights would continue the refinements.

Pete Conrad and his copilot Dick Gordon lifted off from Cape Kennedy on the morning of September 12, 1966. Already circling overhead was the Agena target vehicle they hoped to catch up to on their very first orbit. This was called "direct ascent" rendezvous, an operation considered very important to future Apollo missions. All previous rendezvous in the Gemini series had been accomplished between two craft already in orbit, and took several hours to complete. This was the first time a crew would attempt to launch straight for the target and intercept it on their first pass around the Earth. Conrad and Gordon closed in on the Agena in a record seventy-eight minutes and made a successful docking. Later in the three-day mission, Gordon left the cabin on a spacewalk and attached a hundred-foot-long nylon tether from the Gemini to the Agena. Conrad subsequently docked the two ships, pulling up the slack between the Gemini and Agena, and with a burst or two from the Gemini's thrusters, started the whole dumbbell-like arrangement spinning in a slow cartwheel. The idea was to test a way of stabilizing the motion of the two spacecraft by way of centrifugal force. Theoretically, the rotation of the two vehicles connected that way would produce an artificial gravitational field, along the spinning system that would hold the two craft in steady positions at the ends of the tether. To Conrad's fascination, however, the nylon rope looped and twirled in unexpected ways, causing the two vehicles to wobble in and out of a stable configuration. The gravity field created in this experiment was very weak. Neither Conrad nor Gordon could feel its effect, but they did notice small objects in the cockpit moving toward the rear of the cabin. It was, however, the first demonstration of the feasibility of bringing gravity into the spaceman's environment, an appealing consideration for long-term interplanetary flights.

The Gemini 11 flight ended with the first "hands off," completely automated reentry to a pinpoint landing in the Atlantic. Project Gemini ended two months later with the successful four day flight of Gemini 12.

Three years later, Pete Conrad began his third space flight, this time as Commander of Apollo 12, the second lunar landing mission. On November 14, 1969, he and his crewmates Dick Gordon and Alan Bean set out for the moon, aiming for a spot in a place called the Ocean of Storms, about 800 miles west of Tranquility Base, where Armstrong and Aldrin had made the first landing four months before. The voyage literally started off with a bang. Seconds after liftoff, as the Saturn 5 pushed its way through a low rain cloud cover, a surge of lightning discharged over the rocket in a bright flash. As circuit-breakers kicked in to stave off the overload, an incredulous but poised Conrad saw the instrument panel warning indicators light up like a Fourth of July sky.

"I don't know what happened here," radioed Conrad, "we had everything in the world drop out." The rocket was intact though and kept thrusting upward. The astronauts began pushing buttons and resetting switches, bringing the capsule's electronics back to life again. "I think we need to do a little more all-weather testing," Conrad quipped. The sturdy Saturn carried them on into orbit. Confident that there was no serious damage to the spacecraft, ground controllers gave the astronauts a thumbs-up to head for the moon.

At about 10:00 PM Eastern Time, on the evening of November 17, Apollo 12 arrived on station and settled into lunar orbit. The three Navy fliers stared out the windows, surveying the ravaged surface. "It doesn't look like a very good place to pull liberty," Conrad observed. The next night Conrad and Bean undocked the lunar module "Intrepid" from the command module "Yankee Clipper", fired up its descent engine and started down to the Ocean of Storms.

Their specific target was near a crater formation dubbed "Snowman," three craters lined up next to each other giving the familiar appearance of a snowman outlined on the moon's surface. Conrad and Bean would not be the first Earthly visitors to drop in on the Snowman. Back in 1967, an unmanned American robot scout named Surveyor 3 had landed in the Snowman's belly. Conrad and Bean were hoping to land close enough to be able to walk over to the Surveyor, examine it, and take a few pieces of it back home with them.

They came in right on the money, putting Intrepid down only 600 feet from Surveyor. Making his way out the hatch and down the ladder for his first stint on the surface, the five-foot-seven Commander found the last step to the ground rather steep. "That may have been a small one for Neil, but it's a long one for me," he joked. The two men stayed on the moon for the next thirty-one hours.

Altogether Conrad and Bean spent nearly eight hours on two forays from the lunar module. They deployed a seismometer along with other instruments, collected 75 pounds of rock and soil samples, and retrieved parts from the Surveyor. On November 20th they arced back into space to rendezvous with Gordon in Yankee Clipper. When Conrad and Bean were back in the command module, Intrepid was cut loose and sent crashing down into the surface. The impact produced an artificial quake that rang the moon "like a bell" according to excited scientists who were watching the data come in from the sensors set up at the landing site. It was fascinating new information that would help determine how the moon was formed. The three astronauts then fired out of lunar orbit for the trip home. On November 24th, the flight concluded with a splashdown in the Pacific Ocean.

After Apollo 12, Pete Conrad moved into the Apollo Applications Program, which was planning the first U.S. space station called Skylab. The Skylab station was being built by cleverly converting a Saturn 5 third stage into an Earth-orbiting house and laboratory. The inside of the 45 foot long cylinder was made into work areas and living quarters called the Orbital Workshop. Attached to the front end were an airlock, a docking port, and an array of sophisticated astronomical equipment called the Apollo Telescope Mount. Radiating from the telescope package were four long solar panels, making the whole assembly look like a windmill. Completing the external features were two large wing-like solar panels, one on each side, extending from the Orbital Workshop. Skylab was big, bigger than any spacecraft put up before it or since. The Workshop itself was the size of a three bedroom house. Overall, the station measured 117 feet long, twenty-one feet in diameter (not counting the solar panels), and weighed ninety-one tons. It was designed to host three three man crews on visits of twenty-eight days, fifty-six days, and eighty-four days respectively. Crews would be sent up to the space station in Apollo command service modules launched by Saturn 1B rockets. The principle goals of Skylab were to investigate the medical effects of long term spaceflight on the human body, conduct Earth resource studies and mapping, and make astronomical observations, particularly of the sun.

Pete Conrad was tapped to command the first Skylab crew. Everything was ready to go in the spring of 1973. On May 14th, a Saturn 5 rocket, with the space station sitting on top of the second stage, thundered off the pad at the Kennedy Space Center. Conrad and his crewmates Joe Kerwin and Paul Weitz were standing by to follow Skylab up the following day. But, as the giant Saturn powered through the sky, the rush of air passing over the outer skin of the Workshop unexpectedly tore away a protective shield. As the shield peeled away, it sheared off one of the folded solar wings and immobilized the other by leaving a piece of itself jammed in a hinge. The space station made it to orbit, but was critically injured. With one solar wing gone and the other stuck in a useless closed position, normal operation of the lab was impossible. On top of that, the ripped off shield had left the Workshop vulnerable to excessive overheating that, if not taken care of in time, would ruin equipment and supplies aboard the station and render it uninhabitable.

Launch of the crew was postponed while the engineers worked out plans to save the crippled ship, if indeed that was possible. Conrad, his crew, and the ground experts took up the challenge with staunch determination. In an inspiring display of tenacity and ingenuity, the space team, working around the clock, considered all the options, made their decisions, created the hardware, and worked out the procedures. In just eleven days, Conrad, Kerwin, and Weitz were flying up to make the first repairs in space.

First, Conrad maneuvered the Apollo spacecraft into position near the jammed solar wing. The astronauts opened the hatch and Weitz leaned out to try to free the stuck panel using special tools designed for the job. Nothing worked. Undaunted, Conrad linked up to the docking port for a night's rest. In the morning, the crew entered the space station through the airlock. The heat was unbearable. They solved the problem with a neatly designed, make-shift sunshade fabricated by the ground crew. The "parasol," as they called it, was a large, thin square sheet of aluminized mylar and nylon attached to a folding framework of spring loaded telescoping aluminum spars. The astronauts pushed the folded parasol through a small airlock on the wall of the Workshop. When it was in proper position, the springs were triggered and the sheet spread out over the side of the space station. It did the trick and the temperature inside began to taper off. They had to work around the problem of the unopened solar wing for a while longer, though. Taking a spacewalk later in the mission, Conrad and Kerwin finally managed to get the wing extended, bringing the space station to full function status. Conrad and his crew went on to complete their twenty-eight day flight as planned and left Skylab in good shape for the next two missions.

Skylab I, Pete Conrad's last space flight, came to an end on June 22, 1973. Six months later he left the space program and retired from the Navy with the rank of captain. His achievements in aviation and space have brought him many honors. Among others, they include the Congressional Medal of Honor (space), two NASA Distinguished Service Medals, two Navy Distinguished Service Medals, two Distinguished Flying Crosses, the Cabot Award, the Collier Trophy, the Harmon Trophy, the FAI Gagarin Gold Space Medal, two De La Vaulx Medals, the Haley Astronautics Award, and enshrinement in the Aviation Hall of Fame. He has also received several honorary university degrees.

As a civilian, Conrad worked for two years as vice president of operations and Chief Operating Officer of American Television and Communications Corporation, a national cable-television company based in Denver. In 1976, he joined the McDonnell-Douglas Corporation, the international aerospace firm. He has held various senior executive positions at McDonnell since he has been with the company. Since October of 1986, he has served as staff vice president in the International Business Development section of the Aerospace Group.

Pete Conrad and his wife Jane have four sons. They currently live in St. Louis, Missouri.

Captain Conrad, from your point of view, as one who spent twenty-eight days on the first and only U.S. space station, what are your thoughts regarding the two Soviet cosmonauts who last year returned from over a year in space?

A long time! I mean, the most important thing is that they've had a very dedicated program. They've been building up. You know, they went 170 some days, then they went 211, and 326, and now they've gone to 365. They're obviously building the time to make a Mars mission. They're getting a lot of systems time on their Mir space station. Mir has been up since one month after the Challenger accident, so Mir has been up for more than three years. And as best as I can ascertain, Mir has performed almost flawlessly. And three years is more than enough time to go to Mars and return. I think the only thing that was missing was the heavy-lift booster, and they have flown that now, too. So they have the capability of putting almost the same payload as the Saturn 5 into low Earth orbit now—almost 200,000 pounds.

The significance of all their flying, I think, is that these guys are getting very, very close to having the capability to go manned to Mars. When they will do it, I don't know. There's no heat on them, in the sense that we are way, way behind on anything like that, so they're not racing anybody. I think they're on their way, and that's really the significance of these guys having just spent 365 days up there.

Are you a fan of the Soviet Space Program? Are you impressed with what they're doing?

Well, yes, I'm impressed with the fact that they've obviously had a dedicated program for the last fifteen or twenty years, and we're behind that way. We should have had our space station up years ago.

As you pointed out, they certainly have the capability of sustaining man in space for quite a long period of time. But do they have the technical capability to actually land them on another planet?

Oh, I don't see any reason why they can't develop that. They just brought their shuttle back in unmanned. They obviously are developing the capability to do just that. Now, going to Mars doesn't necessarily mean that they're going to land a man on Mars. There are several ways you could do a Mars mission. One of the things that you might do is put man in Mars orbit, and do the initial exploration by letting him control remote vehicles that go down and come back up. Then, of course, you could go all the way, put a man all the way down.

Do you think they might be going for a landing on the moon Phobos first, rather than the Martian surface itself?

You know, I'm not that far into it, so I really couldn't answer that. I'm not sure that would do them much good. Unless you talk of it as being a better environment for man to operate out of, then they might use that as a staging base. But, I think the ultimate objective is to get on Mars' surface.

What about our moon? Might they go to the moon before going to Mars?
No, but I really don't know. If they are, they've been awful quiet about it.

You commanded the first manned Skylab mission, and we've heard that you actually enjoyed that flight more than you did your Apollo mission to the moon. Is that really true?
Now, you have to be somewhat careful. What I've always said is, I didn't fly the first flight to the moon, and in the case of Skylab, I started to put together the first flight with that. Then, subsequently there was damage, and it changed the whole ballgame. It fell upon us to salvage it. Obviously, if we were not successful we were going to lose the vehicle, or the use of it. But, we *were* able to save it, and I've always said that, personally, that fact meant the most. The fact that we were able to salvage it, and it was able to go on and complete what it was supposed to do, in a sense, gave me greater satisfaction than what I personally accomplished in flying Apollo 12. So, the tendency, in some sense, is that you remember what you did last. So, as time goes on, if people say "space" to me, I don't think about flying to the moon, I think about flying in the Skylab. It was a tremendous vehicle. It was a great pleasure to work in that thing, and to operate it. Again, it was considerably different than flying to the moon. So, I shouldn't say that I enjoyed it more. Apollo 12 was a completely successful flight. I mean, we basically got everything done that we were supposed to get done. It was relatively routine. It didn't deviate from the plans, it unfolded exactly how that flight was supposed to. People don't understand this. People think that you went to the moon, and that's got to be the greatest thing since sliced bread. They don't quite understand when I say, 'Well, you know, I don't necessarily think about going to the moon.' Most people just can't relate to that.

It is kind of hard to believe.
I didn't feel that way about it even before I flew Skylab. I mean, to me personally, we ate, lived, slept and breathed seven days a week for years that we were going to the moon. So I didn't think about it when I did it, in quite the same way an outsider would. Again, I think that somebody who hasn't been associated with the program in that manner, who comes across somebody who's been

to the moon, they have to figure that that's absolutely got to be it. They don't understand that I don't think it's changed me particularly. Again, I'm speaking only for myself. But, I guess it depends on how the individual looks at it. As I said, it was the right place to be at the time, it was a pretty logical place to be. We had worked so hard to get there that I couldn't think about anything else but getting that job done.

Skylab was going along a nice path that way, and it got diverted, especially at the last minute. Then, the whole character of the flight changed. We were there for twenty-eight days, but for the first fourteen we didn't know whether we were going to be forced to come back, or whether we were going to make it. It wasn't until we got the solar wing out on Day 14, and got proper juice back on that we were aware that we were going to be able to save the thing. And, we did save it, and it was going to work.

Why did it take you so long, two weeks, to actually try to get the wing out?

We tried to get it out on Day 1 from the command module, by doing an EVA, and that was not successful. We learned exactly what had jammed it, how it had been damaged. We sent T.V. pictures back to the ground to show them what exactly had happened. A piece of the heat shield had actually rapped into it and it was imbedded in the solar wing. That little piece of metal was preventing the wing from deploying, and it was something that we couldn't break free doing the EVA from the command module. So, we had to give that up. The ground then worked from the TV pictures we sent back, while we were fussing around taking care of other problems. Then, after about a ten day period, they told us what it was. They figured out how to get the wing out with what we had on board once they understood what was damaging it. They put that all together in a set of procedures. They even went so far as to have Rusty Schweickart and his guys in the back-up crew go down to the water tank in Huntsville and actually mock this thing up. They went through the procedures in the water tank simulating the EVA that was required. About Day 11 or so, they sent all that information up to us. Then, we went to work on it, putting together all that we needed to get ready for the EVA. Because we were closer to the situation than they were, there were a few things that I changed in view of the fact that we could see this thing a little better than they could. On day 14 we actually went out and performed the EVA and got the thing out. Day 15 was the first time we could power up everything in the lab the way it was supposed to be running. It was the first time that we had enough juice. We had been losing electrical power as time went on; we were using the solar telescope's power to run the lab, because we had no main power source. We were actually running off something that wasn't even supposed to do that job. Even though we were being conservative and not using a lot of juice, we were taxing the thing so much that it was beginning to fail. We were beginning to lose batteries in the system. It was a question of, are we really going to get the wing out, or is the thing going to deteriorate to the point where there would just be no point in flying anymore and we would have to come home. And, that would have been the end of Skylab. So, we scouted it out and got the job done. On Day 15 we finally got to run everything, and the way we felt about it, after that, it became Day 15 forever. At last we had a nice routine system. We got back into the flight plan, and we just did what we were supposed to be doing.

Without the repair job done by your crew, then, Skylab would have been a costly failure.

That's true. The other unfortunate part about it was that by that time, the program has been so restricted that Skylab was designed not to be reusable after its three missions, and it became a dead spacecraft. That was really a shame because for the lack of a few dollars, we could've had a system that we could have resupplied. It could have served a long and useful purpose over time. But, of course, we had gotten out of the expendable launch vehicle business. The Shuttle was gonna be the save all, and it obviously wasn't. So it was very poor, very poor planning. What people ought to realize is that all that started, ironically with our biggest supporter; questions were being raised about this even before Kennedy was assassinated, but it actually was Lyndon Johnson who was the one that said, 'You boys stay on schedule and go to the moon, but all the rest of this way out stuff, you're gonna have to knock that off. It upsets the picture with the Great Society.' When Nixon came in, he was given the opportunity to look at all the work that had been done, which was not only the space station work, but more importantly, the next objective we tried to sell, which was to go to Mars. Nixon wouldn't buy it. So, that was the end of it. And we had done the work to take a look at going to Mars, and to be there even by about 1983, if I remember right.

Wasn't Spiro Agnew out in front pushing the Mars program?

He didn't last long enough. But, you know, I honestly don't remember. I just know that in '65–'66 the Apollo Applications Group was looking at space stations, a permanent space station, and Mars. Another thing that's forgotten is that by '64–'65, the capability had been paid for, and it exists down there today: a VAB with four assembly bays and two launch pads. It was all purchased to be able to launch one Saturn 5 a week. That facility was set up to handle 50 Saturn 5's a year. Everybody forgets that one. It was almost a foregone conclusion that we were going to go back to the moon on a routine basis. The talk in the Apollo Applications program was what do you do with all of the capability? What you do, we decided, was to build a permanent space station. And you go look at how to go to Mars, which was the next place to go. And, out of the clear blue sky, President Reagan finally says, going into his second-term election, that we ought to have a permanent presence in space. Then he commissions his group to look at the next fifty years and what we're going to do in space, or ought to do. The group publishes this report two months after the Challenger blows up and it says we ought to go back to the moon and have a permanent base, we ought to have a permanent space station and we ought to go to Mars. I said, 'Now, I've heard that somewhere before.' So, when you talk to me about it, I'll tell you right now, we're twenty-five years behind where we should be.

What do you see now as the most important or crucial issue facing the American space program at this juncture?
That President Bush make it a national objective to continue good, funded work in space to carry out those objectives.

Do you think that's a politically viable plan?
I think, if presented correctly, it's politically viable.

Is the President really the only one that can get program going again, like it was in the sixties?
He's got to set the policy. And we have not had a president set any policy worth a shit since Kennedy said we ought to go to the moon, we really haven't.

What kind of things could NASA be doing to popularize and promote a solid space effort in this country these days?
Well, they have to have a president that allows the administrator to speak out. The administrator can only say what is the President's policy. When they put Fletcher in, for example, the first time around, he was a station keeper. Nixon didn't want to be bothered with the thing, but he couldn't bad-mouth the program. It was a little bit like being against motherhood. You know, don't make any waves. That's exactly the way Fletcher operated. Then Frosch was

in there, I think it was Frosch. He was at Woods Hole, under water, and somebody must have told him, don't make any waves, and he didn't. You can go through the time period of 1969 through the Shuttle's first flight in 1981, three years late. If you look at the budget fight to get the Shuttle going, the guys that manned the Shuttle program ought to be given the world's biggest handshake for getting done what they got done, considering the support, the budget, and everything else with which they had to do it. They had a terrible time. You know, I'm surprised it didn't blow up before. If you really read the accident report, and I think they told us very well there what happened, you see the results of the ten years or twelve years or so of just terrible budget fighting, and what the hell it did to the internal organization at NASA. A lot of jealousies and rivalries came up because people were fighting for what they believed in. It was Marshall against JSC instead of the united team.

Do you believe it might take some kind of Soviet space spectacular, like Sputnik back in the '50s, to get the ball rolling right again?
The way things are going today, if the Soviets are going to do the spectacular, I don't see how you can catch them, to be truthful with you.

30 years ago you just missed becoming one of the first astronauts. What was it like being a member of the second group of pilots following the celebrated Original Seven? Did you find it tough or were those first seven helpful and forthcoming?
Reasonably so. Things were moving so that I hardly remember the first days. We got plugged into Apollo pretty quickly, engineering-wise. That lasted about a year, plus we had a lot of general training laid out that they wanted to put on us; jungle survival, desert survival, reviewing geology. We had these Apollo classes and whatever, and then Bango! You're in a flight crew in Gemini and from that point on, I was always on a flight crew. I was either backing somebody up or flying the flight, and our time went pretty fast. Also, we were only there a year, then we had fourteen more guys. Then in another year, we got the scientists next. We got more guys and, after a while, there were about sixty-five people wandering around there. Everybody had something to do, and things were moving.

You were antagonistic toward the doctors, at least early on. In fact, they even said that you weren't qualified because you wouldn't be able to stay in space for very long. Do you feel any

Pete Conrad

satisfaction or vindication that your instincts were right, that they were a little concerned about things that maybe weren't all that important?

I think you're getting two different schools. As for the regular doctors, I didn't like needles. Early on, the doctors that I didn't get along with were the shrinks. They were noticeable by their absence after their first year in the program. I think NASA concluded that they didn't do anything for them either. It was Project Mercury where the shrinks were involved, namely a couple of Air Force guys, who, it's always been my opinion, were two complete assholes. I've never laid eyes on these two guys since 1959, or whenever it was. Now the medical guys, other than the fact that I don't like needles—and I'm not the only one in the office who didn't like needles—they were good, they did darned good work on Skylab—all the food work that we did with them, the bicycle ergometer, and all the metabolic stuff. I think they were good guys who were really trying to understand what was going on up there.

What were the psychiatrists supposed to be doing?

Beats the hell out of me. I don't think the psychiatrists knew. As a matter of fact, back in those days I don't think the medical doctors knew either. That was part of the problem. I was a very curious person, so I would say, 'Why are you doing this to me—needles in my hand and reading oscilloscopes, or sticking my feet in a bucket of ice water? What did that have to do with flying in space?' And they would look at me like I was a dumb shit and say, 'You don't need to know that.' When they couldn't answer the question, my conclusion was they didn't know what they were doing. So, I took that approach with them, especially the head shrinkers. They obviously didn't appreciate that.

You provided Tom Wolfe with a lot of material about that time for The Right Stuff. *Can you tell us about that?*

Tom Wolfe was an amazing guy. During the time I spent with him, the man never took a note, didn't have a tape recorder, and did not miss a stroke. From what I know of his book, not only from my part, but other places I have personal knowledge, the guy hasn't missed a stroke. I think he did a fantastic job. It was great.

How about the movie version? Did you like the way it was brought to the screen?

It should never have been released. It was terrible. In the first place they made NASA people look like a bunch of jerks and that was completely untrue. And, certainly, Tom Wolfe never portrayed those people that way. If you didn't know the history, you would have the idea that Chuck Yeager was flying the X-1 at the same time they were getting ready to fly the Mercury, and they were fifteen years apart. They had the history all jammed together and I thought gave an erroneous impression of the sequencing of things. Technically, there were errors. The sky doesn't change color when you go supersonic. Chuck Yeager certainly couldn't have sat on his horse next to the X-1 with the rocket engines running. He would have been blown into downtown L.A. So, you know, it was bad. A bad movie.

Your first flight was Gemini 5, eight days in space. You weren't able to do much up there, were you? Because of equipment problems, you just drifted along for about eight days.
Yes. We really were in a garbage can and that was it. I could hardly move. I mean, I'm not that big and I couldn't even stretch out full-length in it. Physically, it got painful after a while. Your knees began to get sore. If you don't move your joints, they get sore. I particularly remember my knees bothering me. If you don't get any exercise, then you don't want to sleep. So, we were sleeping only a couple of hours at a crack, and, yes, it was long. It was a long eight days.

How did you keep from getting too antsy, especially with a partner like Gordon Cooper who was so quiet?
It wasn't a big deal. But what are you going to do? There's no place to go. You can't go out, so, you watch the clock.

You once remarked that you'd doubted that space flight would be as fulfilling as flying jet airplanes. What made you finally decide to try and become an astronaut? What made space flight fulfilling compared to flying a plane?
I don't know whether I remember that well. But, Mercury was no biggy as far as flying skills went. Probably from a flying point of view, Gemini 11 was really it. We did rendezvous in one orbit, and that was all manual. We figured it on board; the computers on the ground couldn't keep up fast enough in those days. We hand-flew the machine. I hand-flew the machine all the way through one orbit, through rendezvous and docking and all that sort of stuff. So, that was a great pilot's flight. But after that, it got back to button-pushing. I wound up getting thirty-five, forty seconds, maybe one minute of stick time landing on the moon, and the rest of it was all button-pushing. Of course, there wasn't any flying at all on Skylab. But Skylab was a different field. We weren't really flying. It was

Pete Conrad

getting satisfaction in the other things we did that were not related to flying, like operating the solar telescopes and Earth resources experiments in Skylab or running around on the lunar surface on Apollo or whatever all we did that was completely unrelated to flying. If you actually take Skylab, we were out of our field, but we were doing things that were interesting. You really didn't need to be a pilot to go ride around in Skylab.

This might sound like an obvious question but sometimes you get a surprising answer. Was landing the lunar module the most challenging piece of flying that ever came your way?

Oh, no. Nothing will ever beat landing on a boat at a night. Oh yeah, night carrier operations, night carrier landings—that separates the men from the boys.

You commented, though, after the flight, on the difficulty in bringing the LM in, that it took all the skills you had to make the landing.

Well, I think the worst thing that an aviator can find himself doing is flying halfway between VFR and IFR. I also made the comment that I thought one of the gauges that I had available to me was not working. However, it turns out that the gauge was working fine, and out the window I had, in fact, killed off all the horizontal and lateral velocity, and when I got down to where I wanted to go completely on the gauges, I was satisfied that I had a good landing site from the look that I had at a higher altitude. And, I should have believed my own eyes, I guess, but you don't like to do that, and I felt that the gauge was not at that time giving me the proper information. So, I was continually going out the window to get roll information and a general idea of my lateral and horizontal velocities, and back into the cockpit to set the attitude for landing. It's very bad to land the LM rear skid down and moving forward. That's the most unstable condition. I wanted to make sure that I didn't get that, and, in fact, the landing was a completely normal landing. The remark I made was pointed at the fact that I'd been doing this for twenty years, and one learns to use everything that they have available to them through their experiences. You have to believe your equipment. I had complete faith in the intertial measuring unit, and the information that was being given to me by Al Bean, mainly, reading out altitude and descent rates, and I feel that there is no problem whatsoever as long as you have a good assessment of the landing site before you land on it. They tell me the targeting was 300 feet left of the crater, and I'll bet if I hadn't touched anything, it would have landed us right on top of the

Surveyor. That was my impression all the way down. The only reason I landed as close to the Surveyor crater as I did is I made a very steep approach in the landing site, and I thought I was a little bit further forward. However, had we landed on the wall of the crater, it would have been all right. The spacecraft is designed to land up to 15 degree inclinations, and we had nothing that was exceeding that anywhere in the area.

You did quite a bit of work in the development of the lunar module. As a test pilot, did its performance meet all your expectations when you finally had the chance to fly it?

Sure. The only objection that I remember—and I always thought it was a poor decision—was that the LM was originally at some point, going to carry fuel cells so that it would have up to a seven-day stay time, if I remember correctly.

Somewhere early on in the program they decided, for whatever reason, not to go with the fuel cells. They decided to stick with batteries. I don't really remember whether we were advised of or told these things, or what it was. But, by sticking with batteries there was no way you could spend longer than three days on the moon. That was my objection. That to me was a big, big, change, because seven days sounded like that's where we ought to be headed at the time. You really could explore further, and so forth. As I remember, we were not only going to have a lunar rover, eventually we were going to have lunar flyers. If I remember the original deal, Apollo 17 and 18 were the ones that were going to have rovers because they didn't think they could move quite as fast as they needed to. On 19 and 20 we were gonna have these lunar flyers, and I forget, but I think the lunar flyer was supposed to have about a 140 to 160 kilometer radius. So, you could add 80 to 100 miles, whatever it was, to the range from the LM. it was a vast disappointment to me when we saw that whole program folding up. They started whacking at it just before we landed, I think.

So, when they made the decision not to go with the fuel cells, that changed a lot of things. Batteries weighed a hell of a lot more, so we wouldn't have been able to carry a lunar flyer. The fuel cells were much lighter, and you could have a much bigger payload capability in the landing mode. You could have things like lunar flyers and you could have the extra oxygen and consumables that you needed. The fuel cells were a key element to what capability the LM was going to have eventually, which was more than just a seven day stay time. It was really a shame when all of that was given up.

Pete Conrad

When you arrived on orbit at the moon, you said it didn't look like a very good place to pull liberty. Did your impressions change when you reached the surface? Did you find it to be enjoyable?

Yes, it's a great place. We were in the right place; the Surveyor was there and it was obvious that we would then get everything done that we were supposed to do. So, it was sorta like even before you start, you feel it was done already. That's just the way I felt.

What are your most lasting impression about the surface of the moon?

Oh, I guess its starkness. It's a stark place of really great beauty. And I'm afraid that maybe before the flight I had schooled myself into feeling that I was going to be very lonely and very way out and very remote. And, gee, it was completely the other way around. I enjoyed the lunar surface activities not just for the fun of bouncing around but the real work we could do up there. I didn't know which way I was going to feel when I came back, but I'd go back tomorrow if I had the chance.

Do you see the United States returning to the moon anytime soon to establish a base?

Only if the President decides to develop the spacecraft. Actually, I guess Reagan has done that. I think the funding is there to continue the preliminary look at lunar basing.

Part of the business of being an astronaut includes your family. They have to support you and be behind you. What did you tell your four sons about your missions and why it was important that you were flying space?

I don't ever remember really doing that, specifically. I know we talked about it, but it just sort of evolved as things went on. I would find out I was going to fly Gemini 5, and I'd come back and I'd say that's what was going to happen and this is what we were going to do.

Were they excited, as young boys get, or were they anxious about it?

No, I don't think so. In the first place, they weren't the only act in town, 'cause there were a lot of astronauts around that had children in school at that time. Most of the other children's parents worked at NASA or related businesses. From that point of view, it was fine. Yes, there was a lot of hooplah when the flights came, and you had to get your feet screwed back down to the ground after the flight was over. But, also, fame is but fleeting, and as soon as the next flight went up, why your receded into the background again. I think they recognized that also. If anything, maybe we just tried to make like it was nice and routine and not any different from something else, not a big deal. I don't ever remember having any specific talks with them.

Was the life of an astronaut in the 60's and the early 70's overly stressful on family life?
I don't know; we spent a lot of time away from home. But, then, being in the Navy, I'd spent a lot of time away from home before. It was a little bit different in the way of spending time away from home. At NASA, we were coming and going all the time, while in the Navy, you went off on a cruise and you'd be gone for six to eight months. You'd come back, and you were home for six to eight months. Then, you'd go again. But, I don't know. I didn't really think about it.

Pete, you've made four trips into space—two Gemini flights, a moon landing mission, and you led the first crew up to the Skylab space station. You're one of the most experienced space travelers in the world. How has that experience affected, or changed your life, if it has at all?
It hasn't. I mean, my only problem was that it had to end. It was very sad during the last two years that I actually spent in NASA watching this thing continue to crumble. You know, from about 1969 on it was very obvious that NASA was going to recede. It was very sad to sit there and see that happen. I mean, I would have loved to have been able to stay and keep flying. But, by 1973, I can remember telling George Low and James Fletcher that I couldn't sit around and wait seven years for a ride. They were scheduled to fly the Shuttle in '78, and they weren't going to fly until at least 1980. I can remember George Low saying, 'Stick around and fly. We'll all have a beer over this in 1978.' And I said, 'George, there's no way that's going to happen.' And I was wrong by a year. The shuttle didn't fly until 1981.

No regrets, then, in leaving?
No. I would have had a very tough time staying there, living under the damn ground rules by which those guys had to build the Shuttle.

How do you like your career in the business world?

I enjoy it. I still have fun playing with the toys. They haven't completely shut me out of the cockpit. And McDonnell has always stood out as one of the finer guys I ever worked with, all the way back to when I was in the government, both NASA and the Navy. I've been here about thirteen years now and I really enjoy it. I work across all our aerospace companies, so I don't get bored. I've got my finger in all the pies, from fighters to transports to spacecraft to missiles, and helicopters.

Does McDonnell-Douglas have some exciting things on the drawing board?
Yes, I think so. We're heavily involved in the National Aerospace Plane and we've got the chunk of the contract we wanted for the space station. We're working that very hard now.

Would they ever let you test fly the aerospace plane? Give you a shot in the cockpit of that thing?
I doubt it. I'll be too old by that time. It'll be another four to five years before they'll be able to fly that thing.

You were the only Ivy-leaguer among the Astronaut Corps. Very few of the pilots came from the Northeast, in fact. Most of them came from the South and Midwest. Any idea why that was? Did you notice any sort of cultural bias in their favor?
Nope. I used to have to get Ed White squared away on the kind of shoes to wear, though.

What do you mean?
He used to tease me about tassled loafers. One day, we were going to a reception to meet Jimmy Stewart. I had my tassled loafers on and Ed was telling me I was wearing my fruit shoes. I was telling him he was uneducated, having gone to West Point. Jimmy Stewart was a brigadier general in the Air Force reserve in those days, but he'd also gone to Princeton. Ed walked in the door in front of me, in his normal West Point attitude of being in a full brace. And, I looked down and Jimmy had on the same shoes I did. I said, 'I beg your pardon, General Stewart, but I just wanted to point out to Captain White here that you and I have on the same shoes. And, he was telling me that these shoes were fruity.' So, Ed almost had apoplexy. Jimmy Stewart looks at Ed and says, 'Ed, there's an old saying that says you can take the boy out of Princeton, but you can't take the Princeton out of the boy.' And Ed stiffens and says, 'Yes, Sir!' I told Ed after that, I'd always help him get a pair of shoes anytime he needed them.

Chapter 4

___

ED MITCHELL
Lunar Module Pilot, Apollo 14

A Deep Encounter with the Cosmos

Edgar Mitchell is a soft-spoken, transplanted Texan whose smooth, confident voice carries pleasant traces of the inflection that place his roots in the southwest. On meeting him, one soon realizes that, behind the quiet manner, there is a purposeful and passionate intellect devoted to exploring and understanding the world around him.

Edgar Dean Mitchell was born on September 17, 1930, in Hereford, Texas, a small town in the panhandle not too far from the New Mexico border. When he was five his family relocated to eastern New Mexico. Since then, he has considered Artesia, New Mexico his home town. His father was a rancher and businessman, and Ed grew to become an accomplished farmhand and cowboy.

Young Ed Mitchell went to grade school in Roswell, New Mexico, and later graduated from Artesia High School. That fall, he entered the Carnegie Institute of Technology, where he earned a Bachelor of Science degree in 1952. Soon after college, he joined the U.S. Navy to become a Naval Aviator. Following basic training, he went through Officer Candidate School in Newport, Rhode Island, and received his commission in May, 1953. Now Ensign Mitchell, he was sent to Kansas for flight training. He won his wings in July, 1954, and was then assigned to a patrol squadron based in Okinawa. He enjoyed flying in the military and, when his first hitch was up, he made the decision to stay in the Navy.

He was soon flying jets, and qualified for carrier operations. From 1957 to 1958, he flew A3 attack fighters off of the USS Bon Homme Richard and the USS Ticonderoga.

It was during that time—October 4, 1957—that a new world opened up for Edgar Mitchell. On that day, from the plains of Soviet central Asia, Sputnik I was rocketed into space, its eerie radio signal heralding the dawn of the Space Age. It was inevitable that men would soon be following their machines into space, and that's where Ed Mitchell wanted to go. To get there, he reasoned, he would need more education and more advanced flying experience.

He joined a Naval air development unit and gained practical test pilot experience as a research project pilot. On the academic side, he completed a degree in aeronautical engineering at the Navy's Post Graduate School, and continued his studies at MIT, where he earned a doctorate in aeronautics & astronautics in 1964.

His formal schooling finished, he was sent by the Navy to be chief of project management for their part in the Manned Orbital Laboratory which, at that juncture, was a separate military manned space program headed up by the Air Force. About a year later, he became a student-instructor at the Edwards Air Force Base test pilot school in California. While finishing out at Edwards, he applied to become an astronaut. In April, 1966, he was accepted, along with eighteen others, as a member of NASA's fifth astronaut group. They jokingly called themselves the "Original Nineteen", and Ed Mitchell became their unofficial leader.

His first mission duties as an Apollo astronaut were as a support crew member for Apollo 9, the Earth orbit test flight of the lunar module. He was then named to the backup crew for Apollo 10. That assignment, according to tradition, would have put him in line to be on the prime crew of the ill-fated Apollo 13. But, luck was smiling on Ed Mitchell.

Alan Shepard had become the new commander of Apollo 13, replacing Gordon Cooper. Shepard felt he needed more time to prepare for the flight, and suggested that his crew swap missions with the crew of Apollo 14. Everyone was agreeable, and the switch was made. That friendly accommodation cost Jim Lovell and his crew a lunar landing, not to mention having to endure a hair-raising three day flight around the moon and back in an almost fatally damaged spacecraft. It made it possible for Ed Mitchell to be the sixth man to walk on the moon.

On the afternoon of January 31, 1971, Apollo 14, carrying Alan Shepard, Stuart Roosa, and Mitchell was rocketed safely into space.

The departure was delayed forty minutes because of heavy cloud cover. Four days after liftoff, Mitchell and Shepard would be on the moon, successfully landing their lunar module "Antares" in the vicinity of Cone Crater, a thousand-foot-wide hole dug out by a meteor in an area near the moon's equator called the Fra Mauro formation. Their plan was to hike to the crater and bring back specimens of ancient bedrock blasted to the surface by the meteor that formed the crater.

After a little more than thirty-four hours on the moon, nine hours of which was spent by the astronauts on the surface setting up scientific equipment and collecting close to ninety-five pounds of rock samples, Mitchell and Shepard blasted back up to lunar orbit to meet up with Stu Roosa in the command module "Kitty Hawk". The flight ended with splashdown in the Pacific Ocean on February 9th. Afterward, Mitchell revealed that he had conducted a private series of ESP experiments during the flight, attempting to sent telepathic images back to receiving subjects on Earth.

Apollo 14 was Ed Mitchell's first, and only spaceflight. His last mission assignment was as backup crew member for Apollo 16. In October, 1972, he left NASA and at the same time retired from the Navy with the rank of Captain. After twenty years of dedicated military service, Ed Mitchell was a civilian again.

With his military and astronaut career behind him, he founded the Institute of Noetic Sciences, a private research and educational foundation located near San Francisco. Noetics is the study of mind and consciousness, a subject of deep interest to Mitchell over the years. To quote Ed Mitchell, "We must come to study and know ourselves, our motivations, and our exceptional capacity to become what we dream we can become."

With the Institute solidly established, Mitchell moved on to continue independently his own pursuits as scholar, writer, and lecturer. He travels widely as a speaker, giving a hundred or more presentations a year on such subjects as high technology, military defense, motivational and human resources, management reorganization, and his experiences as an astronaut. He is currently at work on a new book tentatively titled *When the Foxes are Guarding the Henhouse,* a strong opposing view of SDI.

Ed Mitchell's extraordinary and distinguished career has brought him many honors and accolades, among them the Presidential Medal of Freedom, the U.S. Navy Distinguished Service Medal, NASA's Distinguished Service Award, and several honorary degrees.

Ed Mitchell is the father of two daughters. Married twice, and now a bachelor, he currently resides in southern Florida.

Mr. Mitchell, what are you engaged in at present?
Currently, I'm writing and lecturing.

Are you still involved with psychic research?
Not so much anymore. I got the answers I wanted out of that and we've done exciting things with it. We know enough now to move on. The Institute is doing exceptionally well. It's a very prestigious, well-funded institute, international in scope, trying to apply some of the knowledge that we learned in the first ten years to global issues, to global thinking. It's quite respected and does fine work. But, they're not really doing many of the things I want to do. They're more concerned with applications, and I'm still concerned with new knowledge—pure research and the fundamental questions that neither science nor religion have ever satisfactorily answered: How do we human beings process information? How do we get to be like we are? How do our belief systems come about? What role do they have? How does that relate to the way the universe is put together?

You came to those interests as a result of your trip to the moon, didn't you?
It pulled the trigger on a life shift, a change in direction for me. But, I've always been philosophic, I've always been one of those questioning people. And, I always have to know how things are put together. All of my life I've been trying to balance the knowledge I learned through my science and the knowledge I learned from my fundamentalist religious background—and they never matched up. So, I've always been trying to understand that gap. It takes you into the realms of philosophy, world religions, psychic research, psychology, biology, and certainly, cosmology— that is, how it all began, where we came from and how we got here. That's the crucial issue.

You mentioned you had a fundamentalist religious background? Were both your parents very religious?
My mother was very traditionally religious. My father was a spiritual man. He was close to nature. He was close to his animals— a rancher, farmer, and a cattleman. They were fairly prosperous. They battled their way back out of the Depression.

How did you develop such a profound interest in science?

Oh, I don't know. It's one of those things that comes from deep inside you where you just want to know. I was one of those curious people. My feeling has always been to know how things work. That steered me into math, science, and engineering.

Did you tinker around with the machinery on the farm?
Oh yeah, I was always repairing something. We had a farm machinery dealership as one of our businesses and my job was setting up new machinery and repairing old machinery. I wouldn't say I was a motor mechanic, but I was always tearing things apart and putting them back together for profit. And all the new machinery that came in from the factory I set up and delivered. So, as a kid, I was doing all sorts of things.

Do you have brothers and sisters?
My sister is three years younger, my brother six years younger. So, I was the oldest one in my immediate family. I also have an older half-brother. Back then I was driving a tractor and doing a full day's work during the summer and on Saturdays when I was eight or nine years old. I was essentially a foreman on the ranch by the time I was thirteen or fourteen.

When did your attention turn to airplanes and flying?
That was during the Second World War at what is now Walker Air Force Base in Roswell, New Mexico. The training pattern was right over one of our farms. So I became fascinated with aviation—building models and everything. I started flying at the age of thirteen. I soloed at fourteen, then had to wait two years to get my pilot's license.

How did you get the flying time as a thirteen-year-old?
I went out and scrubbed airplanes. The local base operator gave me thirty minutes of flying time for each airplane I washed. So, I earned my way through.

After high school, you left New Mexico to attend college in the East—in Pittsburgh, wasn't it?
Yes, at the Carnegie Institute of Technology—now Carnegie-Mellon University—in Pittsburgh. I started out in electrical engineering and switched to industrial management in the process because it seemed like a broader scope for me. I really didn't think being an engineer and confining my interest that narrowly was really what I wanted to do. Management was really where I wanted to go. And, frankly, it was an economic decision, too. My grandfather

had a heart attack in 1951, so I worked through the summer and graduated in three-and-a-half years to go back to the farm to help out. That was during the Korean War, so I enlisted in the Navy in the fall of '52. I went to boot camp and through officers training, and then into flight training.

Why did you choose the Navy over the Air Force?
I had an affinity—I've always wanted to be near the water. I wanted to be a Navy guy instead of an Air Force guy. And everything just fell into place for me.

Was your desire to be near the water just because you were so far away from it in Texas and New Mexico?
Well, I think I was tired of that dry, arid climate. I wanted to get where there was a little water—tired of the dust storms.

What is it they call them down there—Northers?
Northers. Comin' into the Texas panhandle area.

At that time, had you decided to make a career out of flying and the military?
I didn't really decide to do that until I started getting interesting duty tours. I found out that I really liked the flying. I was promoted early, so when it came time at the end of my four years to go regular Navy or get out, I elected to stay. And once I had done the first tour, I had the opportunity to switch to jets. I was in the first squadron of heavy attack jet aircraft, did carrier qualifications, did two tours in the Pacific, and then came back and worked in a test squadron. Went back to school and earned my doctorate, then was selected for the space program. So, my actual Navy career was about seven years long. From then on it got to be pretty exciting.

When did you first understand, or get an inkling, that you might have a future in spaceflight, or that it might be open to you?
When Sputnik went up. I was at China Lake Test Facility in California in 1957, and I said, 'That's for me. That's where I'm going.'

You knew right then that men would be flying into space soon?

Yes. So that's where I started pointing my career. I was too young for the first group of astronauts and didn't have enough jet time because I had started out in prop aircraft.

And, at that time they wanted only test pilots, right?
Well, I was already a research and development pilot at that point, so I had practical test pilot experience, but I hadn't been through either of the schools. But I decided that I probably needed to get my advanced degrees first. I thought that would be important in the long run of things. So, I went back to post-graduate school at MIT to get my doctorate.

It was in celestial navigation, wasn't it?
That was my thesis. And then I thought I was going to NASA, but, en route, was sent to Los Angeles, to the Space Systems Division as Technical Director for the Navy office there. The military was trying to get its space program together.

Was that the Manned Orbital Laboratory project?
Yeah, that was part of the program, too.

Were you actively involved in that part of it?
I was involved in designing the spacecraft. I was the chief of the Navy technical side of that, and in charge of the technical liaison with the Air Force's Space Systems Division on the design of the MOL.

That was ostensibly an Air Force project, wasn't it?
It was *led* by the Air Force, but it was a multi-service project.

Were you disappointed when they decided not to go with that program, or did you realize as you were going along that it would have problems?
I was already at Edwards Air Force Base when they ended it. I had gone to MOL under protest, really. So, I stayed there for a year, did my job, and then talked my boss into letting me go to Edwards. I applied for Edwards and made it as an exchange student. But, because of my doctorate I was kind of a special student there. I was teaching the MOL candidates in academic work while going through the test pilot school.

Did you feel that the MOL program should have been cancelled, or did you feel that the program should have been continued?

No, I'm glad it was cancelled. The Air Force has been trying to get control of the space program since those days. One of my great distresses these days is that they have succeeded. NASA is effectively an appendage of the military this point. It's a *disaster* for NASA. It's a disaster for the country and the world, I think.

You think the secretary of the Air Force has more influence right now than the NASA administrator?

Of course he does, certainly. NASA is in total disarray. They'll never get their act together staying under the thumb of the Air Force. And space is not going to be dealt with correctly as long as it's viewed as a military preserve.

Let's talk about the Space Shuttle for a moment. Do you think that program has fallen short?

It's fallen short of its potential. We clearly needed something like the shuttle. We shouldn't have placed all of our eggs in one basket, though. On the other hand, the public was not in the mood to let us fund the longer-range programs that were necessary. Part of that was NASA's fault. We never had an administrator that could even come close to what Jim Webb could do. He was the dynamo that made it all happen. A combination of Jim Webb and convincing the administration to put national emphasis on going to the moon really gave us the go.

And having Lyndon Johnson in your corner wasn't bad either, was it?

No, it wasn't, especially since so much of it was in his home state. But, I see NASA's current problem as illustrated by the problem of any maturing organization. NASA and space exploration, by definition, is a high-risk proposition. It must be a highly innovative and creative program. Bureaucracies do not do that well, and the more bureaucratic NASA has become over the years, the less innovative and creative it could be. Success, like NASA had in the early years, brings complacency. Any organization's growth curve is normally going to be an S curve. You start out and go great, and then you level off. And if you're not careful, particularly in a program like this, you fall on your ass. And that's what happened. Complacency set in; we made it look too easy. Everybody got cocksure and knew they knew what they were doing. They didn't listen to the guys down in the trenches sounding the alarm.

How much of a problem was that as an astronaut?

Always a problem. The only way we really got things done was because the astronauts really had clout in those days. We said, 'Look at this or we don't go.'

There was mutual support among the group, then. You weren't going to have your throats cut just to make a flight.
Well, we cut throats among ourselves. But, as far as the contractors and the system was concerned, we stuck together. If we didn't like something, we could raise a lot of hell and get a lot done. I especially give the early guys credit for that.

The Mercury astronauts, you mean?
Yeah. Otherwise, we'd have just been going along for the ride with a few buttons to push here and there. They made it into an operator-oriented piece of machinery by saying, 'It's gotta be that way, fellas, or forget it.'

Didn't that become important anyway, especially in the wake of the problems Gordon Cooper had with the automatic controls during the last Mercury flight?
It's always been important because of the human judgment factor. You just can't design a machine that is going to take care of all the contingencies. And the human ability to make judgments and decisions, and to take corrective action, to think, has got to be in these machines if you're going to have a broad scope mission. Now, if you're going to design a single purpose mission, you can be using unmanned satellites. The early probes of a planet *should* be unmanned. They are single-purpose; they go collect a few data samples along certain lines to be precursors for later investigation. And if they fail, okay, they fail. They are not that expensive compared with a manned flight. So, you send them up and you do the right things with them. Unmanned probes are entirely appropriate. But, if you are going to send men up there then use them to their best ability. And their best ability is judgment, decision making, and encountering contingencies.

What about the ultimate contingency? Did NASA discuss with the crews what should be done in the event of an unresolvable life-threatening failure?
We discussed it among ourselves.

Did you ever come to any firm conclusions?
We were going to make it.

If not, was there a mutual decision to . . . ?
No, that was a private decision.

There were stories that NASA supplied the crews with suicide pills.
No, not true.

It had to have crossed their minds, didn't it?
We had enough emergency and backup procedures that we were pretty sure what we were gonna do. No, we were unending optimists.

You ran into some hairy moments on your flight, Apollo 14. During the landing approach, your radar went out for a time. Were you worried that ground control might abort the landing? How close a call was that?
We were ready to pull our earplugs if necessary.

You were ready to go down no matter what?
We were going down. Everything was right on. We would have gone to the point of pitchover and looked when we were supposed to have aborted automatically. But we didn't plan to abort without looking.

Did you and Alan Shepard talk to each other at this point and agree that, 'Look, we're this close, we're going down. No matter what. We haven't come this far to turn tail and go home'?
No, but it was understood.

So, the crew had to override the abort, correct? Otherwise it would have been automatic.
No, it would not have been automatic. It was a ground rule automatic abort, but it was not a mechanical automatic. Furthermore, we had disabled the abort switch. We had disabled the computer abort because of the prior problem in the abort switch logic which happened on the previous orbit. It would have had to have been a manual abort under any circumstances.

At another point, earlier in the flight, you had trouble hooking up the command module to the lunar module, a very important maneuver since the two craft had to be coupled together to proceed with the missions as planned. What went through your mind when Stu Roosa, the command module pilot, wasn't able to do it after several tries?

Well, I don't think I ever really doubted we'd solve the problem. Stu's main concern and ours, too was that we were using up a lot of precious fuel during that period.

The last time he tried it he apparently rammed it pretty hard, didn't he?
Yeah, it was a pretty good bump.

Were you afraid that you might damage either of the vehicles?
No, that was our plan, that's what we agreed to do. We were going to hit it pretty hard to see if we could jar the coupling mechanism into the right position.

Well, everything worked out fine; you made a safe landing, and set out exploring the Fra Mauro region on the moon. One of the main objectives of your stay there was to hike to a place called Cone crater where you hoped to gather some important rock samples. Unfortunately, you and Shepard didn't quite make it to the crater. "Missed it by that much," as Don Adams would say. You must have been terribly disappointed.
Yes, very disappointed.

Did it bother you to come so close and not quite make it?
Well, it's just ego. Of course, as you know, we *were* at the rim of Cone Crater.

As near as forty feet, wasn't it?
Somewhere like that. I mean, if we had thrown a rock we could have thrown it over the edge. The problem was those undulating dunes, so deceptive as to where you were. That was the most deceiving part of the whole thing. Everything looked the same.

Kind of like lunar "snowblindness"?
Kind of. Very similar. Or like being in the middle of the Sahara desert. Every damned sand dune looks like the next one.

Weren't there benchmarks—surface features you could use to orient yourself?
Well, we thought there were. From a plan view you can see the benchmarks, but when you get down on the surface you recognize that they're in the undulating dunes and you can't see *over* the next one. What you're look for might be two dunes over, right in the bottom of that trench. But you can't see it from where you

are. You've got to be on top of it to see it—and then sometimes you can't even when you get there. Unless it's very distinctive, you look out to see corroborating landmarks around you, but they're hidden. So, you're really only looking at one landmark at a time. There's really no way to get a panorama. And you orient yourself by kind of triangulating, you can say, 'Okay, I can see this crater over here, I know that one, I can see that rock over there, I know that one, okay, here's where we are,' but you can never be absolutely sure. Because of the undulation your vision was always cut off. You could never see more than one subtle landmark at a time.

Was that something completely unexpected?

Yep, we weren't prepared for that. We thought it would be a lot flatter. And these dunes only had to be about three feet high. They weren't humongous, they weren't head high. But it was enough to cut your vision.

Were they piles of sand or actually small hills?

No—that whole area has been pulverized by meteors—billions of them bombarding the surface reducing it to rubble. So the "duning" effect is really from meteor strikes forming ridges of impact rubble and leaving it as a rough surface.

It was very dusty, too, wasn't it? All the astronauts found that to be a real nuisance.

You couldn't help it. All you had to do was walk in that stuff and it just globbed onto you. It wasn't coming loose, it just clung to you.

It was surprising to learn that the moon rocks, some of them, anyway actually smell bad. Michael Collins recalled the foul smell as they transferred the rock boxes from the lunar module to the command module on Apollo 11. He said they smelled like rotten eggs.

Could be. Yeah, now that you mention it, I guess that's right. I didn't recall that. It wasn't a big issue on our flight. I think I thought that at the time, that after pure oxygen, anything could smell bad. The rotten egg smell, well, that would be sulfur. But that would depend upon the type of rocks you were picking up, too. Ours were markedly different from anything else.

Cone Crater might have yielded some very interesting specimens. Now, during your attempt to reach Cone, did you and

Shepard argue with Mission Control to let you keep going a bit longer?

Oh, yeah, there was quite an argument. I argued with Shepard on that, too. He wanted to turn back earlier.

Was that because of fatigue, or just the fact that he didn't think you were going to find it?

Well, he felt it was going to take us longer to get there than we had time for, and I thought he was off on his navigation. I thought we were further up the hill, and further around than he thought. He thought the rim was northeast and I was pretty sure it was straight up the hill to the north. Where we stopped, and where we were to take samples—hell, if I had walked over from here to the edge of this room, I'd have been looking right down on the edge of it. And it was right straight up the hill. By the time we could get there we were just flat out of time.

Were you running out of oxygen?

We were. That was the limitation.

Not being a geologist, were you confident that you were doing as well as professional geologist would be expected to do on a lunar field trip?

Yeah, I think everybody seemed to believe that.

Harrison Schmitt, a professional geologist who later flew on Apollo 17, was one of your instructors, wasn't he?

Jack gave us a lot of help on that, that's true. But, we were not short on good instructors. We did an awful lot of work on that. Our field work was the equivalent of a master's degree in geology, we had that much field work. So, particularly, those of us who were interested in geology, in my case, morphology, were qualified. The thing I was primarily interested in was: How does it form? How did it get here? At least, we were told they were satisfied with the quality of our description. And I was rattling it off and so was Al Shepard about as fast as we could rattle it off with all the knowledge we could bring to bear. And they seemed to think it was good.

Did you find you were pushed too hard?

Not too hard. No, we were pushed by design and by ourselves. We planned a timeline that was about 115–120% of what we reasonably expected we could accomplish. In case of failure of equipment there was no fear that we'd have other things to do. And then, when things didn't fail, we tried to accomplish the whole

115–120%. By and large, we got most of it done. Generally, we were just working our asses off.

Why didn't you have a Lunar Rover on your mission?
It wasn't ready yet. The only thing we had was a two-wheel hand cart.

During your moonwalks did you have the opportunity to stop and reflect, even for a moment, on the awesome nature of the experience you were having, or was your work there so compelling that you had no time for that?
That's right, that's right.

That's a shame, isn't it?
The taxpayer wasn't paying for us to be introspective. NASA wasn't wanting us to be introspective—they just wanted to produce the results. You know, those guys sitting in Mission Control—to them it seems like agonizing hours we're not saying anything or doing anything that they can see because things are so *slow* and we were so *encumbered.* You're working your bloody tail off! They're sitting there just listening, and if the television camera is on they can follow that. But, otherwise, they're listening to you pant and huff and carry on and exchange a few words. You know what you're doing, but they're sitting there for hours on end, impatient as hell for you to get on with the next thing. The whole flight was just one revelation after another. I had trained myself as a pretty calm, dispassionate observer of things. But sure, I was enjoying every minute of it.

One very interesting revelation about the flight was that you performed a series of ESP trials during the mission. How did that come about?
They came about because I was interested and intrigued. And the whole rationale was: If this phenomenon is real, what does it tell us about how the universe is put together. If these things are real, and science won't address them, then we're making a mistake. That's what I was interested in.

How did it work? Did you use the cards?
Yes. I used the normal Zenner symbols, the kind used in the laboratory. Only, I didn't really have the cards. I had a random number table. I simply assigned the symbols to the random number table when it was time to do an experiment.

Ed Mitchell

How was it arranged so that the people on the Earth knew when it was time to try to pick up your signals? Did you pick specific times during the flight?

It was pre-programmed. I told the people that were receiving that I would concentrate on the symbols at the beginning of my rest period each day. We knew when that was. Unfortunately, you see, we had a forty minute delay in launching, so we started our clock forty minutes from what they expected it to be. So, we were forty minutes off all the time. And, furthermore, I didn't get a chance to do it every day like I expected to. I was counting on being able to do it six or eight times and I only ended up doing it four or six times.

Did you do it while you were on the moon?

No. It was only during the flight between the Earth and the moon.

Were Shepard and Roosa supportive, or didn't they care?

They were not aware of it. I decided that before the flight.

What were the results?

Positive. Or, let's say they were statistically highly significant, even though the press has said the contrary for eighteen years. That's because they don't understand statistics.

How open was NASA to this sort of thing, this kind of experimentation?

Totally unopen, totally closed.

Did you try to push for it at all?

No, I wasn't going to jeopardize my flight. I didn't push it because I wanted to fly like everybody else. So, I did my normal work. When I really got interested in the experiment, I did it on my own time. We didn't conceive of it until about three weeks before the flight.

Did you ever try to make suggestions along those lines, or was the barrier absolute?

Well, it was no different than it is today. If you remember, in the early days, even psychologists were banned from the program after they initially predicted humans couldn't survive in space. That was the end of psychologists in the program. So, one of the greatest losses of the entire NASA program, in my opinion, was psychological study at a deep level. I don't think psychology was sufficiently advanced in the 50's to contribute a great deal, frankly. But, nevertheless, it was a fruitful area for study that never took place.

Did your investigations into ESP and psychic research ever bring you into confrontation with debunkers like James Randi?
Yeah, I ran into that whole group of debunkers fifteen years ago.

Randi recently was awarded a MacArther Foundation genius grant and is using the money to support his debunking crusade.
Oh, what a phony! He's made a living on it for the last fifteen years and, of course, he's the biggest phony there is. You've heard of Marty Caidin?

The science fiction and space writer, correct?
Marty's a good friend of mine. He became psychokinetically active here a couple of years ago. And he's just like a kid. You know Marty, he's a *madman.* And he's just like a kid in a candy store with his new discovery. He's set up a room in his house, sealed it all off from air conditioning, and set up targets in there that he could psychokinetically move at will. And he's having a great time being investigated by all these scholars that are doing work on it. And Randi challenged him. And you know Marty, he talks pretty rough. He said, "Get your bleeping ass down here and bring your ten thousand dollars that you're talking about. I'm gonna take it away from ya!" Well, he went on at home like that and Randi wouldn't meet his conditions.

What happened?
All he wanted him to do was come down. "I'm gonna prove it to ya," he said. "Bring your ten thousand dollars!" Randi *knows* it's real. He knows it's real, under the right circumstances.

Why, then would he—
He's making a *hell* of a good living on television and debunking. But he's a bigger phony than anybody I've run into.

Why didn't he come down. It seems that if you could be in on a demonstration that might really prove these things, you'd be even bigger. Wouldn't that be even more amazing?
I don't know what goes on in that man's mind. He's "Randi the Magician" and he's making a lot of bucks in what he's doing. He's beneath my contempt. I really don't even want to waste time with him. And I've seen enough scientists whose reputations and life's

Ed Mitchell

work is based upon *one* theory of reality, and they get terribly nervous, defensive, and upset because you start to threaten, to shake that world-view. I watched it at the Stanford Research Institute. Uri Geller was doing some pretty profound things. And I'd watch as scientists from the National Science Foundation and other prestigious Washington organizations would come in and take a look, and they'd break out into a cold sweat. And they'd be so angry, so furious with us that they couldn't say anything because they were really threatened. They knew it was real, but you wouldn't know it from anything they wrote subsequently.

That must be quite frustrating.
That's the reason I quit allowing myself to be frustrated by it. Because I know it's real. I can do it sometimes. I don't claim to be great at it. I know anybody can do it at times. But, I've quit trying to force my views on people who aren't ready for them.

If your aim is to enlighten people, though, how do you get the message out?
Well, people have to be ready for the message. We're talking about *evolution* here. We're talking about evolution of the species. The question I had to confront ten years ago is: Is this a receding capability that was more inherent in the primitive species or is it an evolving capability. I'm now convinced it's an evolving capability, and that as we become mentally and emotionally prepared, these things will start to emerge more and more. And if you look at those capabilities in a broad, general philosophic sense, what we're evolving are the capabilities we have ascribed, in a religious sense, to God. We *have* all the creative capabilities in mind over matter that we've ascribed to God and this is, in a theological sense, the manifestation of "deity" in an evolving species. In other words, in the universe, if there is deity in it, it is manifesting itself in the organization of intelligent species. Philosophically and theoretically, that's what we ought to look at. We're living in a very crazy time right now, where we're starting to see some of these things emerge in ways we've never seen before. It's pretty fascinating.

Do you think we are backward, as far as species go, compared to other possible creatures that might be living in the universe?
No, I don't think that's so. If you look at the best new work in cosmology and the so-called "anthropic cosmological principle" that's been worked out, it's not likely that the universe could have matured enough in the fifteen to eighteen billion years of its existence to have produced a living species like us, with the

necessary heavy elements and everything that goes into our total reality, much sooner than it has. On the other hand, even if other civilizations preceded us by a billion years, the likelihood of finding us in a billion years—colonizing the universe enough in a billion years to have discovered another occupied planet—is pretty iffy.

Do you discount UFOs, then, and things of that nature, or do you have an open mind about it?

Well, I'm open-minded about it. I was very close to Allen Hynek, the astronomer at Northwestern University who studied UFO sightings and reports. Allen's work you can't dismiss. He was an amazing man. And, of course, we have to recognize that we're dealing with a field phenomenon there, we're not dealing with a laboratory phenomenon. We don't have control over it. His documentation was pretty damn good. However, without having a better feel for where they could have come from, and understanding the time frames developed since the Big Bang and the maturation of the Cosmos, it really poses some tough questions. I'm kind of inclined at this point to put it on the shelf until we have something more tangible. I'm not really prepared to say at this point that I think there were UFO visitations. There is just nothing solid to support that.

What do you make of the cases of people like Whitley Strieber. He's the fellow who lives up in New Hampshire and claims some sort of visitation by extraterrestrials. He wrote a best-selling book about it called Communion. *He doesn't say categorically that they were real. He's willing to admit that it might be something psychical.*

Well, you see, this is the other aspect of my research, this whole role of consciousness and noetics. I know what the human mind can do, I know our capability to create our own reality, and I know that with a little psychological urging, and a little altered state of consciousness, these people can convince themselves of most anything. No, without knowing the vast potential of the human creative capability, I might be more impressed with Hynek's work and questions of the UFO phenomenon. But having also studied Uri Geller, shamans, witch doctors, Eastern religions, bushmen, and firewalkers—and done some of these things myself—I know that the psychokinetic potential of the human mind is unlimited. So, we can create these things.

Do you foresee the results and ideas of the work you and others have been doing in noetics eventually converging with that of physics and the other traditional sciences?

Sure, it has to converge. That's what I've been working at for twenty years. These bodies of knowledge *have* to come together. We're starting to get a fairly good handle on this. Fundamental science. Physicists haven't yet, bit it has to tie in with their work and, of course, it will, probably within this coming century. The universe is consistent. It is not two different things, it's *one* thing, and the processes of the universe work together. There is no supernatural, it's all *natural.* What we see in physics and call "objective" has to be consistent with what we experience at the "subjective" level. It has to be consistent with our experience of the divine, of the psychological, of introspection and intuition. These experiences that we humans have in all our mental states, our states of consciousness, have to be explained in a manner consistent with what we discover in that state of consciousness from which we discover "objective reality."

Are you familiar with the ideas of the English physicist David Bohm? He's come up with a concept that is absolutely fascinating. He sees the universe showing two kinds of order; implicate and explicate. In his view, explicate order is what we experience in the everyday world, what you call "objective reality". Implicate order would correspond to the "deep" structure of the universe, the subatomic and quantum sphere. He hypothesizes that at the implicate level every particle in the universe carries with it the totality of the order and relationship of every other particle in the universe. And it's all a unified whole, like a cosmic hologram.

Modern work in chaos theory is trying to show the so called "butterfly effect." You grab hold of something over here, for example, you pull on that string, and you end up in a whole different level of reality somewhere else. In other words, the butterfly flaps his wings in Peking and it creates a snowstorm in New York. That's the deep interrelationship of the universe, and certainly David Bohm is contributing an enormous amount to all of that.

Do you believe in free will?
Sure!

But how do you reconcile that with these ideas that the universe seems to be an immense, interrelated, and unified kind of machine?
Because it is in the element of choice. The *process* is already set in place and already evolved. It's a trial and error process. The universe started, as best we know, as a Big Bang. At that level of reality, all was plasma. The universe was at its highest level of

potential. It could have evolved into anything. And it might have evolved, there might have been jillions of big bangs, most of them not going anywhere. We can't communicate with them, so we don't know. Our big bang evolved a set of constants and a set of interactions that continue to evolve. If a fine constant in fundamental physics had been slightly different, the universe would have been totally different. We would not have evolved. It doesn't mean that somebody planned it that way. It means that by trial and error, if there were jillions of universes, one of them could have done what ours has done.

But, you always come back to that first principle, the first cause: what started the whole process going?

Well, it could have been noise, noise in the void. You can get Brownian motion, there are a lot of ways to theorize about that, but, see, if you go the other way, if you say it was a planned, deity-created universe, then what created God? You're back to the unanswerable question at that point. But, if you take the notion that the universe evolved and that at each step it either succeeded or didn't succeed, the combinations available from the first instant are virtually limitless—then this infinite number of potential combinations gives you a reasonable starting point. The harmonics of a wave, for example. How many ways can they combine? They augment or they cancel. Some of the combinations worked and some of them didn't work. Those that did work continued to grow and augment and create other forms. So, our periodic table of the elements starts with 1 and goes up to where it becomes unstable at about 230 something. What seems to be missing in the whole of traditional physical cosmology is this: how is the information propagated? And to me, that is the key missing link in science at the moment—how is information propagated. The English biologist Rupert Sheldrake has proposed the "morphogenetic field" as a concept. It's a good concept, better than most. And, essentially, this is the way it ties things together: the physicists from the last century thought that the universe was cooling off, thought it was running down to a state of maximum entropy, or disorder. That it would, according to the Second Law of thermodynamics, disorganize itself, cool, and essentially, die. A better notion, in my way of thinking, is that as the universe organized and cooled off, it organized into the more heavy elements that we now see in all the physical matter around us. In other words, the universe wasn't more organized in the beginning, the way the physicists would say it. It had more potential in the beginning and it organized that potential into certain forms. And information, according to Norbert

Ed Mitchell

Weiner, is the negative of entropy. So, as irreversible processes took place and entropy increased, it spun off information. And that information went somewhere. Now, there are various types of information. There's the patterning information, for example, where an interaction replicates the last, or previous interaction so that you get many, many copies of iron atoms, for instance, and all the other types of atoms and molecules. Then there is the *first* interaction, the first time something takes place, the first time a *successful* interaction takes place. The question is how does the information that this is a successful interaction become propagated itself—and it certainly seems to get propagated—so that it becomes available for future interactions. This is where Sheldrake's hypothesis comes in. He postulates a "morphogenetic field" associated with all types of matter, and information is a field phenomenon. Information from the initial reaction, then, is stored in the morphogenetic field. It creates the impetus, just like a magnet creates a field around it, which will influence the next time the conditions for such an interaction take place. And, it forces that interaction into following that pattern. The universe has memory! Now, you can't observe that, or we haven't observed it, and the physicists haven't looked for it at the fundamental levels. But, it makes sense. The reason it makes sense is that it precisely describes what happens when you get sufficiently organized at the level of living substance, particularly the level of human intelligence. It starts to explain these things of mind, of consciousness that we haven't been able to explain before.

A good example of this morphogenetic field manifesting itself might be in the way an embryo grows and develops. In the case of an embryo, something is controlling and directing all the activity that starts with a single cell and creates a whole new individual. It's absolutely amazing.

Exactly! And my theory—I haven's discussed this yet with Sheldrake personally—but I would say that the morphogenetic field, at some point, became hard-wired in the genetic field, it was set into the genetic code; so the genetic code passes from generation to generation through the molecular structure of DNA. But, *new* thought and choice—you see, we're talking about free will here—new thought and choice goes into the morphogenetic field. So, a choice that we humans make—our thought processes, our choosings, can be picked up by others through the morphogenetic field. That's the basis of intuition; we intuit that information. Jung called it the "Collective Unconscious"; Sheldrake calls it the morphogenetic field. Other members of the species can pick up on that idea and act to create a successful outcome in a particular situation. That's why lower species—ants, termites, whatever—they're programmed strictly according to their genetic information. Now, if they have a sufficient range of behavior genetically programmed, and they encounter a changed environment, a change in their programming might allow them to successfully encounter the changed environment and survive. The fact of *that* process goes into the morphogenetic field and other members of the species can pick up on it. At the human level that happens, too, but we have a broader capability. We can think up a lot of thoughts. And we can choose, we can consciously decide we're going to do something. We're self-reflective, aware of our own thoughts. In the lower species, which are not self-reflective, this sort of thing is a lower-level function. We can choose. And it *is* characteristic of free will that we can evaluate a series of circumstances and make a choice. It may be a bad one, but we make the choice. If it's a successful one, it goes into the morphogenetic field and can be picked up and replicated. If it's an unsuccessful one, it still goes into the morphogenetic field. Maybe it will be picked up, but it'll die out.

Recently, some scientists at Harvard reported a series of experiments that showed that bacteria were somehow able to change their genetic patterns in response to certain environmental conditions. These were not random mutations in the manner of classical evolutionary theory, but seemingly deliberate maneuvers within the bacteria to take advantage of a new environment. That would seem to dovetail nicely with what you've been speculating about.

It dovetails precisely, because if you take Sheldrake's work clear back to the elementary particles—which he has not done yet—it happens there, and it would happen at the bacterial level also. It happens at all levels. So, it's kind of the story of the hundredth monkey. Once a successful event at any level of nature takes place upon which subsequent evolution can take place, that information is instantly known to other members of the species. And they will be biased, upon encountering that set of circumstances, to choose that solution. That's a form of intuition. The morphogenetic field, then, is a causal mechanism, or a propagatory mechanism for intuition.

And you can think of it in terms of evolutionary pressure.
Yes, So, you ask yourself: what is the fundamental thrust to the universe? Is there purpose in the universe? And, you come to the conclusion: it is to organize itself. That's all it is, all it has to be. If

there is an evolutionary pressure to organize and survive, that's all you need. It takes something like Sheldrake's morphogenetic field, and you deduce from observation that there seems to be an organizational thrust to provide the physical mechanism that we seek in nature. But, then, that isn't totally expository, in that we see that the universe isn't random. It is not random, it does have some pattern in it. Chaos theory, certainly, is showing that. Well, what's the mechanism? One of the mechanisms seems to be Sheldrake's morphogenesis, and mainstream science doesn't want to look at that.

Earlier, you said that you started on this quest for deeper understanding of psychic and mental phenomena, information theory—the nature of the universe itself, when you experienced a life shift, a change in direction as a result of your trip to the moon. What do you think triggered this? Was it the experience of walking on the Moon, actually being in a place other than Earth?
Well, I won't say the moonwalk. It was the result of being in space and seeing the Earth in space. I think all of the guys have described that as the profound aspect of it.

The rest of us have only seen the pictures; photographs of the scene you actually witnessed. Images of the Earth hanging there in the blackness. But if you look at them and ponder them, it's possible to catch a glimmer of what you must have felt seeing it out there, how delicate it looks, how beautiful the cloud patterns are.
I think the best way to describe it is to say your reality shifts from Earth-center to Cosmic-center. You no longer see things in terms of Earth-centered reality. And, your time frame shifts from a personal time frame to a universal time frame. I now see things in terms of an historical sweep and an evolutionary position. I live my life *now.* I see things in terms of the long sweep of history.

You once called it "instant global consciousness."
That is the shift in awareness.

When you started out, did you expect anything like that?
No, it was totally unexpected. It's taken me sixteen years to try to figure out what that meant.

When you see the Moon in the sky at night, do you get angry that we haven't returned? That we've lost twenty years by ending the journey?

Angry? No, sad. Sad that we're not learning the lesson. We're pushing ourselves toward the brink; we're backing into the future looking at the lessons of the past. When I think of what this past administration has done to us in that regard, it's heinous. Weapons in space is heinous. It will lead to our demise. I see this period beginning at the end of World War II. What we're going through right now is a transition period. Just as surely as you go from subsonic, to supersonic, you have to go through the transsonic phase. Or, like going from the river through the rapids to a waterfall. That's the turbulent region. It's an irreversible process and you've got to go through it to get to a smoother time.

The book No Man's World, *by Martin Caidin, as a matter of fact, points out that wherever man goes, he's going to bring his frailties, his anger, his greed, his irrationalities, and his weapons. It's a natural process. How do we stop that?*

Well, we don't. But we've got to learn to curb it because we can no longer live with it. You see, we're reaching ultimates. We've already devised weapons with the ultimate destructive potential. You can't destroy more completely than by splitting atoms apart. You can't go any faster than the speed of light. We're starting to design weapons with the speed of light. You can't transport things any faster than you can in space in near-Earth orbit; that's as fast as we can go orbiting the Earth. So, we're reaching a certain level of ultimates. And one of the things that's happened, in fact in several places—the Korean Airline destruction, the Persian Gulf incidents—represent it clearly. Our decision time is getting down so low, so small, that the human mind doesn't have the proper time to evaluate the information to make the right decision. So, we're pushing ourselves to the limit of human capability. When we put weapons in space, for example, laser weapons with the speed of light, your decision time goes to zero.

What can be done about that?

What you can do about it is don't put yourself in that position. Because we know we're against the limit, and it won't work.

As a nation, we can make those decisions for ourselves, but what about the rest of the world?

That's the whole point. If you look at the scenario, we would have to explore space as a species. Clearly, if we are going to explore space as a species, that means cooperation. So, we *have* to start looking at ourselves as a global society. We *have* to learn to cooperate. We *can't* do the things Marty Caidin talked about in his book. We have reached the limit. There are no more frontiers to explore on Earth. We've reached the limit of our population. We've reached the limit of our industrialization because we're destroying our entire habitat with the greenhouse effect, the ozone problem, the clearing away of the great forests, the extinction of species. We've reached the limit of what the Earth can withstand. Now, we hadn't done that before World War II. But, with the power of technology since then, we've entered this turbulent transition phase that we've got to get through and solve the problems we're creating, or else we're going to cease to exist.

In terms of space exploration, should we start thinking about joint missions with the Soviets?
Well, there's certainly a data point in that which says, sure, we can do that. Absolutely. But, it has to be more broadscale than that.

It's a starting point, then?
It's a starting point. Apollo-Soyuz was a starting point. We've got to build upon that experience. We cannot afford, this Earth cannot afford the type of win-lose competition that has been our history since the beginning of time.

Do you think we should start planning to colonize the solar system as a way of assuring our survival?
We don't need to. We've got to solve the problems here. See, this is the reason for all this consciousness research; this is why I went into it. How are we programmed? How do we get these hateful, warlike tendencies that we have? We know how we get them. We know how they're programmed. We know how to deprogram them.

Are you optimistic that we can resolve these problems in time?
Yes, because we have a survival instinct. Now, we may have to scare the hell out of ourselves; we may have to destroy a few million people to learn the lesson. I hope not. But I don't think we'll do it with nuclear war, certainly not deliberately. But, we could do it accidentally—the Persian Gulf incidents again. And, weapons in space—the accident could be upon us before we recognize it, it could get out of hand. But, we won't do it deliberately. I think in all the capitals of the world, all the political leaders now, after forty years of nuclear confrontation, recognize the horror of deliberate nuclear exchange. So, the likelihood of doing that is pretty small. But, if we start tinkering with it and start getting these

systems so they're so hair-triggered, the decision time is so little, that the accident could happen to us. That's the next danger. If we put that behind ourselves, then we've got to start addressing these long-range problems that are creeping up on us—the ozone deple-tion, global warming, destruction of the ecosystems, destruction of species. We can't let that go on much longer or the quality of life virtually goes to zero.

In that context, what kind of space program should we be planning?

If we recognize the lessons I'm talking about, the priorities have to be programs oriented toward life-sustaining capabilities, Earth-sustaining capabilities, cooperative measure to reduce our aggressive, competitive approach to things. In other words, our competitive strategy has to go from win-lose to win-win. Remem-ber that only in the last century we were still facing off with each other man-to-man, shooting each other down. It was win-lose and the loser dies. It goes back to the Christians and the lions; throw them out and let the animals have them. The only places we haven't done away with competition in a win-lose sense and death to the loser is in war and business. In business it's dog-eat-dog, and just as surely as we perpetuate that, the third-party casualties in this are all of us. Initially, it's the environment, it's the whole habitat of Earth that's the victim. That means a fundamental shift is required in the way humans look at themselves and the way they look at this planet. Since we have no place to go—and a relief valve into space is not the answer. If we keep doing what we're doing, we're surely going to destroy ourselves in the next hundred years. There's no choice but to change.

Why not put more emphasis on the relief valve option?

Well, we're going to keep working on it, of course. But, I don't think it's a high priority. We're not going to get everybody off the Earth; we're not going to get the excess four billion people to a colony out in space. That might happen five hundred years from now, but it's not going to happen in the next hundred years. We could, with proper political will and leadership, start changing such things as going from win-lose models to win-win models. We could start cooperating rather than looking to put the other guy down. Those are simple things we could do. We could convert our war industries after we start to reach accord, because we will still have the same number of people to feed and employ and give jobs to. So, we have to convert our military industries into technologies and jobs that are appropriate to the current condition. God knows, we've got enough problems and enough work to do. It's just a matter of converting and shifting, and adapting rather than perpetuating the same scheme that we've been maintaining throughout human history.

It's obvious that the Soviet Union, either in cooperating with us, or on their own, will have an enormous effect on the future of space exploration, to say nothing of their importance on the world political stage. Should we be concerned or fearful of the strong Soviet presence in space at this time?
No, not at this point.

A lot of people are concerned, though. If they are not a threat, how do we go about changing the suspicious attitude we have about them?
Well, that comes from leadership. That attitude has been pressed upon us since right after World War II, in the McCarthy era, by hysteria. And, we've had our political demagogues that have played upon it ever since. Now, that isn't to say that the Soviets didn't earn it. But, the main thing about the Soviets is to recognize that the great socialist experiment of the 20th century has failed. They cannot make it economically in this world. The Soviets are so far behind because the socialist system cannot produce the goods and services the people want and the individual freedom that they now demand as well. So, the socialist system is not a threat. It's got to be dramatically modified. Gorbachev recognizes this. The likelihood is that he'll be able to pull it off, because of the pressure of evolution. Their people can see what the rest of the world has and they want it, too. And there's no reason why they can't have it. So, they've got to open up. To me, political ideology is not the problem right now. It might have been for a few tender years after World War II, but it's not the problem now.

It doesn't worry you that their emphasis seems to be on the military uses of space?
No, I don't think that's true. They can use space for military purposes just as we can. But, they don't have ASAT weapons up there, they don't have weapons in space at the moment. They have observational capabilities. They use a different philosophy, they have more short-range vehicles than we do. They don't design them for long-duration flights, the kind of unattended operation that we do. There's no question they're trying to catch up. They're trying to be a world leader in space and, if we fumble around, they

will be. They're coming along. And they're gaining momentum like gangbusters.

Why do you think space is so important to them?
Well, it's important to all of us; it's the next frontier.

Martin Caidin—again—has an interesting theory. He says the Soviets suffer from the "Viking Syndrome", or more accurately, are doing their best to avoid the Viking Syndrome. The Vikings traveled to North America long before Columbus, looked around, decided it was a vast wasteland and went back home. The Soviets, by comparison, seem to be driven by the notion that there is so much to be gained in space, militarily and otherwise, that they're pressing their effort as hard as they can.
Well, the basic Soviet mentality—and it's shifting—is one of paranoia. It's to protect their homeland at all costs. They've been overrun and invaded so many times. That was the mentality, coupled with the Czarist repression, that dominated Soviet thinking for the first sixty years. You have a new breed of enlightened people over there now. The world has changed, it's not like it used to be. Yes, the old guard is still paranoid about defense, about their borders. But, right now, I think that Gorbachev, at least, is indicating that they're seeing the broader scheme of things. They're seeing that they've got to deal with their people; that they've got to be wrenched into the late 20th century. They've got to provide them with a better economy, they've got to correct their social problems. Alcoholism is rife in the Soviet Union, not drug abuse yet, but alcoholism. And, that comes from personal depression; that comes from lack of drive; it comes from lack of direction in most lives. Psychologists don't miss that these days. You can tell what's going on in that society. There is a hopelessness. Essentially, it's telling you that their way of organizing a social system doesn't work. You've got to give the people more freedom.

Taking into account all that is going on over there, should we offer to share our knowledge and space technology with them?
I'd do it circumspectly. We have to move toward cooperation, but we have to have checks and balances. We shouldn't do it blindly. It is not clear that Gorbachev will succeed. It's not clear that the old guard won't bump him off. So, as long as they have an ultraconservative, angry, hostile group of people over there—just as we've had here—that could assume the leadership, we should move circumspectly. But we have to move toward cooperation, we have to move toward disarmament, we have to move toward

more productive endeavors. You can't do it overnight, and you can't do it unilaterally. And, we've got to realize that they have their hardliners over there, just like we do.

So, you definitely see an important political spinoff coming out of the space program in terms of our relations with the Soviets?

It has helped as one of the bridges. And, it's a catalyst right now because, as you know—I'm taking aim at Star Wars now—as you know, any scientist that is knowledgeable in this area has condemned it as a total fallacy. The Soviets are not dumb; they know it's a waste of time, too. They will do what they have to do to react to us. If we put weapons in space, they'll have to react. The best way to react is to shoot'em down. You don't have to go up there the expensive way to do that; you shoot them down from the ground. Right now, there aren't any ASATs capable of doing that on either side, thanks to our congressmen declaring a moratorium on testing them up there. The Soviets do not want to put any more money into the military effort than they have to. They need to improve their economy. They know, just like we should know, that the money you put into military hardware is not the most useful way to spend your budget.

Then, you dispute the charge that the Soviets have been working longer on their Star Wars program than we have, and are spending more money on it than we are?

They've been working on basics—they've been working on basic research. They've got some very fine technologies in lasers, in plasmas—but they didn't do it for Star Wars. They did it because it's basic research and, yes, it enhances military technology. It enhances other technologies as well. If you look across all of the categories of scientific development, there are only a few in which the Soviets are ahead of us. Our technology is still better; it's still more advanced than theirs, except in two or three areas. Some of the areas that they're more advanced in, by the way, happen to be in ways of preserving nature: animal husbandry, natural wildlife studies, and so forth. In some of these areas they're far ahead of us. That ought to be telling you something. But, in military technologies, in computer systems, artificial intelligence, and so on, we're far superior to the Soviets still. *Those* are the military technologies that you need to worry about.

Let's move from the ridiculous, in your estimation, to perhaps the sublime, from Star Wars to Mind Wars, if it can be called that. There have been reports that the Soviets have been working very seriously on the military uses of psychic power, specifically telekinesis, the ability to move or affect objects, in this case military targets, from a distance. In effect, using the mind as a weapon. Is there anything to that?

They've been investigating that all along, just like we have. Sure, there's something to it. Not as much as some would like to believe, and more than others would like to believe. First of all, these phenomena are very real, but they're also very primitive right now. They're not understood well; there are a few people who can do them. There are some philosophic lessons that come out of it, though. The philosophic lessons are that there are no secrets. The nonsense of trying to close our societies, close our file cabinets, keep our secrets—let me put it this way. If Sheldrake's notion of morphogenesis and information in the morphogenetic field is correct, and it's as good a theory as any right now to explain telepathy, then there is no way you can ultimately hide anything. You can always intuit it. Now, the question is, what is the discrimination of that information, how deeply can you discriminate, or clearly pick up, that information? It turns out that space and time are very difficult to pick up psychically. Emotional content is not hard to pick up at all. But, the discrimination and the discreteness of information is much more difficult. The ability to influence someone, to make them feel good or bad, that's not hard to do. To make them do something specific, that's hard to do.

Telepathically, you mean?
Telepathically, that's right.

Have you had the chance to talk to any of the Soviets about this?
Sure, I know quite a few of them.

Have they made any progress?
They have done quite a bit of work. They can do it because they do not have the social stigma against it. To them it's pure science. But the same thing handicaps them. Let me try to explain what I mean. In this country, much of the work in consciousness or psychic areas is prohibited by a religious tradition that says those are the things of Satan, that it's the evil, dark side of humanity. Thus, it's rejected on theological grounds. That's not true in the Soviet Union. It's pure science to them. And the initial work was conducted because the government became interested in it for military, intelligence, and covert purposes. They only had a limited

Ed Mitchell

amount of success, the reason being that in order to be successful at it, you do have to get into the human being, you have to get into the same spot from which our emotions and our sense of divine reality come. That was an ideological block for the Soviets. They were trying to handle psychic research as a mechanical thing, like you would train a muscle. You can't do it that way, because when you get into that realm of human functioning you're getting into deep psychology, you're getting into the realm of our deepest emotions, our deepest sense of spiritual reality, into our deepest essence. You can't do it any other way, because it all goes together. You're going right in and have to work with the thing that makes us human. So, you can't handle that as objective science. That was the block to the Soviets. The block on our side is the religious sanction. So, we don't make much progress. I'm kind of considered a hero over there in that sense. Many of their scientists have been oppressed in this area, just like ours have. The fact that I've been interested in this field has, in some measure, allowed them to say, 'Look what they're doing in the United States; look what Astronaut Mitchell is doing.' Somehow, it's provided them a little leverage over there, even though I haven't had a close or continuous dialogue with them. I've spoken with them from time to time, and exchanged papers with them.

You've brought up an intriguing point. Can there ever be a reconciliation between "pure" science and the kind of work you have been talking about?

It is fundamentally a subjective area that we're dealing with and, officially, science only deals with objective things. But, if you look at it from another point of view, with a human being there is no such thing as objectivity, because everything has to come through his subjective experience of knowing, thinking, learning, interpreting, seeing, and so forth. So, there is no objectivity. It's really only consensus that you're talking about when you talk of objectivity.

Have you discussed these things with religious leaders and theologians?

Lots of them, but there's not much give and take. They just close their minds. Now, if you go to some enlightened and pretty advanced Jewish cabalists, or if you deal with primitive shaman types or, with the Eastern traditions, they know what you're talking about. They're far more open to these sorts of things than our Western culture is.

That's fascinating. They really do have a much different world view than we do, especially in the Orient. They comprehend the world, and their place in it, as a totality, a harmonized "oneness", the whole Hindu and Buddhist tradition.

Well, some of those in the Buddhist tradition are pretty powerful people. I've watched some pretty interesting and strange things with them.

The Japanese present an interesting case study. Since the war, they've grabbed onto Western ideas and techniques with a vengeance. There has been a real confluence of cultures over there, sort of Buddha meets Thomas Edison. What's intriguing is that at this juncture, they might be in the right circumstance to work out the resolutions between these different ways of interpreting the world that we have been discussing. They might be able to tie it together.

They might. I would tend to think that it might be the Chinese culture. The Chinese have a curious combination of philosophies. They can be philosophic and pragmatic at the same time. That's *exactly* what all this involves. Hinduism and Buddhism are a little too airy-fairy. All religions, major religions, in their theological structures are idealistic. Spirit is predominant over matter, mind is predominant over matter. The Chinese, on the other hand, advocate the yin-yang, the complentarity of mind-matter, the complentarity of male-female. The two go hand in hand. It's more dualistic, not a monadic system. And, that's precisely what I think is needed. You have to recognize that, in Western terms, energy-matter is one side, and information-spirit is the other side of the equation. The two are not dominant, one over the other; information and matter can be seen to be complimentary, and they're related. A way to describe the relationship is that it's the entropy-information exchange; as entropy increases, information increases.

A recent book spotlighted a gentleman who is working on the idea that the universe is a sort of immense computer program that is running through its instructions, playing out its string.

Yes, there's a certain amount to be said for the computer analogy. But, it's really a weak analogy in that the universe is far more complex, it's holistic. It's more of a hologram than a linear program. From a certain distance it looks like a computer, and if you look close you do see bits of information flowing around. But the universe is far more intricate; it's nonlinear. Computer programs are linear.

Information is processed through a computer one piece at a time, like a line of people walking through a turnstile.

Exactly. But, the universe is nonlinear in certain fundamental ways, and that's the difference. So, the computer analogy, even though up to a point it is good for visualizing and thinking, starts to break down when you hit irreversibilities and nonlinear phenomena.

The computer analogy is also insufficient to describe the human mind. Someone once made that point in arguing that it was essential to have a man in the pilot seat. The comment was that man is the only 150-pound, nonlinear computer that can be mass produced by unskilled labor.

It's that nonlinear part that's so important. All of science, you see, up until now, up until the last two decades past Einstein, really looked at the linear function only. They were looking at the universe as being in homeostasis, an essentially static condition. But, it's not. It's an evolving universe; it's got irreversible processes at the macro level, and it's nonlinear. Science has only now, in the last fifteen years, been able to start to confront the nonlinearities in the universe. Before that, all science, up to Einstein, was concentrating on the linear aspects of stable states, working out stable steady-state solutions to problems, and ignoring the waterfalls, the transsonic regions, the birthing process, and all of these examples where entropy is created.

Speaking of entropy, what are your thoughts on what happens when a person dies?

There is immortality. Exactly what that means, I don't know. I think we will find that information principle sooner or later. I don't know that information is always conserved, the way energy is conserved. But, in a sense, no information is lost in the universe. That means that the information-gathering, managing-organizing aspect of the human essence isn't lost either.

It becomes part of the morphogenetic field?

That may be the way we have to look at it. Do we survive intact as personalities? I doubt it.

Our consciousness won't survive, is that what you're saying?

Well, our waking consciousness. You see, we've got a lot of consciousness here. The waking consciousness probably does not survive. That's why we don't remember prior lives, if, in fact, there are prior lives. But, the unconscious and the super-conscious forces probably do survive.

So, after death, our psyches will have no self-reflective consciousness, is that right?
No self-reflective consciousness, that's correct.

What do you make of near-death experiences? People have reported traveling down a tunnel toward a bright white light, and when they reach the light they receive telepathic messages telling them that it's important to learn as much as possible, absorb as much information as they can while they are alive.
Well, that fits right in with what I know. And, the question no one can answer is: does the consciousness and the organized information there represent our essence, our souls? Does that information remain intact as a body of information in organized form or, is it simply part of the morphogenetic field?

Maybe it becomes a sort of raw material for future souls or psyches.
It may be. I think—it's not safe to say, but it's a good theory—that information can't really become manifest except through the physical form. So, to talk of a discarnate being doesn't mean anything. Only an incarnate being has meaning.

But information can be carried by radio waves, for example. You wouldn't call those physical forms, would you?
Yes, but it has to have a physical receiver to utilize it. That's exactly what I'm saying here. The manifestation of the information has to be associated with a physical entity. In other words, I don't subscribe to the idea that floating around up there are ethereal versions of us.

Like the platonic forms of human beings?
Right. I don't think that's true. There might be, in the sense that there is a morphogenetic field associated with me now, with each of us, and it contains the information that we've accumulated and organized—call that mind if you will—and that doesn't dissipate. You know, the reincarnation studies that Stevenson did are awfully compelling in this regard. It seems that an individual might be able to glob onto the body of information from an earlier individual. It's just as though there's a continuation of the earlier person. It's a pretty deep area, but there are not any good answers out at the moment.

That sounds a bit like déjà vu.

It could be. However, the work that Stevenson did was with children, and these children's knowledge of another person who was deceased at the time the child was born seems very complete. They were taken back to the houses in which the deceased persons lived. They can identify everything, they call people by names. So, the reincarnation hypothesis cannot be discarded lightly. But, we still don't know what the hell it means.

Do those kinds of things ever frighten you? Sometimes these deep looks into the unknown can produce fear and anxiety, an existential dread.

The fear in it has to come when you recognize your self-responsibility, that there's really nobody doing it but you. Yes, that's when it comes. I've been through that and it's tough. But, you have to get beyond that and recognize that the way the universe is constructed—and it does almost throw you back to deism or a deity—you have to recognize that the process allows for that as well. That deep night of the soul where you suddenly recognize it, and nobody's doing it but you in your life. Nevertheless, the process is such that we have the capabilities within us to create the reality we want, and it doesn't have to be hands-on, the way science and technology have taught us. We create it within ourselves and it happens out there in the world. God, I've watched it so many times. I can't theoretically explain it. Again, it's Bohm's implicate order.

Let's use this last section to talk about the space program and its future. Are you a fan of the program today?

I'm very critical of the program today.

A lot of people are.

That's right. The whole policy, the whole direction—and it stems from the President's office—is absolutely wrong.

What happened? Was it NASA's fault in any way, by not following through in the right way after reaching the goal of putting a man on the moon?

Well, there is something in that. But, it's just the way politics works in Washington. It was a pretty esoteric thing we did, and the excitement eventually wore off. People aren't interested. We've got too many pressing problems right here. Unless you see things differently, in terms of a philosophic orientation that is shifted from Earth-centered awareness to an awareness somewhere else, the conventional view is that the press of daily problems for America right now is too great. The lower class is sliding lower and lower; the squeeze is on them the worst. The middle class, middle America, is being squeezed hard, too. They're at the point where we're seeing their aggressive instincts coming forth and being exercised. It's a very troubled time, in my opinion.

Was the Apollo program too circumscribed? Was the focus too narrow in the sense that everything was devoted to putting a man on the moon by the end of the '60s and not enough attention paid to plans beyond that?

Politically, it was necessary. We have to be goal-oriented, we have to put responsibility, authority, and money into a very precise direction to make anything work. For science itself, for knowledge itself, yes, it would have probably been better if we didn't make such grandiose gestures and moved more step-by-step. But that's not political reality.

Well, could we have approached the problem differently? The scheme used in project Apollo was called Lunar Orbit Rendezvous. A single Saturn rocket was used to send the spacecraft out to the moon. Early on, Werhner Von Braun argued for Earth Orbit Rendezvous—several Saturn rockets would be used to put all the components into orbit around the Earth where they would be assembled and then head out to the moon. Wouldn't we be ahead of the game now if we had done something along those lines?

That might very well be true. No, it was in order to meet John Kennedy's timetable that it was necessary to do it the way we did it. But, I totally agree with you; the step-by-step approach would have ended with us putting up space stations and learning how to assemble things in space. We might have been more advanced today.

What do you think of the space station that we're planning to put up in the 1990s?

We have to get a goal together. You know, I've been in the Soviet Mir space station and looked at that carefully. It's a pretty sophisticated space station.

Have we a tendency to underestimate their progress?

Yes. They're coming alone fine. In the early days, their spacecraft were pretty primitive—they were like World War I submarines on the inside. But, they're pretty sophisticated now. They're coming on like gangbusters.

We're sitting here talking about moonflights and space stations. Do you still have the urge to go up there again, make another flight?

Sure! If I had the opportunity, I'd go.

You made only one flight, Apollo 14. Why didn't you stay with the program; what made you decide to get out?

Well, I was supposed to fly Apollo 20, but when the series was shut off at Apollo 17 I either had to ship to the shuttle, Skylab or, something else. It was clear to me that it would be at least eight or nine years before I would fly again, and I really wasn't interested in waiting around that long. If I had stayed in, tied to a desk or whatever, I couldn't really confront the bureaucracy. I didn't really want to do that.

Where should we be setting our sights now?

It is clear that in the future what's to be done in space is to more fully explore the solar system and, eventually, more deeply explore the rest of the nearby stellar system—this part of the galaxy. Now that's long-range stuff, there's no doubt about it. But, let's think long-range. The way to do it is to jump to the future, jump a hundred years out, see what has to be done, then look back and say: 'how do we get there?' We're not going to do it parochially, we're not going to do it as a nation. We're going to do it as a species from this planet, as humanity. The question is what are the steps between now and then? What are we looking for when we go out there? Apparently, we're looking for knowledge, we're trying to satisfy ourselves. Are we alone in the universe?

Realistically assessing the present state of the U.S. space program and what is possible in the coming century, where do you think the U.S. is going or, where will we be at the end of the 21st century? And if you were in charge, what would you do to make things happen the way you think they should?

The approach would be three-pronged. I can't assign relative budgets to them, but the priorities would be to emphasize cooperation with other nations in near-Earth orbit, the use of joint resources for solving the enormous global and technical problems we have, to the extent that space is useful for that, and it can be very useful. And to have a certain amount of commercial venture in space, but under treaties and coordinated so that the environment of space, which is more sensitive than the environment down here, is kept clean, because the debris problem is enormous. We're going to preclude our use of space within the next century if we're not careful, just from the junk floating around. If we start exploding weapons up there, it's all over with. So, that's the near-Earth orbit plan. The prime goal of policy for me—near-Earth space policy— is cooperation and solving large-scale global problems, environmental problems. Then, there's the military aspect of surveillance, creating security, keeping renegade nations and madmen under control and making sure we don't have terrorists with suitcase-size nuclear bombs running around trying to blow anybody up. So, there is an appropriate military police effort in space that needs a certain amount of priority. Then, there is deep space exploration. By the end of the next century, I'm sure we will have scientific colonies on the moon. They may be even more advanced than primitive outposts, I can see them as somewhat like what we have at Antarctica right now. We may even have scientific exploration colonies on Mars. I don't know that, if by the end of the next century, we will be able to send men as far as Jupiter or Saturn. We can't send men to Venus—it's too hot there—but we can do a fairly passable job of probing Venus with unmanned craft.

Wouldn't Titan, Saturn's largest satellite, be a wonderful place to explore?
We'd probably be getting close to sending manned missions out there by the end of the next century, if we haven't already sent them. But, since it takes such a long time to make the trip, it will be necessary to send manned probes first to gain the knowledge and set the parameters. Realistically, it will take about a century to get that done, with the sort of budgets we'll have. And, it simply can't be done unilaterally with one nation supporting it all. It's going to have to be a cooperative effort.

Now, that's the ideal. Is there something we can shoot for beyond that?
I don't think we'll be able to do it any other way.

So, in your estimation, what we're doing now pretty much corresponds to what is possible.
That's right. The main thing, the main problem we have to address in the immediate future is resources. We can't afford to have valuable resources rotting in missile silos. Those resources, those materials, that effort, that knowledge must be used more constructively. I don't mean that tomorrow we unilaterally disarm. But, in the long run, it's a use of resources that the planet can no longer afford. We must recognize that we're evolving out of that phase.

You're confident, you're optimistic that our survival instincts are strong enough that we'll make it OK?

Yep. We may make a slip, we may blow ourselves up, but I think we won't. So, those to me, are the pressing problems. Once we've solved them, the rest of it will fall into place naturally.

Chapter 5

ALAN BEAN
Lunar Module Pilot, Apollo 12

The Tribal Storyteller

E ver since he was a boy growing up in Texas Alan Bean has had a discerning and aesthetic eye. He focused a lot of that attention on airplanes, poring over pictures in books and magazines until he knew every shape, feature, and color pattern. He sculpted models of balsa wood and silkspan that he would hang in his room. He remembers them looking "like birds dressed up for a party, in shiny decals and brightly colored paints." And he was a demanding artisan. "Each part had to be fitted just so. Each wing had to be exactly like the other. To me, that perfect symmetry was beautiful. I didn't care if the planes could fly, but they had to be very, very beautiful."

Bean developed his creative talents further during his successful career as a Navy pilot and astronaut. He took art classes and enjoyed painting pictures in his spare time, mostly of flowers and shore scenes. And what was once just a pastime and hobby later blossomed into a surprising new vocation as a professional artist.

Alan LaVern Bean was born in Wheeler, Texas on March 15, 1932. His father, Arnold Bean, was a flood control expert who worked for the government. Alan's mother, Frances, was an enterprising woman who, over the years, ran a grocery store and an ice cream parlor. A younger sister named Paula completed the family. Arnold Bean was sent to where the work was so, as a result, the family moved from time to time; they went from Texas to Louisiana to Arkansas and then back to Texas, settling down eventually in Fort Worth.

Dreaming of becoming a Navy pilot, Alan convinced his parents to let him join the Naval Air Reserve when he was seventeen. He graduated from Paschal High School in Fort Worth, and entered the University of Texas on a Naval ROTC scholarship. During his college days he developed into a star wrestler and gymnast. He graduated from Texas in 1955 with a degree in Aeronautical Engineering and was commissioned an ensign in the U.S. Navy. He was ordered to Pensacola, Florida for basic flight training, then came back to Texas for advanced training at Beeville. He won his wings in 1956 and was assigned to a jet attack squadron in Jacksonville. Four years later, having completed his tour at Jacksonville, he was accepted into the Navy Test Pilot School at Patuxent River, Maryland. After the course he stayed on at Patuxent test flying all-weather aircraft. He also started taking evening art courses at nearby St. Mary's College.

In 1962 Bean applied to NASA as a candidate for the second group of astronauts being selected. He was in the final group of thirty-five under consideration but was not one of the nine pilots selected in the end. He submitted his application again the following year for the third group. In October he received a telephone call from Chief Astronaut Deke Slayton who gave him the happy news that he had been chosen to be one of NASA's fourteen new astronauts.

Although he served as backup commander for Gemini 10, Bean did not get the opportunity to fly in that program, there just weren't enough flights planned. Then, his eager hopes for an Apollo flight seemed to evaporate when, near the end of the Gemini series, he was assigned to the Apollo Applications Office. Apollo Applications was to be the follow-up effort to the moon landings. Its main focus was the Earth-orbiting Skylab space station. Terribly disappointed at having to miss out on Apollo, Bean plunged stoically into his work on the Skylab project. A year later, however, Bean was approached by fellow astronaut Pete Conrad, who happened to be a friend and instructor back at Patuxent. Conrad was backup commander for the Apollo 9 mission and would likely be commanding the Apollo 12 flight to the moon. Conrad had come to ask Bean to join his crew as lunar module pilot, taking the place of C. C. Williams who had been killed in a plane crash. Conrad had recommended Bean for the position to Deke Slayton and Slayton gave his OK. Two years later Alan Bean was on his way to the moon.

On November 14th, 1969 Bean, Conrad, and Dick Gordon started off on their quarter million mile trek aboard Apollo 12. The all Navy crew was barely out of port when their ship was hit by lightning as it passed through some low storm clouds. At first Bean thought their capsule had separated from the rocket. But they kept heading upward and, as far as they could determine, the vehicle didn't seem to be damaged; they were given the go to head for the moon. Four days later Conrad and Bean guided the lunar module "Intrepid" to a pinpoint landing on the Ocean of Storms. They stayed on the lunar surface for the next thirty-one hours, leaving Intrepid twice to gather rock and soil samples, deploy scientific equipment, and pay a visit to Surveyor 3, the unmanned probe that had landed there two years ahead of them.

Having successfully completed the second lunar landing, Bean resumed his work in the Skylab program. On July 28th, 1973 he began his second space flight as commander of the Skylab 2 mission. He and crewmates Owen Garriott and Jack Lousma established a new endurance record by remaining aloft for over 59 days. During that time they covered over 24 million miles and accomplished 150% of the mission objectives.

After Skylab Bean served as backup commander for the Apollo-Soyuz Test Project, the joint mission with the Soviet Union carried out in July of 1975. The Apollo era ended with that flight. Next on the boards was a new, reusable, hybrid design—part rocketship and part airplane. The size of a DC-9 airliner, it had rocket engines to power it into space, and large delta wings to fly back it back to Earth. It came to be known as the Space Shuttle. Bean stayed with NASA after retiring from the Navy and worked in the Shuttle program for the next six years, the last three as Chief of the Astronaut Office's operations and training group. Then, in 1981 he made the remarkable decision to leave the space program and start a new career as a painter.

A friend had given him the idea. She suggested he quit painting flowers and seascapes and turn to moonscapes instead. He became a man with a new mission. "When I left NASA I could have stayed and flown the Space Shuttle", he stated in a magazine interview, "but I made the conscious decision to do this job." His new "job", as he calls it, is preserving the spirit and history of the American space adventure, especially the Apollo moon flights, in vivid, finely crafted paintings. His goal is to leave a pictorial record of our first steps toward the planets, in the same way Charles Russell and Frederic Remington documented the opening of the American west.

"I was fortunate enough to visit worlds and see sights no artist's eye, past or present, has ever viewed firsthand", Bean says. "What I'm trying to do is express my feelings about these experiences and tell these stories. What I'd like to do is become a sort of tribal storyteller."

Alan Bean and his wife Leslie live in Houston. He has two children, a son and a daughter, from a previous marriage.

———————

Captain Bean, after your flights on Apollo and Skylab, you moved into the Space Shuttle program to continue with your career in astronautics. But shortly after the Shuttle's first flight, and before you had the chance to fly it yourself, you made a decision to leave the space program to take up an altogether different line of work. What made you change your mind about going back into space?

I wanted to fly the Space Shuttle, but I also wanted to do the job I'm doing now, telling the story of man's first exploration off this planet. And I felt that it would take twenty or so years to do the art, if I even could to it. I would have to use up to five years to fly the Shuttle so, at my age, I thought which job should I do? I knew there were a lot of people that could fly the Space Shuttle as well, or better, than me. But there was nobody interested in doing this painting job but me. So I felt, in the long run, this is what I should do. My dream is that people thirty years from now will look at my paintings and say, 'Hey, I'm glad this guy did this.' If I'd stuck around to fly the Shuttle, there would be a lot of paintings that would not be here. It was a case of answering the question of what to do with the rest of my life.

You have described your work, at least in part, as that of a "tribal story teller." What is it about your flights and the space program that you want to convey most? What is most important to you to express through your paintings?

I guess I would have to say it's the spirit of curiosity and adventure. What was it that made all the astronauts and all the people that were involved in the space program *and* all the people who supported it in spirit, feel that way? Why they felt that way. To tell stories that, maybe if you add them all up, would connect with people in future generations and inspire them. It's not any one thing; it's generally the overall spirit of feeling of the event or, the forces that caused the event to take place.

It's a bleak visual image you have to work with, don't you think? The emptiness and the colorlessness of the moon; the blackness of space. You don't even see the faces of the astronauts in most of your paintings.

That's right. When I first got back from the moon I didn't paint any moon paintings. I continued to paint things that I'd painted previously—landscapes, flowers, and things of that nature that I thought were beautiful. I said to myself that the moon was such a gray place; the sky is black and the spacesuits are white, and it didn't have the color I was really interested in. And then I began to realize that it was the function of the artist to introduce these into a painting. If you took a look at a haystack, for example, it's yellow or dirty brown. That's it, that's about all there is. If you look at a Monet painting of a haystack it can be golden, it can be blue, it can be greenish, it can be reddish. He took a very mundane shape and a neutral object and created great beauty from it. So, I've got a whole world up there that's gray and black, and people in white suits, and if I can be good enough I can create beautiful paintings of that world, colorful paintings. Yet they'll still look just like the moon, just as Monet's haystacks look like haystacks. That's the challenge of it, really.

On the first mission to the moon, Apollo 8, the astronauts talked about how bleak and desolate, how almost ugly and uninviting the moon looked. Yet, when Armstrong and Aldrin landed, and when you and Conrad landed, both crews were taken with how beautiful it was out there. Are those inconsistent reactions?

No, I don't think so. It depends on how you look at it. When you look at the ocean, you can see a great expanse of nothing there except blue or waves. Or you can see the water and the sun reflecting off it, and you can see the beauty of the fact that it's blue and it's uniform all the way out to the horizon. And you can think of how beautiful that looks. The same way with a desert. I think that with objects, beauty *is* in the eye of the beholder, and showing this beauty is one of the functions of an artist. An artist's function is not just to mimic nature. You can get a camera and do that if you want, or you can paint that way. I think that maybe the job is to idealize it somewhat, or point out the beauty, or enhance the beauty that's there, to make it as you wish it were. It's to create the poetry instead of the prose, and it's difficult to do. It's hard to make something look beautiful but not boring.

An obvious question would be that while you were in space did you have a chance to do any sketches? Alexei Leonov, the

Soviet cosmonaut, was known to draw in space. Did you have a chance to do that yourself?

I had a lot of chances, but I never did it. It never crossed my mind during the space flights to do any art. I've always been sort of single-minded all my life, as I am now, and my mind was on the space flight, doing the things assigned, and flying as well as we could. Now, I don't do any flying, and I don't even really miss it. My single focus is painting and that world. It's just the way I am. I wish I had, but it never crossed my mind at the time.

Not even during the Skylab mission, when you were up for 59 days?

No. I never felt like I had the time to do that because I really needed all the brains I had to perform the mission as well as we could. I felt that was my duty, that I should not be doing other things.

Do you feel NASA would have discouraged you from doing your art work while on a mission?

Oh, no. They selected us because they thought we were the best people around and available to do the job. They took us because they thought we had the discipline and knowledge to do things the way they should be done. That's why you have the selection program and you look at the person's history to see how they've behaved in the past, which is a good index of how they're going to do in the future. So, I don't think it would have bothered them a bit. I mean, I could have done it or not, and they'd be happy either way, I'm sure.

Let's talk about your flight to the moon. After missing out on a flight in project Gemini, you were very hopeful you'd get to fly in Apollo, but you were switched to the Apollo Applications Program. To your great surprise, however, Pete Conrad came over to you one day and said he wanted you on his Apollo crew. Is that really how it happened?

Yes. Just like that. I was coming in from a flight and he was going out and he said, 'I'd like to talk with you, come over here a minute.' I didn't have anything on my mind about the moon; I was busy trying to do Apollo Applications. I didn't *want* to be doing it, but once I realized that was where I was assigned then that's what was on my mind. So we talked, and of course, it changed my life right there and then. Of course, I was really happy and satisfied. I hadn't been planning on it or anything like that. I'd been kind of wrapped up in single mindedly doing this other job.

Did he tell you why he picked you or why he wanted you to go with him?

He probably did. We'd been friends now off and on a long, long time. He'd been my instructor in test pilot school, and I guess he knew what kind of person I was, and he wanted me on his crew. He must have said some things, but I just don't remember them. We like each other and had a lot of confidence in each other, and we knew what kind of people each other were, so that was about it.

Is that generally how it worked, the commanders got to pick their crewmates?

Oh no. He had gone to Deke Slayton, who was our boss at the time, and he was the person who really picked the crews. But, as the Commander you could make a request. If he assigned someone that you really didn't feel like you ought to be with, I'm sure if you talked with him, he might change his mind. Or he might say, 'No, I want you all to work together.' One of the things that you had to be able to do, and were selected for, was to get along with people, to do your job and not let personal opinions get in the way of professional performance.

Even though you were highly competitive, and there were thoughts you had about each other that might have interfered, your discipline took care of that, is that it?

Well, now that might have been true for other people, and we've seen from some of the books that have been written that that was the case. But that wasn't the case with Pete, Dick, and me. We were fortunate, we were a natural group together. We liked each other, we thought the same way, we were interested in the same things. We had the same professional ethics, so we seldom had disagreements that were anything more than just different ideas about the best way to do a particular thing. We didn't have any personal problems. We're good friends today. We just liked each other.

36 seconds after lift-off, your rocket was struck by lightning. Did the crew feel that you were in mortal danger at that point or, did you feel that well, we'll probably survive, but the mission will have to be aborted?

Well, we didn't know what had happened because all we saw were a bunch of warning lights. We didn't imagine that it was lightning. Nobody'd ever thought about the possibility, or they never would have launched us into the clouds. We just thought some failure had occurred, a short in a main circuit, or something like that. I thought the command module had separated from the service module. I didn't know of any way how that many warning lights could come on unless the command module had separated from the service module. There wasn't any one failure that could affect all those systems. We had simulated all these failures over and over again and there wasn't anything even approaching the magnitude of that. And of course we were lucky because, if it had been that, it would have been the end of the mission right there. But, it wasn't, and it was only about staging time that Pete began to realize that maybe we had been struck by lightning. He had seen a flash and heard a noise; he had the only available window. Dick and I weren't able to look out yet, so we didn't see the flash, of course, and the noise was just another noise with all the noise that was going on. We had no idea whatsoever what had happened. We were concerned that our spacecraft might go off in a funny direction, and we'd have to abort. That's what we were thinking: do we abort now, or do we keep riding this thing? You see, that was the question.

Were you amazed that you made it through all right; that the back-up systems worked so well under those circumstances?

Well, when the lightning hit I didn't know the back-up systems were taking over. I didn't know exactly what had happened. Looking back, it shows what a great design the command module was because the batteries assumed the full launch load. They were really never designed to do that, yet they kept the voltage up at a critical level. If the voltage had dropped below that level, then everything would have gone out. So, the batteries were strong enough to hold up with no fuel cells on the line. That was amazing to me and I was just gratified. It's a tribute not to us, but to the designers and builders of the command module. There was nothing that we did to solve the problem initially. The back-up systems saved our ass.

Were you afraid that you might have to come down anyway, even though you made it successfully to orbit? Could you be sure that everything was still intact before it was decided to commit, to the go to the moon?

We had certain things to check. The ground asked us to check a few others. Our biggest problem was that it dumped our inertial guidance platform. So, we had to get an alignment. We were busy getting ready for that. And we got that alignment and it worked okay, and we could see that everything that was measurable was working okay. The big question was, if the lightning hit us on the nose what did it do to the recovery system—all the pyrotechnics,

Alan Bean

the parachutes, the cone that's got to come off so that the parachutes get out. There's a lot of pyrotechnics up there, small explosive charges that activate the parachutes. Nobody knew the answers, so the thinking was, first of all, that *we* didn't worry about it. We had other problems, mainly getting the navigation system alignment and getting ready to go. We had a lot of work to do even if nothing had gone wrong. We had to leave it up to Houston to worry about the other things. And, they decided that there were two cases: either the parachutes are going to come out and they're going to get down in the water when they come back, or something went wrong up there and they're not; but we can't determine that. And there's certainly no reason to rush back to Earth to see that, so we might as well send them out to the moon and let them do all that stuff, and when they make the regular reentry, if the parachutes come out, great. If they don't, well, they lived ten days longer. That was the thinking on the ground, but we didn't worry about it. It wasn't our part of the job. It's sort of like being on a football team. You've got certain jobs, and you need to do them right, and you need to let the other people do their jobs.

Could you really put something like that out of your mind?
No problem. It was something that you have to learn to do as a test pilot and astronaut. You have to be able to take dangerous situations and kind of set them in the back of your mind and perform, or you can't do it. You're not born with the ability, you sort of develop it over the years. That's why they selected people like us, because we could do it. Some people can never learn to do it, and some people can learn to do it a lot better than we can. But we just happened to be some that did develop it, and they were able to measure it by our careers as pilots and test pilots. They could see that we could do this.
When I was up on Skylab, we lost one of the thrusters during the rendezvous, we lost the next thruster when we were docked, and they had to get the rescue command module ready in case they had to rescue us, in the event we lost another thruster. We were up there two months and I can safely say I didn't think of it five or ten times. We'd say, 'We're going to have to do these experiments and everything else we've got to do; let's don't think about that. Let's let them worry about it on the ground. We've got our own problems up here.

Back to Apollo 12, then. Aside from landing near Surveyor 3, we were wondering why they picked the Ocean of Storms as your landing site?

When NASA was laying out the missions they called together all the different scientific organizations that were going to be interested in what we did on the moon. They asked these organizations to form working groups of the best people interested in these things, and had them work among themselves, and together with the other groups to try to figure out what they thought were the best places to go on the moon, and why. Then it was our job to figure out how to get there; which places to go to first, the easy ones, and which ones to go to later, the ones more mountainous and rocky. That's how it was figured out. They wanted to go to Tranquility Base first because of the ease of getting there, the flatness, and a lot of other things. It was primarily for ease of navigation, landing, and radar tracking, so they could launch off the moon and get a lot of tracking before they went around the back side of the moon for the rendezvous. So, it was picked out completely by being the easiest place to go. They, we said, 'Of all the places you guys want to go to, what's the next easiest?' I guess that was the Ocean of Storms. So we went there. We just gradually built up that way.

Pete Conrad said that when you guys were landing, there was so much dust being kicked up that it was an IFR landing, an instrument landing. Did you really have to go in blind like that?

Well, now you've got to realize that dust on the moon doesn't kick up like dust clouds on Earth that are caused by the air. On the moon it goes sailing out almost like water jets in all directions from the rocket engine. So what it looks like is not like you're in a cloud, but if you look down to see the ground you can't see it. What you see is this little thin layer of dirt flying out away from you. So you might say it's like having a teeny layer of clouds under you just before you land. It's very disturbing because you see this stuff moving away from you, which makes you think you're going backwards. It's like being stopped at a red light and the car next to you moves ahead a little, and you think you're moving back. A natural way to try and correct it is to move the spacecraft forward so you can zero it out, but you can't do that. What you've got to do is learn to ignore that and look at the rocks that are sticking above the dust layer that are still visible; or use your instruments that'll show you that the ground's not moving 'cause the radar picks that up. It's different than an IFR landing in an airplane.

Did the dust being blown around by the engines make it a more tense situation than the simulations would have you believe?

Well, it makes it more difficult. But, Neil Armstrong got to see this, so we were aware of it when *we* went, and so we actually practiced on a simulator at Langley. They sprayed water jets below you to kind of get you used to seeing that. It was much more difficult for Neil because he was the first one to see this and overcome it. It's more difficult than without it, but not extra-special difficult. It's just part of the job.

Did you feel that yours was the first real scientific mission, since Apollo 11's main objective was the landing itself, whereas your flight had more scientific objectives?
Well, no. But I know that for each mission, the public relations people were always trying to find and make it a first of something. So, I think that was their effort to make the second landing a first at something. But, I think probably the greatest scientific mission was the first one, because they brought back unknown things, and we just refined their information. Exploration is a lot like that. In general, the first people there discover the most things and everybody else kinds of adds or subtracts from what they found out. I did think we did a good scientific job, but we had more time on the surface. I wouldn't call it the first of them at all, even though I've read that about it off and on.

Did you have enough time while out on the surface, or could you have used more?
Pretty much. I thought our training was excellent. We saw that things were a little different but it couldn't have been any more thorough. One of the things I wish we had done, and we didn't, was ask for another extension. We asked for one extension and got it. We probably could have asked for another one and gotten it, too, but we didn't do that. So, I think we really could have spent more time on the surface, only we were afraid we wouldn't be working together with mission control correctly. Now, I think they'd wished we'd asked for another, too. The time was there, and we were doing really well, and everything was going great. But, like I said, we had one extension and so we felt that was about fair.

Was your landing the best of the series? You were shooting for the Surveyor, and came within 600 feet. Was that the best of all of them?
I don't know. Even if we hadn't touched anything we would have landed right where we were targeted. But I don't think that's a criteria that's a real accurate measure of success. That's like asking

a pilot if he landed on the first hundred feet of the runway, or the first thousand. You know, it's not important. The important thing is did he make a safe landing. That's what's really important. I would say that probably they got closer and closer with each mission. The ability to navigate got better and we knew what we were doing better.

Was there a competitive aspect to it? One of your colleagues said that he wanted to come in the closest to the prescribed site, that it was important to him.

I don't personally see that as measure of profession skill, so, I didn't feel that way. However, that's only my opinion. If he feels that way, then that shows that he feels differently from me.

What was it like flying to the moon with Pete Conrad and Dick Gordon? Pete Conrad has the reputation of being a very feisty, ebullient character, and Gordon was a fun-loving kind of person, too.

Well, it was great. Both of them are just exactly like you describe them. Pete is very much the leader and very much the fun-maker, and, in my opinion, he's the best astronaut that's ever been there. Not because I flew with him, but because he seems to have the balance of instinct, attitude, skill, and everything that makes him, across-the-board, able to do things, influence people, and lead crews, which other people can't do. He just has a certain way about him that helps him get along with everybody. His IQ is big, and he just knows things. So, you always felt good, you always felt like Pete could make things work out. He was a good leader. There was never a question that he didn't have the best ideas. We might disagree and give other suggestions, but we usually felt like his final solution was the best of the bunch, and it did turn out that way.

Dick Gordon had a lot of equanimity. He's really the nicest possible guy. He could fly the command module beautifully, and he was easy to get along with. I'll give you an example. After we'd come back up from the surface we spent an extra day in orbit doing photography. It was Dick's responsibility, even though I happened to be shooting most of the film at the time. I was fooling with the Hasselblad camera, and all of a sudden the back comes off the camera. I had been flipping it around, you know, and finally I'd made the thing come loose. Dick saw it, and I could see that he was disappointed because it was his experiment. He didn't say, 'You dumb ass, why didn't you quit doing that?' He said nothing. He just turned and floated down toward the lower equipment bay and started doing something else. I put the camera back together and felt real bad. It turned out we'd lost only three frames of 250 shots. But at that moment we didn't know that we hadn't lost them all. Yet, he never did more than just try to busy himself doing something else. He understood, and he never has mentioned it since then. That's the kind of guy he is.

Did anything particularly funny happen to the three of you up there?

Well, one of the funniest things I remember was on the way to the moon, about a day out and Pete says to us, 'Look, I don't want anybody having to take a crap on the moon. We don't have time, we won't have time. I want you guys to get down there in the lower equipment bay and take your clothes off and get your little plastic bags and I want you to crap now so that you don't ever have to do it again, until we're headed back home.' We said, 'You're nuts, Conrad. We don't want to do it, we can't do it, we're not gonna do it.' So he said, 'Get down there.' He probably sent me down first because I was the junior man. He said, 'Get down there and get your clothes off and crap in that bag.' I went down there with my clothes off and they busied themselves looking out the window and stuff, and pretty soon I did. Then I folded mine up, you know, and did everything you did, and put it where it goes. So Pete then sent Dick down and he did it. And then he got down there and did it himself, and sure enough we never did have to crap until we were on the way home. So I've often laughed, 'cause we almost had a mutiny when he told us that. We thought he was a nut.

That was his truest test as a commander, right?

It really was because we thought, 'Are you kidding us? I mean you're gonna start regulating nature here?' But he made up his mind that we weren't gonna crap on the moon. He never mentioned it in training, but he did then. So, I've laughed about it lots of times.

When you were out on the surface, Conrad fell over and you had to pick him up. Was that an anxious moment?

No, and he picked me up. It was nothing. You could pick people up with one finger. It's kind of fun to reach down and just get one finger under the other guy's finger and pull, and up he would come. It's easy, and if they'd wanted to they could get up themselves, but it was less energy if you just helped them up. We're always in the business of conserving energy up there so we would have enough to do the job.

The NASA people must have worried about somebody falling down, and how they would get back up, because the pressure suits made it a little bit tough to bend over and move easily.

We worried that you could get stuck on your back like a turtle. Of course, even then you could probably get up, but it would take a lot of kicking around. So it could be done, but you'd get tired and you didn't want to do that. You wanted to save your energy for exploration.

When you were training, what kinds of things did you want to find out from the astronauts who had been out there before you? What kind of information were you looking for from them?

We were all getting ready for our missions in the same way. We would be using the same techniques to get to the moon. What we wanted from them when they came back was to tell us which things that we were using had to be changed, which ones to emphasize. For example, should we quit using this simulator and devote time to that one? Should we modify this simulator so that the sound was greater, since we found out that the sound was distracting. Maybe in this simulator just eliminate the sound because the sound wasn't a real factor. We wanted them to come back and just essentially say, 'If I had to do this over again, here's what I would do now that I've been to the moon.' Then, we would take what they said and do it.

Were there any real surprises that they came back with?

One of the surprises they came back with was the difficulty they had of knowing where they landed, and knowing exactly where they were, even knowing now where they'd landed for sure. The people at mission control began to realize that they were going to have to find a better way to navigate and land on the moon more accurately. They began to develop this, and that's when they began to say we want the second flight to be real accurate. Someone said, 'You can't be accurate if there's nothing there, just some crater. Who the hell knows what that is? So, we've got to send them to some *thing* that's on the moon that's not just a crater.' Then, someone said, 'How about the Surveyor spacecraft?'

And then the problem came up that they didn't know where the hell *it* was. They didn't need to know which crater it was in. They had a lot of photographs but they still weren't sure which of the craters that Surveyor was in. And it's interesting that the way they finally did it was that the scientists took the television from the Surveyor on the surface, pictures that it had taken of other craters, and then used that data to kind of figure out what crater it would have to be in to see these other craters at that distance and size. They never did figure it out from the navigation data, they figure it out this other way. We didn't know after we landed whether Surveyor was in the crater. We knew by then what the crater looked like that we were going for. So, we landed there and we said, 'We know it's the crater, I wonder if Surveyor's in it?' So, the first thing Pete did when he got out was to walk over and look in the crater to see if Surveyor was in it. It was behind us, and it had been in the dark when we landed. Sure enough, there it sat. But, nobody had known until several months before the mission which crater it was in.

We wanted to ask you, did you ever get a chance to figure out exactly what those small conical mounds were that you found near the landing site?
We didn't, but later on they felt they'd been ejected from a crater and they'd been big boulders, and over time the meteorites beat them down to be those mounds. So, at one time they were like rocks and over millions of years all of the little impacts wore them down enough so that they didn't look like boulders anymore, they looked like little mounds of dirt.

They caught your attention almost immediately, we assume.
Yes, because they were feature that we'd never seen in photographs or anything. I don't think anybody else saw any of them either. I think those were the only two things like that that were seen in all of the explorations. I'm sure they're all over the moon, but nobody else happened to see any other big things that had been kicked out in that same time period. If they had been kicked out earlier, or maybe made of softer material, then the meteorites would have worn them down and they would have been like little hills. Or, if they were harder and had kicked out more recently, it's quite possible they would look just like boulders.

Did NASA prepare the astronauts for any psychological changes they might undergo as a result of going to the moon?
They didn't do any of that. That's not NASA's way. It's up to the individual to look out after something like that, although I'm sure they'd give you help if you asked. I think the changes that did occur were a surprise to everybody. I don't think anybody changed to a different person. Everybody became more like they were when they were on a day off, you know. More relaxed, thinking about other things. At the same time, I think it was a surprise that some people really had difficulty afterwards.

One of the moonwalkers has mentioned that, after coming back from a voyage to a whole new world it became a little difficult to accept taking orders from generals and flying a desk.

I think that's true for a lot of people but we never thought about it. And people have difficulties all through their lives, so that's OK. We didn't expect to come back and be perfect. We expected to come back and have the same amount of problems we had before we left, just different ones maybe.

Did you find that your outlook changed in any appreciable way from your experience on the moon?

I feel more self-satisfied and happy. When you achieve your life's dream, then that frees you up to feel successful about your life no matter what happens after that. It also lets you go on to new dreams and try to satisfy them. Most people never do satisfy their dreams, so you've immediately been luckier than they are. And I feel lucky a lot, I feel blessed. I feel like somebody up there loves me, even though I don't believe in that sort of thing. I still wonder about it sometimes because it's like I've had a lucky life.

So there was never an uneasy sense that you couldn't top that, that somehow your life had peaked with your voyage to the moon?

No. Don't forget that even though that was an amazing achievement, the things we did individually weren't all that amazing. When you ride a rocket to the moon, *that* is amazing. But, the things you do, guiding the rocket, and eating on the way, and making navigation sightings, all that isn't that amazing. It's like flying on an airline; it's amazing an airliner can fly from London to New York in six or seven hours. It's amazing when you look out at the engines on the wings. Yet, the pilots aren't doing anything all that amazing. They're just flying their systems, and keeping the plane level. It's amazing that technology can let you do that, but the individuals aren't doing anything spectacular. So, we as individuals weren't doing anything that spectacular in terms of skill level. It's not like setting a record in the Super Bowl for a quarterback. We were doing things that we could easily do.

It's not the isolated elements, but the circumstances, the whole situation, that we're referring to. It's not hard to imagine someone having that kind of exceptional experience and finding it difficult having nothing like that to shoot for anymore.

I think they confuse what they personally did with the achievement. Sometime they begin to believe that *they* flew to the moon, let's say, when they really didn't. They made navigation sightings, they watched the gauges during launch, they did much less magnificent things than the total *thing* that was accomplished. I think that's something people have to bear in mind when they do something like this. They didn't just do this on their own. Let's take the Russian space shuttle. We certainly appreciate our shuttle astronauts. However, the Russians flew their shuttle unmanned. So, you've got to say to yourself, well, they can go the moon unmanned. So maybe we're not doing anything that incredible, if they can just do it with machines. It's not like the guys that flew Apollo to the moon and back built it and flew it themselves. It's more like they're sort of part of the whole team. I think that helps you keep in perspective what you've accomplished and in what is new. Because it seems to me that a person can do much better than that in the future. I probably can't, but some people can do much better than that in the future, in different fields. It may not be as spectacular looking or as dangerous. But as far as personal difficulty, I thought it was much more difficult, and required much more self-discipline and training to fly a 59-day Skylab mission than it did to fly to the moon. I liked going to the moon, but I thought it was more a test of a good astronaut to fly a good Skylab mission and do it right.

You spent 59 days in Skylab and the next crew spent 84. The Soviets have been up for almost a year now. Can you extrapolate as to how much a man can take in weightlessness, loneliness, and homesickness?

First of all, it depends on the individual. But, I think physically, as long as they exercise hard, an hour and a half a day, it looks like maybe they could spend years and years in space.

Even with the bone loss and other physiological changes that take place?

Bone loss doesn't mean squat! It's only a tiny percent of what you've got. It doesn't appear that there's any limit for the time that a person can spend in space physically. If they don't exercise, they probably won't survive when they come back to Earth. The exercise is to make you survive when you get home, it has nothing to do with being in space. Now, some people will want to stay a year, while others will want to come home after a day. We're going to take people up to the space station whom I'm sure we'll have to bring down within a week; they're not going to be able to stand it.

Then, we'll start to figure out how we can separate them out, right now I don't think we can. But, some will want to go up there, and someday, they'll say we're going to send some people and we want them to live there ten years. There'll be a lot of volunteers.

With your experience on Skylab and your experience with space stations, do you worry that the Soviet Union is opening a lead in that arena that the United States may not be able to close in the near future?

I don't worry about it very much. I think I would like it if we were the leading space-faring nation in the world, but we're not. And it doesn't appear that we're going to be. It's not something that seems to have the national priority that I would like to see. I think maybe this is going to be true for a number of years to come. Barring any sort of real emergency, or something, with other people, like getting mad at the Russians or their getting mad at us, I would say that we are just not prepared at the moment to spend the kind of money that they are. But it could change. It could change for them. Things are looking better for them over there, but who knows?

Do you think part of the problem is with NASA? Has it lost its way?

No. The problem is that the administration listens to the American people very carefully, and the space program is something everybody wants, but nobody wants to pay for it. So, it's easy for somebody like Reagan to talk about how wonderful it is. I heard him say it and I was thinking, well sure, you don't have to pay for it. You can talk about it all you want. Where were you when you had to pay for it. This is not a negative to Reagan, I think this is going to be the new administration too. We all want a Rolls Royce, but I'm not going to buy one, I can't afford it. I think maybe the space program fits in there somewhere.

In your opinion, does the continuing progress of the Soviet space program or their space station program pose any kind of threat to our security here in the United States?

Of course, they are taking a look to see what they can use the space station for in a military sense, just as we are. At the moment, there doesn't appear to be any short-term great advantage to it. It's not like if they suddenly got up there and had a laser weapon, if they could shoot our cities from up there or something like that, we'd start getting worried, and want to get our laser weapons up there, and vice versa. It doesn't appear to me that in the short term that is going to happen. I think we're doing our research, too. I never feel short-changed by our own research. We could have orbited a satellite before the Russians, and people proposed it. But, politically, nobody was interested. I think we've got technology that can beat them, and we will have that for the foreseeable future. We just won't be spending the money to implement those things. I want to work with the Russians, I want to compete with them, but at the same time, you try to do cooperative things. I want us to go to Mars, and when we go, I want to go with Russia and Europe and Asia all together. I wouldn't want to see us go by ourselves. I want to see us go with *them*. I want to see us go with England and France; maybe have a five-member crew: one American, one Russian, one European, one Asian, and one African, or something like that. I think the time has come, and the space program is a field where we might be able to do things that, although they're just symbolic, and people will say they're political, they can still change people's attitudes. If we went to Mars with the Russians, and you took a poll after that, people would think the Russians were less threatening and a lot nicer than they do now.

You worked with them on the Apollo-Soyuz project, didn't you?

I sure did. And I liked them. I liked them and I felt that they were trapped in a political system that's very difficult. Certainly, we've got to be ready to defend ourselves against that political system. But, in the long run we need to make friends with these people. They're nice people, they're honest, they're reliable, they work hard, and they've got a lot of characteristics that we like in other people. And, if we can just find a way so that their political system is more in tune with ours, or at least not at odds so much, we'd be much better off. The biggest threat to the world is a nuclear confrontation. Anything we can do to lessen that threat is the thing we should do. If they wanted to go to Mars and we wanted to spend the money, I'd say that's the best money we could spend, period. Anything to lessen the international tension is important. The French have nuclear weapons, and submarines. If a French submarine captain shot a nuclear weapon over here, accidentally, or a captain did it on his own, or something, I don't think we would go to war with France. We'd wait and try to figure it out, and then make a decision. Well, that's because we feel that way about France. I don't think many people feel that way about Russia, particularly people that haven't been around them, maybe, very much. Certainly, the old-time military people don't feel that way. We need to have a situation so that if some Russian submarine skipper sometimes does send one over here, or one of our skippers sends one over there, that we don't blow up the world without talking about it for a while. Now, there would be a feeling among a lot of people that, well, that's them, that's the Russians. Let's get ours airborne and kill them all even if we die trying. We wouldn't do that to the French. That tells you something.

What is your feeling about the use of space for something like Star Wars?
My feeling is, first of all, that you can't do it now, it's technically impossible. But, if you want it to be technically possible someday, then you've got to take the first step, which is what they're doing. But it'll never be able to do the things they promise, it's just impossible. Compare it to just launching the Shuttle. I mean, launching the Shuttle is child's play compared to SDI. So, think of what could go wrong there, think of the difficulty. I think that the Russians are going to be looking at space for weapons for defense and offense; we've got to be ready, too. We've always got to protect ourselves. Even though we extend the hand of friendship, if they decide to swing at it, we better be ready to do something back or they're going to take our place.

But, you've got to try to make it a better world, meet them more than half-way. They seem to be meeting us more than half-way now. It's kind of embarrassing. At the same time, we've got to protect ourselves in case they're lying. We used to be at war with the French, we used to be at war with the English. Well, we're not any more. Times change. We've got to make it so that we feel about the Russians like we do the Canadians now. And that's the way it ought to be 50 years from now. People will say, 'The Russians shoot something at us? You're crazy!' The same thing we'd say about the French now.

Before we finish, we'd like to get your opinion of the proposals set down by Sally Ride in her report on future space policy.
I like it, but it's not as adventuresome as I tend to think. You know, she wants Mission to Planet Earth. And I think it's probably practical and logical, and all that, but emotionally it doesn't have much for me. If I wrote the report, I would have said let's start getting things going on the way to Mars; we can't do it yet, but let's get the space station ready. Let's build a space station with its primary goal to be served as a launch platform to Mars. Let's start

doing all the research to get to Mars and let' go that direction. And if we can do any mission to Earth along the way at no extra expense, okay. It's a difference in philosophy. I don't say her way is wrong. It's my own personality; I want us to go do things that are more adventuresome, maybe not even as hard.

ARMSTRONG, ALDRIN, AND AN AMERICAN EAGLE

The Eagle with Neil Armstrong and Buzz Aldrin aboard are just about to touch down on the Sea of Tranquility, July 20, 1969. The descent engine is firing to slow the descent rate for a gentle landing as Neil flies the lunar module beyond some rough terrain searching for a level area.

The Eagle was designed to fly like a helicopter even though it has a rocket on the bottom rather than rotor blades on the top. The reasoning was that controls and techniques for operating a machine that could move up and down and sideways and even stand still were needed. The helicopter was such a machine and the controls and techniques had been proven over many years.

Neil is looking out the left-hand window, Buzz out the other. Between them is the square hatch Neil will use to exit the lunar module. After crawling backwards along the platform, he will descend the ladder to the surface; a small step for a man, but a giant step for mankind.

Many space enthusiasts say the eagle was the first true spaceship because it could land and then take off again. It was an incredible vehicle on an unbelievable mission. That was okay because we all knew that every worthwhile endeavor is at first impossible. It had to work right or Neil and Buzz wouldn't be bringing home any moonrocks. When we Americans put our minds and energy to it, nobody, but nobody, can do the things we can do. The Eagle did what it was supposed to do and more. I believe the Eagle (and her crew) could only have been made in America.

--Alan Bean

AN AMERICAN SUCCESS STORY

I have painted Astronaut John Young as he stood proudly on the moon, but for a while it didn't look like he and Charlie Duke would even land there at all. Earlier, as they had been orbiting the moon in their lunar module preparing for descent, a call came from Ken Mattingly in the command module reporting an unexpected oscillation in the backup steering system for the rocket engine. They all knew that if this oscillation prevented the backup system from controlling the rocket properly then all three crewmembers would have to return to earth as soon as possible. This would be the only prudent course of action because if the primary system should fail at any time there would be no way to steer the rocket engine. Apollo XVI and her crew would orbit the moon forever.

Immediately engineers and technicians at mission control in Houston and at other key locations were alerted. Could they determine if the oscillations would prevent the backup steering system from doing its job? From North American Rockwell in California to the Kennedy Space Center in Florida records were searched, simulations were run, and tests were conducted. In less than six hours the results were in. The oscillations would damp out as rocket thrust built up at engine start. The mission could continue. We all breathed a collective sigh of relief. As John Young would say later, "It was a cliff-hanger from where we were sitting in the cockpit. But the ground, who were calling in data from all over the country, really came through. With a couple of clutch hits they put us right back in the ball game. It was a superb performance."

--Alan Bean

MOONROCK—EARTHBOUND

Collecting a moonrock was more than just reaching down and grabbing one we happened to like. The first problem was to know which rocks of the many that can be seen are worth the time and energy to document, collect and return. We learned a lot about rocks in the six years of geology training on earth prior to going to the moon.

It wasn't easy for "hot white stuff test pilots" to sit through the hours and hours of classroom lectures and laboratory demonstrations. We did, however, take right well to the field trips to Arizona, Oregon, Iceland, Hawaii, etc.—locations where the geology was thought to be similar to the moon. The field training was where we honed our skills.

Usually, the first rock we selected was one that looked most like all the other rocks in the area. This typical rock was photographed from two positions before we disturbed the ground. Picking up the rock was not simple either, and I have painted John Young using the long tweezer-like tongs at a site near where Apollo 16 landed.

Charlie Duke is inspecting the rocks, making specific comments to earth, then placing it in a numbered sample bag. This is a big day for the selected rock, as it has probably been sitting right here for at least 3 billion years, just waiting for some human being to single it out for a quick trip to Planet Earth.

--Alan Bean

TRACY'S BOULDER

Gene Cernan and Jack Schmitt have finished their work at Station 6 and are loading the lunar roving vehicle with their rock samples and experiments. Although our planet earth is not visible in this painting, we know it is some 240,000 miles away in the direction the rover antenna is pointing.

This panaramic view of the Taurus-Littrow Valley with South Massif to the right and East Massif to the left gives some an idea of majestic vistas that wait to be seen by earthlings of future generations. This might someday be the location for a scientific station, or maybe a shopping center or housing development.

When I showed this painting to Gene Cernan, he told me about how he had scooped a dirt and dust sample from the left side of this massive boulder. He said he wishes he had thought of writing his daughter's name in the dust but the idea didn't come 'til he got back home. The sheer romance of such a thought was so appealing that as Gene's friend, I have employed artistic license to save him the long trip back to Station 6, not to mention the monumental savings to all US taxpayers.

--Alan Bean

LOAD 'EM UP . . . MOVE 'EM OUT

The highest priority task Pete Conrad and I were scheduled to accomplish during our first moonwalk on Apollo XII was the deployment of an unmanned geophysical station. We called it ALSEP, an acronym for Apollo Lunar Surface Experiments Package, and it consisted of a cluster of six experiments all connected to a Central Command and Control Station and powered by the first thermonuclear electrical power generator on the moon.

I have painted myself attaching the ALSEP components to either end of a light-weight metal bar. This "High Tech Barbell" was the best way we could think of to carry all this hardware to a relatively flat spot 300 feet away so the experiments wouldn't be blown over or covered with dust when we blasted off the moon the next day. The wastebasket shaped object on the near end of the bar is the seismometer. It measures moonquakes or meteoroid impacts; and, as surprised scientists discovered, our footsteps as we moved about our tasks. The magnetometer with its gold foil covered sensor arms is just below.

In my right hand we can see the bottom of the thermonuclear electric power generator. I can distinctly remember feeling the intense heat from the decaying plutonium fuel element—even through my heavily insulated suit. I wondered if the dedicated and able suit makers on earth had anticipated this heat and built the suit to withstand it. But I didn't have time to worry about it then. We had to get on with our work. It was time to "load 'em up, and move 'em out."

—Alan Bean

DRILLING FOR KNOWLEDGE

Apollo 15 Astronaut David Scott is using his new lunar surface drill. He is planning on drilling two holes, each 10 feet deep, to be used in an experiment that will measure the rate of heat flow from the interior of the moon. Knowledge of this heat flow rate may allow scientists to understand why we see evidence of volcanos on the moon yet we see no volcanic activity.

Dave is having difficulty, "When I got the first two borestems in, it was apparent I was hitting something very hard. The first three feet or so was quite east to drill and then it was difficult to get it in any further. We'd never seen this in training nor had we ever seen any material that was compacted as hard as this material". Although Dave could not drill either hole to the planned ten foot depth, they were deep enough to allow Dave to partially insert the temperature sensors.

Results from this experiment indicate that the heat generated in the interior of the moon is about one-fourth that produced by our planet earth. This is completely consistent with our observation that there was abundant volcanic activity during the early formation of the moon, some 3 to 4 ½ billion years ago, but as the natural radioactive elements decayed and the moon cooled to its present level there is no longer sufficient heat to provide for volcanic erruptions. This is unfortunate for us earthlings. Wouldn't it be exciting to look up at night and see the bright fires and dark smoke plumes of active volcanos scattered across the moon?

-- Alan Bean

Chapter 6

JIM IRWIN
Lunar Module Pilot, Apollo 15

Walking with God in the Mountains of the Moon

Exploring amid the airless mountains of the moon in the summer of 1971, Apollo 15 astronaut James Irwin felt the presence of God. "I felt his spirit more closely than I have ever felt it on the earth," he later recalled in his 1973 autobiography *To Rule The Night.* He was deeply moved by the stark, serene beauty of the moonscape. Like a pilgrim in Jerusalem he sensed he was in a holy place. "It has remade my faith," he affirms. "I had become a skeptic about getting guidance from God, and I know I lost the feeling of his nearness. On the moon the total picture of the power of God and His Son Jesus Christ became abundantly clear to me."

On the last day there, when his partner Dave Scott took a moment to point out the beauty of the sunlit mountains, Irwin responded by quoting from the Book of Psalms. 'I will lift up mine eyes unto the hills, from when commeth my help.'

James Benson Irwin was born in Pittsburgh, Pennsylvania on March 17th, 1938, the first of two children of James and Elsa Irwin. He has a younger brother named Chuck. The family moved several times as Jim was growing up, first to New Port Richey, then to Orlando in Florida. It was in New Port Richey that Jim made his commitment to Christ. Walking down the street one evening with his mother and brother they chanced by a Baptist church holding a revival meeting and decided to go in. Jim was eleven years old at the time. At the end of the service he stepped forward to accept Jesus as his Personal Savior.

Escaping the Florida heat the Irwins moved west in 1944 to Roseburg, Oregon, living there only a short time before resettling in Salt Lake City, Utah. The family home in Salt Lake was near the base of the Wasatch Mountains. Jim developed a deep love for the area. His great pleasure was climbing, hiking, and skiing in the nearby hills and canyons.

In school Jim was a diligent student and made good grades. He graduated from East High School in Salt Lake City in 1947. He had his heart set on going to West Point, but a low mark on one of the substantiating tests put him out of the running among the candidates from Utah. He then decided to try for the Naval Academy, and was accepted. Irwin did not care for the Navy, so he put in a bid to transfer to another branch when he finished at Annapolis. He graduated in 1951 and chose a commission in the Air Force. He was sent to flight school in Texas, but felt uncomfortable flying because he found no interest in it at the time. He even made an attempt to get out of it, going to the Commandant of Students with his reservations. No dice. He had to stick it out.

The turnaround came when he made his first solo flight and experienced, in his words, "the great charge of exhilaration from being absolutely alone up in the sky." He eventually made the transition to jets, then set his sights on test pilot school. To prepare for that he attended the University of Michigan where he received dual Masters degrees in Aeronautical Engineering and Instrumentation Engineering in 1957. Three years later he entered the Test Pilot School at Edwards. He completed the course in 1961 and was assigned to the top secret Lockheed YF-12A Blackbird project. Irwin was only a month into his new job when his test pilot career nearly ended. He suffered head injuries, two broken legs, was badly cut and bruised, and almost lost his right foot when one of his students from the base flying club crashed their light plane after takeoff during a weekend lesson. He was grounded for over a year.

Fully recovered and flying again, Irwin went through the Air Force Aerospace School in 1963 with the idea of becoming an astronaut. He applied for the third and fourth groups but was turned down both times. In 1966, at the upper age limit for new astronauts, he put his application into NASA for the third time and was selected as one of the nineteen Group Five pilots.

In June of 1968 Irwin was crew commander in an important series of lunar module systems tests in a simulated space environment. He went on to serve as a member of the support crew for Apollo 10, then was named to the backup crew of Apollo 12. Late in 1969 he and his backup crewmates from Apollo 12, Dave Scott

Jim Irwin

and Al Worden, were given the nod to man the Apollo 15 flight scheduled to fly in 1971.

On July 26, 1971 a Saturn rocket rose from the Kennedy Space Center shooting Apollo 15 on a trajectory to the moon. On the afternoon of July 30th Irwin and mission commander Scott swooped down towards the moon in their lunar module "Falcon". Their destination was a small, relatively smooth lava lake in the Apennine Mountains on the eastern rim of the Sea of Rains with the decidedly unappealing name of Palus Putredinus, or the Marsh of Decay. Despite its ugly name, it was a breathtaking spot. Two huge mountains, one towering over 14,000 feet high to the north-east, one rising more than 11,000 feet and to the south, stood sentinel over the landing site. Snaking across the plain was a 3000 foot wide, 1000 foot deep lunar canyon called Hadley Rille. It was as though Jim Irwin was returning to his back yard in Salt Lake City.

About a hundred feet from the surface the LM's braking rocket started kicking up a lot of dust, obliterating the astronauts' view. Guided by instruments, Scott brought Falcon to within a few feet of the ground and turned off the engine. The lander hit on an upslope, banging down hard with a shuddering recoil. "It was a tremendous impact", Irwin remembers. "I was sure something was broken. . .We just froze in position as we waited for the ground to look at all our systems." To their great relief the LM was intact and they would get to stay.

The two astronauts spent the next three days roaming the landing area. They made their forays in style using the first lunar automobile, Rover 1. They drove to different sites and formations, including Hadley Rille, where they would give descriptions of what they saw, take pictures, and collect geology specimens. On the second day, near the rim of a crater, they noticed a white rock perched on a small mound. Its appearance was different from other rocks they had seen in the area. They picked it up with excitement, sensing that it might be an original piece of the moon's crust. It turned out to be very old indeed and became known as the "Genesis Rock".

On August 2nd, after 34 hours on the moon, Irwin and Scott flew back into orbit in Falcon's upper section and hooked up with Al Worden in the command module "Endeavor". They circled the moon for another day then fired out of orbit for the journey home and a splashdown in the Pacific Ocean on August 7th.

The voyage to the moon had awakened a new life in Jim Irwin. Back in Houston after the flight he was assigned to the backup crew of Apollo 17, but found the work uninspiring. He started speaking to church groups on weekends about his spiritual revival and became increasingly preoccupied with his new role as a Christian emissary. At about the same time, a controversy erupted around Irwin and his Apollo 15 crewmates when it was learned that they had taken some unauthorized postal covers to the moon and sold them to a West German businessman. The astronauts returned the money before the story broke but the affair left them under a cloud. Under those circumstances Irwin decided to leave NASA, and retired from the Air Force in the summer of 1972 to pursue his ministry on a full time basis.

With the help and encouragement of some friendly religious leaders he established High Flight, a nonprofit foundation with the purpose of "leading man to his highest flight in life, to realize his greatest potential, using all his gifts and abilities to the highest degree." Despite a heart attack in 1973, Irwin has kept up a busy travel schedule bringing his message to people all over the world. In addition to spiritual and motivational programs, Irwin and his group embarked on a series of expeditions beginning in 1982 to search for relics of the biblical period including Noah's Ark, and the Ark of the Covenant. In August of 1982 he was seriously injured by a falling rock while on the slopes of Mt. Ararat in Turkey investigating reported sightings of Noah's Ark.

Jim Irwin and his wife Mary have five children. They make their home in Colorado Springs.

Col. Irwin, you've been to the moon and have come to regard it as a holy place. In what sense, exactly, do you mean that?

Well, it was holy, as far as I was concerned, because I just sensed that God was there.

Did you, or do you, have any sense of it beyond that? Was that a surprise to you?

I shouldn't have been surprised, but I was. And I should not have been because you realize He's everywhere, as long as we're conscious. I was so tied up with the details of exploring the moon that I thought *that* would be my prominent thought. But, it seems like the Lord invaded those thoughts to the point where I was more aware that He was there.

Did you actually sense His presence?

Yes, I did. He was guiding our activities, our exploration.

As a corollary to perceiving the moon to be a holy place, do you also feel that space exploration is a kind of holy enterprise itself?

I think that, clearly the heavens are the domain of the Lord, of God. We go there with His permission really. So anything that we do out there ought to be to glorify Him and to humble us. We do it, as a service to Him and a service to others, to mankind. The words on the plaque on our spacecraft that landed on the moon, were very appropriate: we came to the moon "for all mankind". We went out there to be of service to others, that they might be enriched by our experience. Because we were enriched in a new dimension, in a physical dimension, a psychological dimension, and also a spiritual dimension.

That brings us to an interesting point. You saw yourself as kind of a nuts and bolts type, a test pilot and engineer, someone concerned with the job at hand. How did you find the process of turning from that into someone who felt compelled to go out and share these experiences and bring this message to as many people as you could?

At first it was a great challenge, but I think an everyday challenge. I sensed it as a golden opportunity, to communicate some worthwhile information to other people on earth. And I came to realize that communication is the most important thing that we have going for us as human beings. If we lose the ability to communicate, we might as well be dead. So, I've been trying to communicate ever since I came back to the earth. Communicating not only the fact that we'd been there, but that my life has been changed by the new perspective. I came back with a new appreciation of things that I had taken for granted. So, as a result of that new appreciation, life became more precious and life became richer. But, life became a littler shorter, too. I just realized that life continues to rush by, it goes faster and faster. Each day and each year disappears. I'm aware of that because I've had some close calls. I'm lucky I'm here. I'm thinking of the—you know, I've had a lot of heart problems. I had a heart arrest two years ago. And I had that rather serious injury on Mt. Ararat. It was a miracle that I even pulled through that one. So the Lord has given me plenty of warnings that life is fragile, that life is precious, that the end of life is probably fairly close. So, I realize that I'm here to serve others.

We might be getting a little ahead of things here, but since you mentioned it now, do you think that your journey to the moon, and your moonwalks in particular, could have been re-sponsible in any way for your heart problems?

I don't know that directly—Indirectly it probably did, because it precipitated the arrhythmia that I'm plagued with even now. Dave Scott suffered the same irregular heartbeat but, fortunately, he's been able to correct his and so, as far as I know, he doesn't have that problem. I think the stress of the moon adventure, the severe dehydration, precipitated that arrhythmia so, the doctors suspect that the arrhythmia that I suffered brought on the heart arrest that I had two years ago. But, the heart attack that I had in 1973 was the result of blockage in the coronary arteries, atherosclerosis, which most of us are affected by just because of the rich life that we live, the so-called "good life." I should point out that the "good life," in this sense, isn't a *good* life.

We're all becoming more aware of that these days. But didn't some of the other Apollo astronauts, too, have similar symptoms while they were on the moon? The medical people became concerned about them losing too much potassium, wasn't it?

Yes. That's what brought on our problems. It's a thing called "heavy electrolytes," and potassium is a very important one.

Getting back now to the change you experienced by traveling to the moon; was it fair to characterize you before that as being introverted, somewhat of a loner?

Well, I guess that would be true.

In your book To Rule The Night, *you described your upbringing in very fond terms. You had a close family, you lived in several different parts of the country, you were very active and enjoyed the outdoors, hiking and camping. How do you think you came to develop such an independent and self-reliant kind of character?*

Oh, I don't know. I think I got that from my father. He was very independent, a little cocky Irishman. He was resilient. I think I developed a lot of my character from him. I loved him. Some of my fondest thoughts are of the times that I spent with my father. Yes, I think that probably came from my father's side, although my mother sometimes had some of the same characteristics.

In that same vein, you mentioned the particular joy you have of being alone when flying airplanes, and that when the Apollo moonship slid behind the moon out of radio contact with the ground you said it was the kind of privacy that you liked.

Yeah, there was kind of an isolation. But, it is a tendency that, maybe, we were somewhat more in charge than when we were on the front side of the moon where Mission Control had communication with us, always giving us instructions on what we should do.

Was that something that you thought of as kind of a nuisance? Maybe nuisance might not be the right word but, you know, the constant stream of messages from the ground?
It's certainly a necessary way to run a mission. You realize we needed that help, that observation. All that information is vital to the success of the mission. I never objected to that at all. It was great that we had that communication.

What about the astronauts themselves? Were you close, was there a genuine comraderie?
We were very close for our flight. Then some problems came up after the flight that kind of divided us on a few things. I think the most divisive thing that came out of all of that was the publicity on the first day covers.

Were you eventually able to rectify those problems?
No, I don't think it's ever been completely rectified. There were some disagreements that have never been resolved.

You also had some uneasiness on the personal side, didn't you? An unsettled feeling, a period of adjusting, or sorting things out.
We were very busy when we got back. There was very little time to really get away and meditate on things for any extended period. We'd been recovered southwest of Hawaii, put on a giant cargo plane at an Air Force base, and brought back across the Pacific. During the flight we tried to get our thoughts organized. We knew that once we got back to Houston, we would be expected to have our personal reflections summarized for the New York Times article. That gave us the opportunity to get our personal thoughts pretty well prepared and organized for that.

We're not referring so much to the hectic times immediately following your return, but the situation you talked about in your book where you described having a feeling of being in a new life, of being a new man, and being afraid at the same time. You said you didn't understand what was happening inside you. You wouldn't face it.

I kind of dreaded public speaking and I think that was a fear that I had. I felt more comfortable with something tangible, a piece of equipment, a button, or a control, than public speaking.

You also had this sense of a personal change talking place, a certain transformation in your view of life, your outlook. Can you give us some insight into your emotions during that time, what you were thinking, as this change was taking place?

Well, that was seventeen years ago; I don't think I can recall specifically. I think what I said is probably all I remember at this point.

You also had kind of a rough period two years or so before you made your flight, an upheaval in your family life brought on by the demands of your training and preparation for the mission. You almost gave up the flight at one point. Did you eventually expect that, once the mission was successfully completed, you would be able to return to the semblance of a more normal life?

I thought so. I think my wife had the feeling that once I got all this flying stuff out of my system, we could look forward to civilian life at some point, a "normal" life, whatever that might be. And I think that *was* a conflict. Today I'm more content with myself and the world, more content not to be so achievement and goal oriented. I just realized that I'm here to serve others as best I can.

Let's talk about exploring the moon for a bit. Now, you were the first crew to use the Lunar Rover. You and Dave Scott drove it around to different spots in the vicinity of the landing site. It looked a little like a go-cart. Were you ever concerned about maybe getting into an accident, or was it just a lot of fun?

Oh, we had a good time. It was exciting to have the Rover, being the first to use it on the moon. There was some concern that perhaps the vehicle would actually roll over—you know, flip— because there were many times when we were coming up over a rise and there would be a crater, or we'd bump into a sharp stone. If the car hit that obstacle, it would go up off its wheels, and we wondered it if did roll over how we would release ourselves. If it rolled over, it would be lying on top of us.

Did you wear seatbelts?

Oh yes, we had to or else we'd fly right out of the seat.

You had to end your first excursion a little sooner than planned. Did you and Scott find it more strenuous working on the moon than you had anticipated?

More strenuous than we anticipated? Yes, I guess we did, but it was exciting. We didn't notice the stress or know there was concern, until we got back in the spacecraft and were told about the heart murmurs.

Did you and Dave talk at all while in the LM, between the times you were out on the surface?

Of course. All that is monitored and saved for the mission record.

What about just between yourselves? Did you talk about your impressions, how things were going?

Oh, I'm sure we did. I don't recall exactly what the conversation was. In other words, once we got back into the spacecraft it must be—I'm trying to think—it was probably about twelve hours before we got out again. Once we got in, we debriefed, ate, slept, got up again, then ate again, and went out. Plus we recharged the backpacks. So it was a pretty busy time, all the time we were in the spacecraft.

You and Scott found and brought back a large white rock that, because of its type and age has been dubbed the "Genesis Rock". What was it like discovering such a specimen? Can you tell us a little about it?

That was a moment of great joy, of great satisfaction. We found an object we came looking for in the mountains of the moon. I'm just surprised there weren't many other white rocks sitting around because, if you look at the mountains of the moon, you can see they're almost white. We thought we were going to find white rocks. But, it might be just the reflection of the light on the slopes of the mountains that gives it that color.

Wasn't the Genesis Rock over four billion years old?

Yes. The last figure that I heard was 4.15 billion years, plus or minus .25 billion. It's also interesting that the green rock that we brought back has an approximate age of about a half a billion years older than the white rock. So, really, the green rock should have been called the Genesis Rock, rather than the white one.

Let's shift from the ground to the sky. A lot has been made of how the Earth looks from the moon. What about the stars and the rest of the sky above the moon? Does it look much different than it does from on the earth? Can you see the Milky Way, for example?

I say there is no sky. The sky means, for me, an atmosphere. You have no atmosphere above the moon, you just look out into the blackness of space. And there's so much reflected light that you can't see the stars.

You can't?

I could not, no. If you get into a position where you're on your back, then you might be able to see them. But I could not see any stars, just the blackness of space. The place where we really view the heavens is on the dark side of the moon. As we circled the moon, we had about one hour of almost perfect viewing when we were on the dark side. It takes about two hours to go completely around the moon, one one hour in the light, one hour in the dark.

How much different do the heavens look from that point of view?

Well, you can certainly see the Milky Way. It looks just like, well, perhaps more distinctive than it does from the Earth. But, the thing out there, when you're in space, above the atmosphere of Earth, is that the stars no longer twinkle. They're just steady lights. So, it's very difficult to distinguish between the stars and the planets.

Because of its environment—no atmosphere, low gravity, and so on—the moon would be an ideal place to set up observatories and other kinds of scientific stations. Should we be concentrating on getting back to the moon now, rather than pushing other programs, or thinking about going to Mars?

I think we'll have to look at the status of our program—our capabilities, or technologies, and our funding possibilities. You know, it would be nice to do all these things, but I think, though, that if we have a desire to go back to the moon, we should establish a base very much like the base we operate at the South Pole, in Antarctica. There'll also be a desire to reach out even farther, to go to Mars, because Mars holds a lot of promise. It's more like the Earth. I think that men and women will feel much more at home on Mars than they will on the moon. The only problem is it's much farther away and much more expensive to get there.

Do you see the moon as a logical stepping stone in terms of establishing manned outposts in space, in the solar system?

It might be, particularly if we look at the mission to Mars.

Looking at it economically, would it be better to launch from the moon, or would it be better to launch from a space station out of earth orbit?

I'd have to look at the requirements in terms of power, the size of the spacecraft. I think it could be just as economical, in fact, to launch from a space station in Earth orbit as it would be from the moon. Because, if you go to the moon, of course, then you have to assess again the power needed to fly there first, slow all that stuff down, and eventually land all the equipment, and launch it off again.

When we finally do get to Mars, do you think we'll find life there? How about in other parts of the solar system? The universe?

I don't think they'll find any life on Mars, though there is some speculation that maybe there was an ancient civilization on Mars. I don't know whether you've seen some of those pictures of the so-called "face" on Mars. It's probably just a lighting artifact, just a peculiarity, a natural phenomenon. But, it could be the result of some ancient civilization. It would be fascinating, I think, to visit that particular area of Mars to find out what it is. But, as far as life somewhere else in our solar system or beyond our solar system, I don't think so. We've already explored our solar system, except for some of the remote moons and the outer planets and we're pretty sure that there's probably no life existing anywhere but here. The only place where life is, is the Earth. So, we ought to feel very special for that. On the other hand, if you look at the vastness of the universe, I'd say the probability would be greater that there's life out there somewhere. Whether we'll ever make any contact with that life, I tend to doubt it. Frankly, I doubt that there's intelligent life out there.

Would it change any of your religious views if we were to come in contact with an extraterrestrial civilization?

Not really. But, I should preface that by saying that it depends on what form of life we find and what the state of that life is.

Assuming it was advanced, maybe even similar to our own, would that make a difference?

I'd like to talk to them, to that so-called advanced life form, and find out if they have a concept of God. Do they know God in a personal way? Maybe they've had a chance to know Him more personally then we do. Maybe they've actually seen Him.

To extend that even further, a really fascinating question would be would they have a concept of Christianity the way we understand it here on earth? Would that be a part of their theology?

That also would be a kind of follow-up question. But, I think that Christ came to the Earth because of man's depravity, for man's acceptance into Heaven, and his redemption, for reconciliation, that we might be brought to God. And, that relationship to Christ that we have—that they might have—depends upon their status; have they fallen, have they become sinners? I don't know; I think it could be that there *are* other civilizations out there, that maybe the Earth is considered off limits because of our state of affairs here.

That's a fascinating conjecture. In pondering our position here on the Earth, our situation, do you think that maybe God created the rest of the solar system for us, as a gift, to use and explore?

I think that He's given us intelligence, He's given us inspiration, He's given us resources and technology. I think that He wants us to use it. He wants us to use it to serve Him by serving others. He's given us a dominance over the resources of our solar system for the benefit of all mankind. It says in the Bible that He's given us dominion over the world, over nature. I think that our solar system was, clearly, the work of His hand. So, we have the dominion, we have that responsibility that we've got to exercise, or I don't know why He fashioned it.

After your return from the moon you created a public service foundation called "High Flight". It took its name from the title of a poem written by a young flyer named John Gillespie Magee. Before we talk about the foundation itself, can you tell us the story of John Magee and his poem, and the effect it has for you?

It's a very beautiful, inspirational poem that I remember first seeing as a young pilot, and I think I've always had a copy of it. I had the chance to take several copies of it with me to the Moon, as others have done. It's well known by pilots in our country and around the world. John Magee, you might know, was the son of missionary parents serving in China. John was actually born in Shanghai. The family was forced to leave there, and they came back to the United States. His mother was actually English, his father was an American, from Pittsburgh—my own hometown. In fact, I was born in Magee Hospital, so there's also a close connection there. Anyway, when John and his family returned, World War II was breaking out, and John wanted to serve in the war effort. He wanted to serve, somehow, both countries, England and America, and he decided the best way to do that would be to go to Canada and join the Royal Canadian Air Force. He trained to be a fighter pilot and was shot down in the Battle of Britain at the age of nineteen. Before he was killed, he was inspired to write the poem "High Flight":

Oh, I have slipped the surly bonds of Earth
And danced the skies on laughter-silvered wings;
Sunward I've climbed, and joined the tumbling mirth
Of sun-split clouds—and done a hundred things

You have not dreamed of—wheeled and soared an swung
High in the sunlit silence. Hov'ring there,
I've chased the shouting wind along, and flung
My eager craft through footless halls of air.

Up, up the long, delirious, burning blue
I've topped the windswept heights with easy grace
Where never lark, or even eagle flew.
And, while with silent, lifting mind I've trod
The high untresspassed sanctity of space,
Put out my hand and touched the face of God.

You're right, it is very beautiful. It's not hard to understand why so many pilots treasure it and keep it with them. Tell us about the High Flight Foundation. What are its goals? Has it met your expectations in terms of success? How is it doing?

We have been successful, I think. The High Flight Foundation was formed, to share the good news of Christ around the world. It's goal is to pull everyone close to God, to an awareness of Christ, so that everyone can enjoy a "high flight", that they might be prepared for a flight through life, a flight to eternity, a flight, through Christ to Heaven; that they'll be ready for their highest flight, their ultimate flight. We hope that everyone in some way, has been lifted up through the work of High Flight, that we've been a inspiration to the world.

You've told us how you were inspired by feeling God's presence with you on the moon. Was that kind of spirituality shared by any of the other astronauts?

I think you know that we have the support of several of the retired astronauts. Those that are active in the program, I don't know how much they've been able to think about the spiritual things. Because, when you're in the program, you're tied up so much with the technical preparations for the flight. Many times you forget the spiritual aspect. It's not until you retire or leave the program that you have the chance to look back and realize what were the results, what the effects that technology, that achievement in your life were.

What are some of the programs or activities carried on by High Flight?

Mostly, I'm traveling and sharing, essentially, and giving them a new perspective on the earth, a new appreciation for it, I hope. I speak everywhere, almost everywhere I'm invited. I spend a lot of time in schools. We've also had retreat programs for various groups over the years. We've had crusade programs. For the last ten years, we've been involved in the search for biblical artifacts like Noah's Ark, and the Ark of the Covenant. This last year we spent a lot of time trying to retrace the Exodus route, trying to find the point where the children of Israel crossed the Red Sea, trying to find chariot parts from Pharaoh's army. Most of my time is spent in traveling around the country, and around the world, sharing the message of Jesus Christ.

The search for Noah's Ark has been going on for some time, not only by you, but by other people and groups. Were you confident that you could find it, or that it even exists? What kind of evidence did you have, what kind of research did you do before you actually set out on the expeditions to locate it?

We based our search effort largely on the eyewitnesses over the last hundred years who say they have been taken to the site of the Ark at Mount Ararat. That's been the guiding light of our effort. But, so far, we have not found any evidence that the Ark is on Mount Ararat. I recently received in the mail an article that says "Discovery of the Century: Noah's Ark Found". It says the Soviets have found it up in the Caucuses Mountains at 12,000 feet.

Not on Mount Ararat? Doesn't the Bible say it came to rest on top of Mount Ararat?

No the Bible doesn't say it came to rest *on* Ararat. It just says it came to rest in the *mountains* of Ararat.

You also mentioned looking for the Ark of the Covenant. That received a lot of attention when the movie "Raiders of the Lost Ark" came out a few years ago. Do you think it exists, and can be found?

Oh, I'm hopeful that it will be found. We were looking in a cave on Mount Nebo. I think it probably is in either Jordan or Israel. It's well hidden, though. The reasons we were on Mount Nebo was because the Second Book of Macabee says that Jeremiah took the Ark and hid it in a cave on that particular mountain.

The Ark of the Covenant is supposed to contain the tablets of The Ten Commandments. What do you think that would mean to mankind if it were found?

It would be a great discovery, one of the important archaeological finds, almost as important as finding the Ark of Noah.

Have you found that it's easy to share the experience of being in space and on the moon, or is it something that's hard to get across to someone who hasn't done it himself? Do people get an accurate sense of what you tell them about, of what it's actually like being there? Is it really possible to get that feeling across?

I think they do. At least they have a much better feel for it. They're very appreciative, and in most cases respond to the message and the challenge to get their life right with the Lord.

You mentioned the idea earlier that, in broad terms, you and the other astronauts made your voyages for all mankind, that you were emissaries for everybody here on the earth, and not only the people of our own country, but those in the rest of the world as well. We all shared vicariously in your missions and want to know what it was like. Do you have the impression, from your going out to these people, that they have a true sense of the experience that you had firsthand?

Yes, that we went out as their servants, as advanced senors for all of mankind. I think it's our responsibility to give them a report if they're willing to listen to that report. We all have a responsibility to encourage others that will go on after us.

We were intrigued by a comment you made once that you felt alien being in space, but you felt at home being on the moon. Can you elaborate on that a little bit?

Well, I really felt like an alien when I was outside the spacecraft during the spacewalk 200,000 miles from Earth. Stepping out into the blackness of space I felt quite lost, and I was eager to get back in and close the door.

But you were comfortable, you felt at home while you were on the moon?

Sure. We gained from the confidence of the earlier missions. And, ours was such a special flight anyway, because we had the comforting influence of the mountains that were around us. We were in a little valley in the high mountains of the moon, and I've always loved the mountains of earth; it seemed providential that I'd be living and exploring in the mountains of the moon. I felt right at home there. I felt almost like I was above the timberline in the Rocky Mountains. It was a combination of the desert, which I love, and the high mountains, which I also love. I was really in my element.

You talked about the responsibility to encourage others who will follow in the exploration of space. What are your feelings about the program now, and what should we be planning for in the years ahead?

I think the steps that we're taking now are the proper ones. To demonstrate once again reliable transportation into space using our Space Shuttle; I think that's a wise approach. Unfortunately, it's not as economical as we'd hoped, and I think there's clearly a need now for heavy-lift vehicle such as the Soviets have developed with their Energia. We don't have that heavy-lift capability since we don't have our Saturn 5 any longer. But, I think that there will be a need to boost heavy loads into either earth orbit, or high orbit. So, there's a need to develop that type of capability. I think we also have to be particularly careful that we don't pollute the space above us, because that could cause great danger to future travelers in space.

What do you mean by polluting space?

The debris that's up there that comes from launching rockets, particles that are up there that can pose risks for those that might be out, say, in a spacesuit. Or, it could pose a danger even for a space station.

At the tremendous orbital speeds of thousands of miles per hour the collision with even a tiny particle could be catastrophic, is that it?

Sure. It could penetrate a spacesuit on someone that's out there on a spacewalk, or it could puncture a spacecraft.

Given our American free enterprise system, do you think somebody might be able to start a space garbage company and start hauling away some of that stuff?

It's too difficult, almost impossible, to collect it, unfortunately.

In the context of the view of earth brought back from deep space by the Apollo astronauts, you mentioned once that you would very much like to compare that experience you had with someone who had seen the earth from a much farther distance, from as far away as Mars, for example. What would they see, what would they feel? Can you foresee a time when space travelers would ever become immune or jaded in their response to being so far away?

No, I wouldn't think so, because you're looking at you home, your roots. You're tied, whether you like it or not, you're tied to that home planet. To be taken out, say, as far as Mars, where the Earth is just a little blue speck in space, I think would be tremendously moving, a great effect on those that travel out. I was hoping that I'd be alive when that journey is accomplished, but now we're talking about a fairly long time, probably fifteen to twenty years. I just don't know whether I'll still be around to see that.

What would be the effect, on human culture, on people who may never see earth people who are born in space, or on another planet let's say. Would that create a fundamental and dramatic change in human civilization?

I'd be interested in what they look like, and also how they feel. I think humans would change depending on where they're raised, where they grow, where they draw life. I think even a person that's, say, born on the moon, who would live there for a lifetime, would be different from an earthling. I think they'd probably grow taller, their circulation systems would probably develop a little differently. They would be changed in several ways.

So, we might be influencing our own evolution in a very fundamental way by expanding out into the universe?

That's right. Very much so.

The legacy of all this, the legacy of you and your colleagues who flew the missions, might not be fully understood or appreciated for a long time. From your point of view, though, as one of those who first went to the moon, how would you characterize, or summarize the meaning of Project Apollo.

The meaning of Project Apollo? Well, I think the purpose of Apollo was not only to reach the moon, but explore the moon. And, Apollo was successful. You can look at the results, and I hope they're well documented. You know, we have 850 pounds of lunar material here now for analysis by present and future scientists. We probably have over 10,000 photographs taken on the surface of the moon. We've left six scientific stations there, and three automobiles. We have a wealth of new knowledge about our closest neighbor in space to a point that makes us want to go back. And I'm hopeful that we have the capability to go back. I hope we haven't lost the plans to do that. So, I think it was an investment in knowledge of the moon, and I hope that future generations will look back and say it was wise that we did it, that we invested the money, and that we accomplished what we wanted to accomplish.

Chapter 7

JACK SCHMITT
Lunar Module Pilot, Apollo 17

In the Footsteps of
John C. Fremont

Harrison "Jack" Schmitt has the distinction of being the only "Scientist-Astronaut" to walk on the moon. While that title might be technically accurate, it is not one with which he is entirely comfortable, especially when taking into account that Buzz Aldrin and Ed Mitchell preceded Jack Schmitt to the surface of the moon— two scientific heavyweights if ever there were any. Aldrin has a PhD from M.I.T. in Astronautics, and Mitchell has a PhD from M.I.T. in Aeronautics and Astronautics.

As much as Jack Schmitt may have been uncomfortable with the title of Scientist-Astronaut, a number of his fellow astronauts were just plain uncomfortable with him. Some felt that he was forced on the Astronaut office because of intense pressure by the National Academy of Science to have a "scientist" walk the lunar surface. The fact of the matter is that he *was* forced on them. NASA had finally given in and agreed to bring in a true scientist. And what better scientist could they send to the moon than a highly trained and accomplished geologist?

It turned out to be a good arrangement for all concerned, except for Joseph Engle.

Joe Engle was the man bumped from Apollo 17 to make room for Schmitt, and it might have been tough to convince him that it was a good thing. Although, he did get to fly later aboard the Space Shuttle, it was a far cry from walking on the moon.

All in all, it worked well for NASA because Jack Schmitt did a fantastic job. And, NASA could take even more credit for Schmitt's success since they had to teach him how to fly, literally from the ground up. Because, until his tenure with NASA, he'd never piloted an aircraft of any sort.

Jack Schmitt possesses the varied experience of having been a geologist, scientist, astronaut, pilot, administrator, educator, writer, and United States Senator.

Schmitt was a teaching fellow at Harvard in 1961; he assisted on a course in ore deposits. Prior to his teaching assignment, he worked for the Norwegian Geological Survey in Oslo, Norway, and for the U.S. Geological Survey in New Mexico and Montana. He also worked as a geologist for two summers in southeastern Alaska. Before going to the Manned Spacecraft Center, he served with the U.S. Geological Survey's Astrogeology Branch at Flagstaff, Arizona. He was project chief for lunar field geological methods and participated in photo and telescopic mapping for the moon; he was among the USGS astrogeologists instructing NASA astronauts during their geological field trips. He has logged more than 1,665 hours flying time.

Dr. Schmitt was selected as a scientist-astronaut by NASA in June 1965. He completed a 53-week course in flight training at Williams Air Force Base, Arizona, and, in addition to training for future manned space flights, had been instrumental in providing Apollo flight crews with detailed instruction in lunar navigation, geology, and feature recognition. He also assisted in the integration of scientific activities into the Apollo lunar missions and participated in research activities requiring the conduct of geologic, petrographic, and stratigraphic analysis of samples returned from the moon by Apollo missions.

Schmitt served as a backup lunar module pilot for Apollo 15, and, ultimately, he served as the lunar module pilot for Apollo 17— the last Apollo mission to the moon.

Schmitt's studies of the Valley of Taurus-Littrow on the moon in 1972, as well as his earlier scientific work, made him one of the leading experts on the history of the terrestrial planets. As the "only scientist" to go to the moon, he was also the last of twelve men to step on its surface.

After organizing and directing the activities of the Scientist-Astronaut Office and of the Energy Program Office for NASA in 1973–1975, Schmitt fulfilled a long-standing commitment by entering politics. He was elected to the U.S. Senate from his home state of New Mexico in 1976.

In his last two years in the Senate, Senator Schmitt was Chairman of the Senate Commerce Committee's Subcommittee on Science, Technology, and Space, and of the Senate Appropriations Committee's Subcommittee on Labor, Health, and Human Services, and Education. He currently serves as a member of the Army Science Board and as consultant to the National Strategic Materials and Minerals Program Advisory Committee.

Harrison Schmitt is consulting, speaking, and writing on a wide range of business, foundation, and government initiatives. His principle activities are in the fields of technology, space, defense, biomedicine, geology, and policy issues of the future. He brings to the consideration of complex public and corporate concerns a unique breadth of experience ranging from the scientific to the practical and from the administrative to the political.

Jack Schmitt is a bachelor and lives in Albuquerque, New Mexico.

Will you tell us about how you came to be a geologist, what influenced you along those lines; then how you became interested in lunar geology, and how you eventually became an astronaut?

My interests in geology grew from being exposed to it all of my pre-college days via my father, who is a well known mining geologist. I worked with him summers and weekends a lot, so I was pretty well exposed to geology and what it was all about. When I got to Cal Tech I found out very quickly I was not going to be the world's greatest physicist, so I decided to pursue geology, which was easy and a lot of fun for me. Basically, when I got out of graduate school at Harvard I was looking around for a job in the middle of what was a geological recession not unlike today, and the only interesting opportunity was working with the U.S. Geological Survey out in Flagstaff, Arizona where Eugene Shoemaker had set up a branch of astrogeology. Now I think it's called the Center of Astrogeology. Gene and I happened to be looking at each other and it was easy to come to an agreement; I went out there and started to work in lunar-geological pursuits, and within a month or two, NASA asked for volunteers. So, I decided to volunteer.

Nobody suggested that you apply? You took it upon yourself?

Yes. I just happened to be in the right place at the right time. Like all the early astronauts, we were accidents.

You can thank the recession!

Yes, although the timing was right wherever I'd have been. If I'd heard about it during any other job, I have a feeling I would have still volunteered. I'd already developed an intellectual interest in the Space Program for other reasons, and this just happened to give me a chance to get involved personally.

Do you consider yourself a different type of astronaut from the traditional fighter test-pilot?

There wasn't much of a tradition, even in our days. There had only been two selections of pilot astronauts before the scientists were selected, so it wasn't that much of a tradition. We were the third group selected; three of us had to go to pilot training, which delayed us about a year from getting directly involved with NASA. But really, the idea of scientist-astronaut appeared fairly early in the program. I'm not sure how enthralled NASA was with the idea, but certainly the National Academy thought it was a good one, and they put a lot of pressure on NASA.

Did you feel there was any kind of prejudice against you because you went into the program as a non-pilot?

Oh, I don't know; a little bit. One can say it was understandable prejudice. When we were brought into the program, NASA still didn't know whether they could do this thing or not. They had the confidence of professionals that they were going to figure out how to get to the moon and return people safely to Earth, but nothing had yet been demonstrated that, indeed, it was going to be possible. So, here were these scientists appearing on the scene who obviously were not going to fly the early missions. And, there was no guarantee that it wasn't going to take an awful lot of missions before we finally landed on the moon. The probability in 1965–66 of NASA being successful on their first landing attempt was really very, very low. So, there were lots of pilot astronauts and lots of vehicles were ordered and being built on the assumption that it would take quite a number of flights before we actually were successful. As soon as we were successful, then the pressure started to rise to put a scientist on one of the early missions. Unfortunately, at the same time, the Nixon administration was trying to get out of the whole thing. The press was losing interest rapidly as they do on anything that's continuously positive, and the Nixon administration and even Congress were losing interest as a consequence. They were not seeing any political mileage in it anymore. So, those two things were competing with each other, and indeed, Nixon's people cancelled the last three missions that were already planned, or being planned. That was Apollo 18, 19, and 20, and my normal cycle would have been to be on 18 since I was a back-up crewman on Apollo 15. When 18 was cancelled, while we were in training for

Apollo 15, actually, it became clear that NASA had a tough decision to make. It was not unheard of to break up crews and reconstitute them, but it was not usually done. The assumption was that Joe Engle would fly with Cernan and Evans on Apollo 17.

He was an X-15 pilot, wasn't he?
Yes. He had been an X-15 pilot. But, the pressure was very high to have at least one scientist-geologist go to the Moon, and I was the only one in the program, and so they ultimately made the right decision, from my point of view.

Was that an uncomfortable situation for you—replacing Joe Engle?
Well, it was uncomfortable, but the decision was made to assign me to that crew, and I wasn't going to argue with them. It was very uncomfortable for Joe and it took him some time to get over it. He has subsequently flown on the Space Shuttle, and had his trip in space. I'm sure Cernan and Evans for a while, though you'll have to talk to them, may have felt some resentment that the crew they had trained with for some time before had been broken up. But, I think it all worked out.

Were some of the astronauts more willing to accept you than others in the program?
I never had a problem that I could detect in being accepted. I brought something to the table for all of these guys that they couldn't ignore as a possible factor for their own selection. That is, how well could they do the job of being geologists as well as pilots going to the moon? So, when I began to organize a new training program in geology for these guys with Al Shepard's blessing, I had a lot of good cooperation. I was pretty well accepted as one of the people who was part of the team trying to help everybody do a good job on the moon, whether I ever went or not. I never sensed that problem. Other guys did. Some did not have a clear skill entré into the Apollo lunar program.

The other scientists, you mean?
Yes, the other scientists felt that they were having a problem, and indeed there was even one pilot-scientist who tended to iden-tify himself more with the scientists than the pilots. Don Lind felt that, I'm sure, he was being discriminated against as a result of his interest in science. He had a Ph.D. in physics. Finally, part of the fall-out of the whole loss of political interest in Apollo was the reemphasis of the Skylab program. For a while it looked like there

would be several opportunities for scientists to fly Skylab; that finally collapsed into three opportunities because they cancelled the second Skylab vehicle, which is now a relic in the Smithsonian. Joe Kerwin, Owen Garriott, and Ed Gibson were assigned to those three Skylab missions as scientists, Joe Kerwin being a physician. There was another scientist-astronaut who decided he could see the handwriting on the wall, and it would be a long, long time before he had a chance to fly, so he left the program. Also, in that period when they were building the Shuttle, and the shuttle was delayed, several other people left, though most of them came back. It was quite a bit of in and out there for a while, while they waited for the shuttle opportunity to develop. Some in the second group of scientist-astronauts waited, I think, seventeen or eighteen years before they flew. Thornton, Allen, that whole group. They all flew, including Don Lind. Don had not only put up with the problems of personal relations with the pilots, but he had a terrible bicycle accident, also. He was badly injured, and still got to fly after he had been rehabilitated from that.

After your mission, did you find that it was essential to have all the jet training you were required to have to become a crewmember?

I was an advocate for that for Apollo. The Apollo spacecraft was really designed, and appropriately so, to have three people who had background and experience in flying aircraft, in using machines and putting their confidence in machines. Scientists don't really have that except for their research. But, putting your physical well-being in the hands of the machine is something that is not normally taught to scientists.

Did you find it hard to gain that level of expertise and confidence?

Yes. Flying did not come naturally to me, principally, I think, because I was ten years older than the age when people normally learn to fly jet aircraft. I had a lot of habits ingrained that were appropriate to scientific research, maybe, but not appropriate to flying aircraft, particularly instrument flying. I was as good as anybody in the visual flying, but instrument work required learning a new set of habits, psychological as well as visual. That took me longer than it probably would take other people. In fact, Gibson and Garriott mastered it much more quickly than I did. But, ultimately, I found that as long as I flew a lot, I could keep those learned skills sharp and fly as well as anybody. If I slacked off for a while, they would start deteriorating quite rapidly.

Jack Schmitt

It has been written that you came in second in your class at the Air Force flight school. Is that correct?

No, no. Ed Gibson did. I was down in the middle of the pack. No, Ed did very well.

It's interesting that Ed Gibson led what he called the first mutiny in space. The scientists didn't handle easily the rigors and routine that the military style imposed upon those space missions.

Well, another way to look at it is that they may have handled them too well, and they'd started to overload the crew on that mission. They were trying to pack too much into the routine, and appropriately, the crew said, 'Hey, enough, back off.' Sometimes that's what you have to do; if you're going to utilize the talents and capabilities of human beings, those human beings have to be part of the team and be able to tell you when you're trying to ask too much.

With the strong military background of NASA, was it important to you to be the first true civilian to walk on the lunar surface?

Well, I think that strong military background has been over-rated. NASA was and is a civilian agency. They have military people TDY; the vast majority of the engineers, though, had no military background. If they did, they were enlisted personnel, or they were already out of the military. They were just young engineers. NASA was an extraordinarily young agency during the Apollo period. You had people who were in their early twenties with the responsibilities that you wouldn't find today in the space program at all. That's maybe one reason why we did it so well. At the time I flew, I think about two-thirds of the astronauts corps were military while they were in NASA. Most of the rest, except for the scientists, had received their pilot training in the military. But, people like Neil Armstrong and Jack Swigert, for example, had been out of the military for many, many years. Neil had been out for fifteen years, I think. So, there was a military orientation within the astronaut corps in terms of how it was organized, pilots' needs, and things like that. But, it wasn't that there wasn't a very strong civilian influence. People like Al Shepard and Deke Slayton may have regret-ted that, but nevertheless, I don't recall very many of the scientists being reticent about expressing their opinion. Some of them did not do it very diplomatically, but that's true in any endeavor. You can be forceful, but you can do it in a way that doesn't make other people resent you.

So, you wouldn't be comfortable being called the "first true civilian" to walk on the moon?

You can say it however you want. I was the first astronaut on the moon that had not received pilot training as a professional military pilot. I had never flown until I joined the program and was sent to pilot training with the Air Force, but I was a civilian; it was a very different kind of environment. I didn't go through a military kind of environment while I was learning to fly. The other way you might say it is that I was the first professional scientist, civilian or otherwise, to go to the moon.

How much of a difference did it make, do you thing, being a professional geologist with respect to the scientific work you had to do on the moon?

There's two parts to that. Having scientists in the Astronaut Corps upgraded the total skill-level of the Astronaut Corps. For example, in my case, I just took over the lunar geological training program and reorganized it, brought in professional instructors, people who understood how to teach people, rather than just try to make geologists out of these astronauts. What we did was focus on the kind of skills and knowledge they needed in order to do as good a job as they could do given the time we had to train them.

Is that something you started yourself, or were you asked to do it?

No, I started it. I already knew something about it because I'd been exposed to it in the USGS and knew what was going on. And when I got in the program, I just told Al Shepard, 'It's not being done right; we're not going to be sending people to the moon who can really do that job well, and here's what I propose.' He agreed, and I started finding people on the outside of NASA, people I knew who were outstanding scientists, but even more important, were outstanding teachers. And I got them involved. People like Lee Silver, Nick John, and Bob Sharp were brought into the program at that time, and they were tremendously well-received by the crews. The crews could recognize people who knew what they were doing. Also, we cast it in a much more operational sense. We just didn't try to teach them names like, unfortunately, much of geology is taught. We put it in concepts of what they needed to know to do the missions. We actually ran rough simulations of the missions while they were getting their training. We changed the whole thing, and it worked out very well for them, I think, and we got a lot more out of each of the precursor missions before Apollo 17. The other part, though, is true. When you put somebody who's a professional in doing specialized tasks in space or anywhere else, you gain the years, sometimes decades, of experience that person has in sorting out was is trivial and what isn't. When you're merely exposed to geology or any other discipline, flying included, it's very difficult in the first few years to decide what is a trivial issue, what can be ignored, and what cannot. That's what being professional is all about.

Do you think much was lost by not having persons such as yourself on other missions, the earlier missions?

Scientifically, it was lost, but that was never a question. First of all, the National Academy Committee didn't send enough names and people to NASA to pressure them to fly more scientists earlier. I fault the National Academy for that, particularly Gene Shoemaker, but this is nothing he and I haven't yelled at each other about before. His argument is that we just didn't want to take the chance of sending a dog or a lemon to NASA. They erred on the side of sending too few. I know an awful lot of people who applied and were not selected by the Academy to take the physical. They were outstanding scientists, certainly as good or better than some who were sent, in my judgment, and there was certainly no need to filter those people out. At the least, NASA should have been sent 50 or 100 names that they would have to weed out on the basis of physicals and put that onus on NASA. But, that's a political issue long under the bridge and it's just unfortunate. Given the deck that was dealt, I think that I got to the moon about as fast as one could ever have expected, although I was disappointed each time a crew was put together and I wasn't on it. But, they had an awful lot of commitments to other astronauts who came into the program at a time when it wasn't clear how many astronauts it would take before we landed successfully on the moon. There were long-standing professional commitments to these people, and I can understand why they were flown.

What scientific and geological value was served by sending men to the moon? Can you give us a capsule summary of the six missions?

Through those six missions, we gained a remarkably detailed, first-order understanding of the evolution of the moon and the planets. We know as much—in fact, we know more—about the early history of the Moon than we know about the early history of our own Earth. I won't go into why it worked out that way, but that's a statement of fact. It is a level of understanding, a level of deep wisdom about the moon and the relationship to the Earth and

Mars and other planets, that could not have been gained, I believe, without the use of human beings, skilled, trained human beings. Not to mention the fact that on the last mission we had a professional geologist. But, even without the last mission, we had gained a remarkable understanding of the moon. We refined that significantly with the last mission and gained new insight and details of it. But a lot of it had already been put together by missions other than ours. To do that with an automated unmanned system would have been, I think, impossible, and second, would have been extraordinarily expensive to even come close, far more than the 22 billion dollars we spent for Apollo. Unfortunately, nobody ever forces the advocates for unmanned exploration of space to sit down and really show the cost of duplicating what we did with Apollo. I would be willing to bet an extraordinary amount of money if I had it, that they couldn't do it. If they tried it would cost far more than Apollo cost, particularly at that time, when we just didn't have the automation techniques that we have today. Even today, the thing you will always miss is the qualitative supercomputer, the instant reprogrammability that you have when you put human beings into space.

Ed Mitchell likes to point out the nonlinear function of the human mind.
Well, that's certainly part of it.

One of the most striking characteristics of the moon is the difference between the near and the dark side. Did you learn anything about why there is such a difference in the two sides.
You should say the far side. People make the mistake of thinking that the far side is always dark.

That's the layman's term. Did anything we learn from Apollo give us any greater understanding of why there is such a difference? Does it tell anything about the origin of the moon?
No, it doesn't tell us anything about the origin of the moon. I think we can explain why there's a difference; for one thing the center of mass of the moon is offset about two kilometers from the center figure of the moon and that offset of the center of mass is roughly toward the Earth, but not even close to being exactly toward the Earth. The line between the center point of the moon and the center of mass actually points through Mare Tranquilitatis, the Sea of Tranquility. That is a physical explanation of that phenomenon. It means that the liquid maria, the dissolving maria that formed the dark parts of the moon, rose to levels that would be

above the surface on the side facing the Earth. Where, for the most part, it couldn't reach those levels on the far side. So, we can explain physically why it's the way it is, but nobody's really fully explained, at least to my knowledge, why moons and sometimes planets like Mercury, lock themselves into a rotation rate equal to their orbital rate. The Moon goes around on its axis once every twenty-eight days, which is the same period it goes around Earth, so, we always see the same face. Mercury does the same with respect to the Sun.

What did you discover about the moon that told you about or gave you insight into the origin of the solar system, where it came from, or how it formed?

Not as much as everyone had hoped. On pertinent thing, I think—and this is controversial—but the evidence is fairly clear that the moon and the Earth formed in the same part of the solar system by a related process. What that process was is still subject to a lot of debate. The chemistry is similar, very similar, the differences being easily explained by other phenomena. At least, it tends to help constrain the distribution of elements within the original solar nebula. Beyond that, the planets are not going to give you a lot of information about the origin of the solar system; they are gross in terms of their chemical compositions as related to the composition of the original nebula. What gives us information about the origin of the solar system are really two other areas: that's the study of meteorites, particularly the one that fell in Mexico called Allende. We found some little grains in them that appear to be material that was not fully assimilated by the solar nebula, and actually have isotopic compositions that indicate it was debris that was around before the sun was formed.

What do you mean by "isotopic"?

Isotopes are slightly different forms of the same element. They differ by atomic weight. The ratio of isotopes of oxygen, magnesium, and calcium, for example, are not related to what we know of the isotopic ratios of the solar nebula. They're different, strikingly different. So, the interpretation is that they are grains or extra-solar material that had not been fully assimilated.

Were you disappointed that the orange soil that you discovered on the moon was not as young as you first thought it might be?

Oh, not disappointed at all. I mean, we were hoping to sample young material. There was photographic reason—obviously insufficient—but still photographic reason to suspect that there was young material at Taurus-Littrow. It turned out there was not. Geologists are very philosophical about finding that their original working hypothesis is wrong. The orange soil turned out to be such an important part of piecing together the whole evolutionary history, as well as the structure, of the moon as it is today that nobody worried about whether it was young or old. Its chemistry is the important thing. The fact that it probably came from two to three hundred kilometers inside the Moon gives us information on the internal makeup of the moon that we would not have had otherwise. The fact that the orange soil was not young really finally put a cap on a growing interpretation of what we had seen from all the missions on the moon. That is, the moon ceased to evolve in any significant way about three billion years ago, about the same time the Earth was really beginning to evolve in its crustal and upper manal components. That really make it possible to begin to use the moon as a model for the evolution of an Earth-like planet— and that includes Mercury, Venus and Mars—in the first billion and a half years of the history of those planets. The orange soil put a final cap on that interpretation. The fact that we went to a place expecting to find the youngest material that we could find, and it was still 3.5 billions years old—that pretty well told us that we could use the moon without any doubt as a model of how these planets formed, or how they evolved after forming in that first billion and a half years. So, the orange soil was really one of the singular discoveries of the whole Apollo program. There were a lot of these, but it was one of the major ones. And it could not have been done, really, by a robot. It would have been extraordinarily accidental and fortuitous to have a robot that would have detected that subtle difference in coloration.

As a scientist-astronaut, did you have a hand in picking the landing sites and devising the EVA scenarios?
Oh, yes. I was very deeply involved in all of that.

Did you actually pick out Taurus-Littrow?
All the landing sites were picked as a team effort. There were a lot of people involved in the site selection. If I remember correctly, Taurus-Littrow appealed initially to a minority of the scientists and even of the operational people.

Too dangerous? Do you mean the landing site was too small?
Well, some people were concerned about being able to land in there. Too constraining; they couldn't get their error margins down to where they could justify committing to it. It represented

a major challenge to those people, which they were able to meet. That was the excitement they felt about it; here's another challenge, let's see if we can get in there. It's a valley deeper than the Grand Canyon. That stimulated the flight control, the mission planning, and the analysis people a great deal. On the other hand, by that time all of the scientists had favorite places where they wanted us to go to verify their ideas. It was principally the field geology team and others that said, 'Hey, let's go to the place that gives us the widest variety of features and the greatest three-dimensional exposure of those for which we have operational photography. Let's go there particularly since we have a geologist on board.' Taurus-Littrow was an obvious candidate. I had suggested early in the game that we ought to go to the far side. That was examined very briefly by a few people, and rejected by NASA management; once they heard we were looking at it. I thought we could land there.

Would that have entailed putting communications satellites around the moon?
We had figured out a way in which you could do it without that, but it would have entailed significant periods of time when the Earth wouldn't know what was going on, and of course the Earth can't accept that. Not yet, anyway. Until we go to Mars, they won't accept not knowing what's going on. Then, we looked at the option of putting a communications satellite, two of them, actually, one for back-up, two with one launch in the libration point directly behind the moon, and that looked like it would cost an additional 80 to 100 million dollars.

It would have been to big to bring with you on the Apollo?
No, we couldn't have put it back there. It would have taken a separate launch, an expendable launch vehicle.

As someone who'd spent time working on the photo-telescopic maps of the moon, how different was the reality for you?
Down to the resolution limit of the photographs the reality was very comparable. The exciting part of Apollo was that with our eyes, we got down to the submillimeter resolution in the samples that we took. The best photography that we had even after Apollo 17, I think, the theoretical resolution was only a meter. Anything inside of five meters was new information. We'd made guesses, but there were plenty of surprises inside that five meters.

You and Gene Cernan made up one of the most exuberant crews ever to explore the moon. Can you tell us something of the exhilaration of that time, and what went through your mind as you climbed into the LM for the last time?

Of course, we had the benefit of the experiences of plenty of successful flights before, several actually, so it was obvious from the very beginning that we had an excellent rock and spacecraft people who had been working to test and check out Apollo 17's systems had done just an outstanding job. You could see the motivation of those folks everywhere to make sure that this one, like all the others, was the best possible. It was, there just were no systems problems, and we had had no problems up to the time we arrived on the surface of the moon; there was no reason to expect any beyond that. So, we really had no worries nagging us about systems or anything else like that. In addition, for all the crews, being in 1/6 gravity is just a very, very pleasant experience. It's a lot easier than training; all the crews had a tendency to whistle and sing while they were up there because it was fun, literally pure, unadulterated fun. And, it was very stimulating for me, scientifically.

In your post-flight remarks, you talked about the need to step back once in a while and take in the majesty of the place. Can you describe that?

We didn't do that very much, except when we were sitting on the Rover, driving from place to place. Then we had a chance to at least look straight ahead and see what was there. That really was the only opportunity at the time. Many years before Apollo 17, when we were training for Apollo 15, Dick Gordon said to me, 'One thing you'll find is that time is relentless.' And it is. You hesitate to take any personal time, so to speak, away from doing as much as humanly possible, and from absorbing as much as humanly possible while you do those things. At least, that's the way I felt, and I've done most of my thinking about what I saw, and did, and experienced after the flight rather than during it. You just hesitate to take that time.

As a member of the crew that spent the longest time on the moon, what went through your mind when you climbed back into the Lunar Module for the last time?

You have to remember that in a moment like that, the main thing you're trying to make sure of is that you are working in a timely way. We were already over the amount of time that we should have been outside, I think by half an hour, because we kept finding more things to do. The last thing I did before I went up the ladder was to use one of the last core tubes we had left right underneath the Lunar Module. As I got this core sample, I was still thinking of how to maximize the return of the missions. At some point in doing it, a thought passed that it was too bad I hadn't been successful in persuading NASA to give us an extra day. But, that was something that I had tried to do long before the mission actually flew. It was too late to change those plans in midstream. NASA had become very conservative about a very liberal enterprise, with Apollo 17, and they just didn't want to stretch anything any further than they had to. Everybody was thinking that this was not the time to lose a crew. I argued that one more day on the moon doesn't raise the probability of losing a crew to a much higher level. If you're willing to commit to the moon, you ought to be willing to commit to another day there. But, that didn't sell.

Gene Cernan mentioned that, on your way back to Earth, you mostly talked about the color of the moon. Is that really what happened?

Oh, the day we left lunar orbit, we had a beautiful view of a full moon, close enough for me to make out what I later called the color provinces of the lunar maria, the subtle shades of blue and brown in the maria. As we left the moon, I actually mapped them on some of the charts that we had on board, and later published a short paper in "Geology" magazine. At least during that first day, I'm sure that in the process of my mapping, we all chatted a bit about what one color was versus another. But, the mapping I did at the time was based on what my eyes said were the various hues. We did have that kind of conversation. But, I wouldn't say that's the only thing we talked about. As a matter of fact, it was a significantly quieter trip than you might expect going back, somewhat faster by half a day, and there wasn't an awful lot to do. The first day, we had to occupy ourselves looking back at the moon. The second day, Ron Evans had an EVA, so that took up most of the time, and I guess it was really the third day that things got a little bit dull. We were just coasting, accelerating toward the atmosphere. In fact, Gene got so bored he started playing with the computer keys, and actually fired some thrusters.

You're a trained scientist, and there's a whole legacy of scientists who have made spectacular expeditions, Charles Darwin among them. Did you study any of the lives of some of the great explorers that had preceded your mission to the moon?

Through the years I had studied that to some degree, focusing during my astronaut days more on the equivalent group of men called the Army Corps of Topographical Engineers. They were attached to Army expeditions into the American West in pre-Civil

War days. There were, as I recall, 26 of these men, commissioned officers trained at West Point, both in military science and physical science. They were primarily surveyors, but many of them, including Fremont, who was the first, and Emory, who explored the southern part of the West, were far more than surveyors. They collected samples, they sketched, they described, and really created quite a record of the physical science of the American West along with the expedition route. They were in communication with the scientists both in the Eastern universities, including, as I recall, Agassiz at Harvard, and people like Humboldt in Europe. They had very much the same background and, of course, were aware of Powell and his work in the Grand Canyon and other parts of the West. I was generally aware of them just because of the nature of my profession. The Corps of Topographical Engineers were of particular interest to me. A fellow at Princeton, I think, did a thesis on them, which was later published as a book.

Were they colorful characters like the astronauts?
Oh, I'm sure they were, Fremont of course, was a major political figure.

He ran for president more than once.
Exactly. Probably the best of the group from a scientific point of view was Emory, and he turned out not to be a good officer; he had to fight the Spanish I think, at the end of his expedition once, and probably didn't do too well at that. But, he was an outstanding surveyor, geographer, and scientist. I think the individuality they displayed was comparable to the astronauts!

What propelled you into politics?
I had begun thinking about that when I was in graduate school, well before the space program. The opportunity to volunteer for the astronaut program just came along while I was pursuing a career, which I felt any politician ought to do first, at least show you can be successful at something besides getting elected. Unfortunately, that's not the rule. I couldn't see any reason why I shouldn't volunteer for the astronaut program; it didn't seem to be inconsistent with anything, and it was obviously a great opportunity. Since I didn't have plans to get into politics immediately anyway, I just went ahead with that career first.

Did someone approach you, or did you make it known that you were available to run for the Senate?

Jack Schmitt

I had my own plans. People came to me and suggested it simultaneously, but literally I was looking ahead. It became obvious that I was not going to have a chance to fly in space again for ten years, in my estimate, which turned out to be more realistic than NASA's. Then, I decided to go to Washington. George Low asked me if I would consider coming back and managing the creation, for a year or two, of an energy office for NASA. I saw that as an opportunity to go back to Washington to learn something about the way the government works. Again, this was not inconsistent with whatever else I might want to do. At about the same time, in 1973, some Republicans approached me to consider running against Harold Reynolds, the congressman from what is now the third district of New Mexico. Harold, who since has died, was a conservative Democrat, very well liked by both the Republicans and Democrats in the district. It didn't take me very long to figure out that he was not the guy I ought to run against. So, I said, no thanks; but, I would take another look at politics in New Mexico, at some future time, and that future time in my own mind was 1976 when I knew that Senator Montoya would be up for re-election. He had already, I think, displayed significant vulnerability even as incumbent, which is unusual.

He got sort of caught in the backlash of Watergate, didn't he?
Yes, he did not do well, but that was only part of it. He'd just worn out his welcome in New Mexico, and everybody knew it. I mean, I thought everybody knew it. But, most of the advice I received was not to run against him. But, I judged for myself, and said I thought that was a good opportunity, and I began to point in that direction. When I went to Washington, I got my little notebook, and every once in a while I'd go talk to somebody, Democrat and Republican, about political campaigning, what it took. Gradually, I built enough of an understanding to throw my hat in the ring. After resigning from NASA in August of 1975, I began to campaign in New Mexico.

Did you also plan to be a Republican?
I never thought about it one way or the other. I had been a Republican, it was my family tradition, it was generally consistent with my political philosophy.

How would you compare a political campaign with the preparation of going to the moon? Are they similar in workload?
There are a lot of similarities, as a matter of fact. For the first campaign we actually pert-chartered the efforts, which means that

you start on election day in 1976 and say, okay, I've been elected; what does it take to do the job? Then, you start to separate the various components of the campaign and work backwards in time, integrating what had to happen for that election to take place. That's the standard process of planning that has been used in a variety of technical activities, and for us it was an exercise that made us think about the campaign. Indeed, for the first two to three months we followed that plan pretty closely. Gradually, things got so hectic, that we didn't pay that much attention to it, but it had already imposed its discipline on us. Once or twice we had to go back to it to find out that we're doing what we wanted. It took good scheduling, good staff work, and good implementation. The one thing you have to depend upon, at least in a challenger's campaign, is that practically everybody's a volunteer.

So, you'd recommend to a future candidate that he become an astronaut first?

No. Just that he become successful at something. If you know how to be a success, it always helps.

Where was the frustration level higher, in political campaigning or training?

There was no frustration in campaigning or training, either one. I don't know that I'd ever use the word frustrated. If you're frustrated, you're doing something you shouldn't be doing. I was disappointed at the inability to do things in Congress. Congress turns out to be probably the least productive place for a person to spend six years of his life.

Would you ever think about running for office again sometime in the future?

Never say never, but I think there are more important problems right now to be addressed, and they can't be addressed within the current political system. I think the political system is so controlled by short-term special interests that the longer-term issues that are going to get us into trouble are not being addressed. We're going to have to figure out ways to address those outside the political system until one can build the constituency necessary to change the focus of politics more towards the future. You can't ignore the present, you have to have compassion in the present, unfortunately, right now, we're doing that at the expense of addressing any of the major issues.

You saw the Space Program from both sides of the fence. You were an astronaut, you went to the moon, and on the political side you became a senator, one of the people that made the Space Program possible, through appropriations. Did you find a lack of understanding or vision among the people in Congress? Was it hard to get them to see the importance of the Space Program?

No. I think you could get them to see the importance of it as individuals, and they all believe in it. Congress has always been supportive, up until the Mondale candidacy for president. Even then, they have tended to be supportive. The problem has been getting administrations to articulate or to be leaders in space; the Congress is a follower for the most part. For things like space, Congress is not going to try to lead. They're going to follow whatever the administration proposes. Oh, they'll modify little bits and pieces, but they're unimportant to the overall question of vision. That has to be supplied by the administration, and it has not been supplied by an administration since John Kennedy died.

Is that just a function of the particular president, or is there some institutional responsibility needed?

It's both the function of the president and a function of whether there's an organized political constituency for space. It's become more and more of the latter. In the days of Kennedy, a president could lead and the Congress would follow. Now if a president tried to lead, I'm afraid you have to be sure that there's a political constituency that's going to give Congress backbone on that issue. Mainly, congressmen and senators have to believe that their reelection may depend on how they vote on space as an issue of the future, and actually how they vote on other issues as well.

Do you think that the future programs that are being talked about, the mission to Mars, are too far-ranging, are they too far in the future to excite the people the way they were about going to the moon?

Of course they are, because nobody has articulated a vision and gone to the public and to Congress and said, 'This is what we're going to do.' The moon excited the American people because Kennedy said, 'We're going there, and I'm going to go for the bucks and fight for the bucks to do it.' And nobody's done that for anything else since then.

But that was a rather short-term goal, eight years.
You can get to Mars in a decade.

You feel we could be on Mars in a decade?

If that's what we wanted to do. With leadership and a political constituency, there's no question we could be on Mars by the end of this century. The technological hurdles have largely been taken care of. It's a lot less of a challenge technologically to go to Mars from where we stand today than it was to go to the moon from where we stood with Kennedy when he expressed that vision.

What would be your vision for the next 20, 30 or 40 years. Would you envision the "Millennium Project" or something totally different?

I think we ought to commit to the settlement of Mars, and in the process utilize the lunar resources to enhance and accelerate that process, as well as provide the Earth with energy resources.

Were you upset that the Apollo program was scuttled at its peak; that we didn't exploit it to its maximum?

Of course. What thinking person would not be, when you look at an 80 billion dollar investment, then watch it basically be thrown away after it was used half a dozen times only to explore the moon and to put up one Skylab? That's crazy. The Apollo technology base had a lot more that could have been done with it than we did. We could have grown from the Apollo technology to a lunar-based technology without too much difficulty. We couldn't go to Mars with Apollo technology, but we could have easily amortized that investment to establish a permanent scientific station on the moon that would then lead to a rapid exploitation of the resources. We could have had Skylab-type space stations all around the Earth. Skylab still represents a more sophisticated space station concept that the Soviet Mir.

Do you look on the current United States space station "Freedom" as being too little, too late?

I think ultimately we have to do it. It fits neatly into a strategy for the settlement of Mars. It will help us do that. It also is important that there be a permanent presence of U.S. citizens and their allies in orbit around Earth. Unfortunately, the lack of support by the Reagan White House—Ronald Reagan was certainly supportive, but nobody followed up on his policy statements—has further delayed the space station. Now, we're literally ten years behind the Soviets in having comparable capabilities.

If the next president called the NASA people in, the day after he's inaugurated, and said, "Listen, I want a space station in five years. No ifs, ands, or buts," could it be done?

With enough money, yes.

So it's a matter of money, not really time.
Considering what we've gone through, five years would be a tremendous challenge. But, I think it's a doable challenge, provided the money and people were made available and that NASA could streamline its procurement process. The thing that slows the hardware systems down today is that the government bus the procurement rules and regulations. We have made that system almost impossible to work. If you could go back to the Apollo procurement, then there's no question we could build a space station in five years, no question in my mind, anyway.

As someone who has served in the United States Congress, combined with an astronaut's point of view, you have a unique understanding about foreign policy. Where do you see the Soviet program in ten or twenty years from now?
The Soviets have committed to a very mature vision of what they want to do in space. Their principal objective is the expression of Soviet sovereignty in space. It's a political objective, and it's correctly tied and integrated with their military doctrine, something that has been there right from the very beginning. Even today, their space program is run by their military. Whatever other people may think, it is run by their military. We like to think of it in the image of our own, where two programs are separate, but that's just not true with the Soviets.

Do you believe they are going to Mars?
I think they're clearly focused on Mars, and began that focus probably around the late sixties, when it became obvious with the Saturn 5 and the Apollo 8 missions that we were going to win the race to the moon. They changed their internal vision or policy focus to Mars, and have taken very systematic steps to ensure that they have that capability. I suspect that we will see a Soviet expedition to the vicinity of Mars, not to its surface, but to the vicinity of Mars before the end of the century. I don't think there's anything that would prevent them from doing that right now, outside of a major catastrophic disaster or an internal revolution.

They would probably land on the moon Phobos?
Maybe a visit to it, yes.

Now with the new policy of glasnost coming out of the Kremlin, do you see any joint cooperation in doing that?

I don't think we'll be asked. Maybe some little this and that, where they think there's some technology they can siphon off, they'll offer a chance for us to cooperate. But, they're not going to ask us to work as an equal in a major space endeavor until we have made it absolutely clear that we're going to do it whether they do it or not, then you can get cooperation. That's true of any foreign policy, not just the policy that relates to space. Both parties have to be committed to a joint endeavor, and both realize the benefits from that cooperation. Right now, we're not committed. Why would anybody want to cooperate with the United States in a major space activity? There's no commitment here. Those nations that committed initially to work with us on the space station have watched its delay, delay, delay. Now, they are turning to work with the Soviets. Yes, they still sign the agreements, but that doesn't mean that they're going to cooperate with us exclusively. They're going to hedge their bets.

Were there plans on the drawing board for modification or extension of Apollo-type technology or were they planning to go right into the Shuttle?

In 1970, and even before that, there was a program called the Apollo Applications Program.

That basically became Skylab.

Well, there were many other aspects. There were longer duration bases on the moon, mobile laboratories on the moon. There was the AAP program which was very broadly based and Skylab was just the only thing that was implemented, and it was only implemented once, whereas the original plans were to have at least two Skylabs operating. No, NASA and its centers let that fall through. Unfortunately in 1970, the Nixon administration lost interest in manned space flight. We almost didn't even have the Shuttle. If it hadn't been for Jim Fletcher being willing to buy into the Shuttle, we wouldn't have had it. We wouldn't have a manned space flight program, either.

Senator, do you think that when you have U.S. senators and U.S. congressmen flying on space shuttles, do you think that's more a stunt, or is it something that NASA can gain from and Congress can gain from?

Oh, I think the country gains from having as many people from non NASA activities fly, if there's any kind of reasonable justification. And having members of Congress in space to understand more about the process as well as the risks is perfectly legitimate. Teach-

Jack Schmitt

ers, journalists, as well as geologists and other scientists all have a legitimate place in space, and I don't think they have to be NASA employees to go. The current philosophy is, somehow or other, the lives of NASA employees are less valuable than the lives of non NASA employees. I just don't agree with that. I think everybody has to understand that anything worthwhile results in some risk. Everybody has to understand that you get a lot more bang for your buck if you take the trained geologists to the moon than if you try to train test-pilots to do geology on the moon. I thought we had crossed that hurdle, but apparently the current NASA, as a result of the Challenger accident, has regressed back to the early 1960's.

Wasn't that due to the major public relations problem for NASA because of Christa McAuliffe?

A major public relations problem because they made it a problem. They didn't know how to handle it. Christa McAuliffe knew exactly what she was doing, she knew what the risks were. The first teacher that went west in covered wagons probably didn't make it either. NASA just didn't know how to handle it. They were leaderless at the time. Bill Graham was thrust into a situation he could not comprehend. He did not know how to handle the accident, even though NASA itself knew how to handle it. the Administrator, or Acting Administrator at the time was unable to make the decisions required to handle that appropriately.

Then you didn't think she was sent up too soon?

Oh, of course not! No! She had more impact on education by being involved in the program than any group of astronauts has had in the whole history of the program. No, she had a tremendous impact, and definitely her life was not lost in vain. There are risks to doing things, and everybody who's gone in space so far that I know of has fully comprehended those risks.

Well, how do you think Congress would react to another Shuttle accident?

I have no idea. The country and Congress reacted very positively to the Challenger accident. Much more positively than I expected, I'll be very frank with you. Whether that would happen again, I don't know. If there was very broad-based grassroots constituency for space, then I think there's no question how Congress would react. They'd continue to support it. If Congress would find some excuse like an accident or other excuse not to support space, well this is going to be a very difficult time for this country and for freedom in the next century.

Are you optimistic that the United States will be able to pull together, both in terms of scientific exploration and national security?

I really don't have an answer to that. I guess I'm hopeful. Objectively, I have no reason to be optimistic, because I see absolutely no comprehension of the major issues of the future in our political process.

Do you think another Jim Webb would make a difference?

No. Jim Webb would not be able to do it. What you need is a president, and a constituency behind that president, who believes that this country ought to have a role to play in the future. We haven't seen that yet. We get lots of rhetoric, but we've seen absolutely no commitment to address opportunities, the challenges, and the problems that will be present in our next century.

Looking back, how would you characterize the meaning of Project Apollo?

At what level?

Let's say an historical level.

In the history of science, the meaning of Apollo is that we gained the first order of understanding of a second planet, which has enabled us to more fully understand our own Earth, and also more fully understand the origins of life on Earth. With the history of technology, we saw probably the greatest explosion of know-how that humankind has ever seen, and one of the few times when that explosion occurred as a consequence of peaceful activities, rather than as a consequence of war.

Would you call the space program the moral equivalent of war?

No. That's silly.

Not even in terms of the kind of the Cold War conflict from which the Space Program grew, that tension between Russians and Americans?

There was that kind of a challenge, but the Russians dropped out of the race, and we continued. So, that challenge really faded into the background to be overshadowed by the challenge to the men and women of Apollo, 500,000 of them, supported by most of the American people. They felt that it was still worth doing, that the most important thing they could do with their lives in the

1960's and the early 1970's was to put men on the moon, and return them safely to Earth—to begin that great adventure in space.

You don't see part of that impetus as being the cold-war back in the early 50's?
Of course it was the impetus, but the competition with the Soviets disappeared after Apollo 8. They were no longer in the race, so why did we continue?

Apparently we didn't. We started slacking off.
We didn't slack off until we had landed on the moon.

That was the ultimate goal, and once that happened, didn't things just slow down?
That was due to the media and the politicians. It wasn't the American people.

But, as you said, the Soviets didn't drop out of the race, they dropped out of the sprint.
They just changed their focus; they realized they had screwed up, they'd bitten off more than they could chew, and so they started to do it in a much more mature fashion.

They gave us the sprint and then they took away the marathon, perhaps?
That's an after-the fact analogy. We just did not follow through. We were in the marathon; we just dropped out of the race, and we haven't reentered it for all intents and purposes. But, going on in the history of nations, Apollo, I think, symbolizes what free men and women can do when faced with a challenge such as that presented by the Soviet Union, and what they can do to continue even in the absence of such a challenge. For the human race, the history of the human race, we have seen the first movement of the species into the solar system, and into the universe for that matter. It's a clear psychological commitment of the species to settle other planets. There now are no psychological barriers that I know of between the human species and their settlement of Mars, and indeed of the moon. That's what Apollo demonstrated. It is a new evolutionary status now to leave our planet and to live elsewhere. And we've yet to take advantage of that.

Chapter 8

DAVE SCOTT
Commander, Apollo 15

Space Entrepreneur

I f there were a stereotypical "All-American Boy" among the twelve moonwalkers, it would have to be Dave Scott. It is a description that fits him like a hand in a glove. One that he may not like, or even accept, but nonetheless, accurate in its basic concept. Simply put, he was then and continues to be now, one of the really good guys associated with the space program.

Today he is a successful businessman in California, who cares deeply about the future of our nation's space program and is not timid about letting his feelings be known.

Since 1977, Dave Scott has been the President of Scott Science and Technology, Inc., Lancaster, California. Scott Science and Technology, Inc., through its subsidiaries, provides specialized research, engineering, and technical services for the development and implementation of commercial applications of advanced technologies. The company's services have been directed toward two specialized areas: (1) Design, engineering, development, and missions operations for space-oriented government and commercial projects primarily those related to the launch and space transfer of satellites, using as an option the patented "Satellite Transfer Vehicle," and (2) Research and engineering services in connection with development of vicarious applications of the patented "Structural Information Detector," a microprocessor based opto-electronic sensor which measures with great precision the bending or internal stress level of structures to which it is attached.

Before starting Scott Science and Technology he was the Director of NASA, Hugh L. Dryden Flight Research Center, Edwards, California, responsible for the overall management of the prime NASA aeronautical flight research facility. This included both programmatic and institutional aspects of an autonomous field center conducting as many as seventeen separate research and development projects with up to fifteen types of aircraft. Center resources included approximately eight hundred engineers, scientists, technicians, and administrative personnel, and an annual budget of forty million dollars. During this period, the first successful flight tests of the NASA Space Shuttle (Approach and Landing Tests) were conducted at Dryden. He retired from United States Air Force as Colonel in April, 1975.

As a NASA astronaut, Scott flew on Gemini 8, Apollo 9, and was Spacecraft Commander on Apollo 15. He has logged 546 hours and 54 minutes in space, of which twenty hours and forty-six minutes were in extravehicular activity.

In 1972, Scott was named as Technical Assistant to the Apollo Program Manager at Johnson Space Center. Prior to coming to the Dryden Flight Research Center, he was Special Assistant for Mission Operations for the Apollo-Soyuz Test Project. He retired from the U.S. Air Force in March 1975, with the rank of Colonel and over 5,600 hours of flying time.

On the Gemini 8 mission in 1966, Scott and Command Pilot Neil Armstrong performed the first successful docking of two vehicles in space. In 1971, Scott commanded Apollo 15. He was responsible for the overall flight crew mission operations, planning, training, and implementation of the first extended scientific exploration of the moon. As Commander of Apollo 15, he spent nearly three days on the moon, more than eighteen hours outside his spacecraft, and explored the vicinity of Hadley Rille in three long excursions using, for the first time, a Lunar Roving Vehicle.

During the flight of Apollo 9, Scott was responsible for all command module flight operations and preparation of the first inflight demonstration of the complete lunar orbit rendezvous spacecraft configuration consisting of the command module, lunar module, and other systems. His specific responsibilities included the first docking of Apollo spacecraft, first solo rendezvous operations in the command module, first solo extravehicular activity, and first in-flight demonstration of manual thrust vector control during main rocket engine powered spaceflight.

Scott received a Bachelor of Science degree from the U.S. Military Academy in 1954, standing fifth in a class of 633, and the degrees of Master of Science in Aeronautics and Astronautics and

Engineer of Aeronautics and Astronautics from M.I.T. in 1962. He was awarded an Honorary Doctorate of Astronautical Science from the University of Michigan in 1971. He has graduated from the Air Force Experimental Test Pilot School and Aerospace Research Pilot School.

Among Scott's special honors are three NASA Distinguished Service Medals, the NASA Exceptional Service Medal, two Air Force Distinguished Service Medals, the Air Force Distinguished Flying Cross, and the Air Force Association's David C. Shilling Trophy, the Robert J. Collier Trophy, the Federation Aeronautique Internationale Gold Medal, and the United Nations Peace Medal.

Born June 6, 1932, in San Antonio, Texas, Scott is the son of Brigadier General (USAF, Ret.) and Mrs. Tom W. Scott of La Jolla, California. He is married and the couple resides in Manhattan Beach, California. They have two children.

Can you tell us what you're doing today? Can you describe for us the kind of work you're involved with?

I'm running a little company that supplies a turn-key satellite delivery service for commercial communication satellites right now.

What does turn-key mean in this case?

Turn-key means you do the whole package. Turn-key includes everything from the launch vehicle, to insurance, to financing the launch services. In other words, a communications company that needs a satellite normally doesn't have the expertise or the experience to get one launched. They're experts in using them and, after the last three years, we have found that most communications companies would prefer to just buy a switchboard in the sky rather than go through the black art of rocketships. So, we handle the black art. We package everything necessary to put a satellite on orbit. We don't build anything, and we're not really brokers, because by controlling the various business elements, we can make trade-offs to the benefit of the customer.

In what way?

Well, it's a systems integration job, really. You have control of all the subsystems in the system, and you can match wires, match plumbing, do the software, and make everything fit better. It's been done with airplanes before.

Do you provide a part of the satellite, or do you just handle all the arrangements of the deal?

We'll arrange the whole deal. But, as an option, we have designed an upper-stage, which was originally designed for the Shuttle as a commercial upper-stage. But, when the Challenger went down, and the President said the shuttle will no longer be used commercially, why, it turned our lights out. We had to go get a candle to get them relit. So, we'll have as an option in the turn-key delivery service, the use of our upper-stage, when we get it funded, to complete the development.

What satellites have you been involved with?

What we did after Challenger went down was to look around to see what got bumped, who was sitting on the ground. Several had, and these people were looking for rides. We recently signed a letter of intent with a little outfit in Florida that is planning to put up a couple of direct broadcast satellites. Other then that, we're negotiating with a couple of fairly substantial companies with satellites sitting on the ground. It took us a while to develop the concept, and it's just now really materialized to where we have the whole team in place and we can handle all the pieces.

Are you negotiating with the Europeans and the Russians for launch vehicles?

Yeah, we've talked to Ariane, we've talked to the Chinese, all of the U.S. guys. We just take the launch vehicle that is most appropriate for the customer's satellite and timing, and also the economics.

Do you still do any work for NASA at all? Do you still have any ties to them?

Well, NASA got us started on the upper-stage business. In 1983, NASA made an announcement that it wanted the private sector to become involved in space. They wanted the private sector to develop an upper-stage for the shuttle and NASA said that they wouldn't compete with government funds. That's how we got into this business. We were basically consultants before that. We provided payload integration services to the Air Force, Martin, TRW, and so on. We decided that it looked like a good idea to get involved in a piece of the hardware. We took it a step at a time, and got a couple of rounds of financing to get it going. Since the Challenger went down, we've been trying to get NASA interested in the President's policy. And what can I say, they certainly don't always understand it.

Are you involved at all with Deke Slayton and the work he's doing?

No. It's a totally different vision. He's trying to find some little payloads that he can stack on top of used Minuteman rockets, things like that.

No more work in manned space flight for you then?

Well, no. Right now there isn't much for the commercial or the private sector to do in manned space flight. The President has established, I think, a super policy, but the government doesn't seem to know how, or want to implement it. The government is totally fragmented. The last time I counted, seventeen federal agencies have space budgets, and they have no boss. There are a lot of folks in the boat with oars, but they're all stroking in different directions. So, there's just no implementation of the policy.

Do you believe the next ambitious mission for the United States program should be a manned landing on Mars?

Well, it depends on what you call ambitious. That's a fairly broad and generic term. The space station is ambitious, yet it's somewhat benign. But, it's still a big job. And that's not going to Mars. I think I would reflect on the Ride report, and I would say that the next step, really, is going back to the moon, and setting up a base so that people can learn how to live in a hostile environment a long way from home. Trying to go to Mars without doing that is taking too big a step. Although, Mars is in the offing somewhere, twenty, thirty years down the road.

Do you see the private sector, through venture-capitalists, for example, getting involved in the commercial exploitation of space?

No, not for a long time, not until the government does something to stimulate them, if you will. You know, they have a very bad taste for it right now. I've spent a lot of time with the generic venture capitalist institutions in London, Hong Kong, New York, and whatever. They just don't have a taste for commercial space. Frankly, when commercial satellites got bumped from the Challenger, that left a pretty bad taste in the mouths of those in the financial community that had actual contracts and money down. That was a real blow. Nobody's made any money commercially in space other than communications satellites. Ariane is making money because they started out commercially, so they're doing pretty well. But, none of the microgravity research is far enough along yet to be a product, and from our experience in the financial world. the financial community would rather do a nice, simple leveraged buyout. They don't want to learn anything about space. We're talking to a couple who are into it. But, for the most part, space does not attract the financial community because there's no payoff. It's all long term, and you can't figure out what the multiples are.

I'm surprised that there isn't a space-age Henry Ford out there ready to jump in.

We've tried them all! Boy, we have sure been beating the bushes. Our basic project was an upper-stage, and, we can show some pretty good market analyses. It doesn't cost much to finish the development. We've got to dig up another partner to do it. We have an agreement with TRW to do it. But, the reason we went to this turn-key delivery service was because we couldn't find any money for an upper-stage. Nobody in the financial community could understand what it was. Nor would they take the time to learn it. I have a partner who is my investment banker who came out of the oil industry. He's used to, I like to say, "big bucks, long-term investments, and dry holes." He knows the business; he started out in a British merchant banking firm. He's American, but he started out in England, and one of his first clients was J. Paul Getty. He was a close, personal friend of J. Paul Getty for six years. So, he's been in the big leagues. He owned a New York member firm in Beverly Hills, and he ran an Australian energy company that did over a billion a year. He's been working this problem with us for two and a half years. He's convinced that there's something there. But he, too, is frustrated because the financial community just doesn't respond. I can tell you, we have pounded the streets. Every dollar is hidden. There's just no support for commercial space.

What do you mean by the government having to stimulate this sort of thing?

For example, in a National Space Directive of February 1988, the President said that the government should purchase, when it can, commercial services and commercially developed hardware. As an example, we have an upper-stage that we designed. We have patented it, and we have spent only private money on it, about six million dollars. It could be built, manufactured by TRW and sold to the government. If the government would order twenty of those, we could go to the financial community and we could find the money to develop it. We have TRW, Inc., and that's credibility, but the government won't order any because they don't know how to do that. The acquisition procedures are scrambled, they can't

understand that, and there's no leadership within the broad definition of government to implement the President's policy.

The Shuttle accident brought the U.S. space program to a
virtual standstill for over two years. Do you think that maybe
the Space Shuttle was developed a little too soon? Was it the
appropriate next step after the series of moon landings and
Skylab?

When the shuttle was conceived it was the logical next step.
Then, unfortunately, NASA ran into a lot of budget crunches, and,
the Shuttle wasn't developed right. It wasn't what was envisioned.
They didn't build enough spare parts, so it came out sort of half
way. If you had one on the pad and had a problem, you had to go
cannibalize parts off another one. You didn't have a storage shelf
of spares, or a development program. Under the circumstances,
though, I think NASA did pretty well. Unfortunately, the NASA
management system broke down, and the Challenger went down.
Again, hindsight is really terrific, but conceptually, I think the
shuttle was the right thing to do. Also, if it were operated properly,
the cost wouldn't be so high. It's not operated properly, because
in my opinion, it's being run by a bunch of R & D guys. I think
they're terrific, but you don't have R & D guys run operational
squadrons. You have to shift the culture; you finish your development, and you have to go to a new culture, to people who are
operationally oriented rather than development oriented. The
group actually didn't really do that.

The Challenger explosion was the first fatal disaster in the
program. There were no inflight casualties up to that point. Your
flight on Gemini 8 was the first close call, an immediate life-
threatening emergency. Can you explain what exactly happened
to you and Neil Armstrong?

Sure. But, before Challenger, Apollo 1 was a failure, a catastrophe. We lost three guys. And, we had no experience in Apollo
flight. We had to go back and redesign the whole system. We
recovered, and started flying again in *half* the time it took to
recover from the Shuttle, and the Shuttle had twenty-five flights. So,
it shows me that the system, the management system or oversight
system, in the country is stalling. Bureaucracy is grinding us to a
halt. We recovered from a more tragic failure earlier in the game
more quickly. Why did we do that? Why were we able in 1967 to
recover as quickly as we did, compared to 1986 when we just
stumbled and dragged along for what, thirty-two months?

Do you have an answer to that?

No, I really don't. Somebody ought to look at it someday. I think one answer could be that in '67 there was a more clearly defined goal—man on the moon by 1970. And, you had all first stringers in there. The people running the program then were all committed and dedicated to space, and they had been there since the beginning and were the first team. With the Challenger, most of the first team was gone and a lot of the second team was gone. So, you didn't have the capability. They have good guys down there, but you just didn't have your first stringers in there. If you try to recover from a disaster, and if you don't have your first stringers in there, boy, it's tough. Back then, at the time the country was more space conscious. More people were involved, and there was more oversight. In 1986 you had this giant bureaucratic machine grinding away, and it just takes a long time to get to an answer. It's a good answer because it works. On the other hand, Apollo worked pretty well, too.

Is that just the nature of the beast, that organizations just develop like that? Or could something have been done earlier to prevent that?

It is sort of the nature of the beast; when an organization gets twenty-five years old dry rot starts setting in. That's classic. NASA got twenty-five years old. Something should have been done to revitalize it. That, in my opinion, is one problem. Another problem is there just has been no focused space leadership in this country for many years. There's no boss. You cannot run it with a committee, in my opinion. That's what the government's trying to do. In the Apollo days, by God, they had some leaders. They took the bull by the horns and said, 'GO!' The culture is different these days.

Do you think that they should separate the R & D from the operation side? Run them separately?

Yes. I don't have a vote, but, I would vote to break up NASA into three pieces. In fact, there was an article in *Forbes* a while ago that said it's time to break up NASA. It had many wrong reasons, but the conclusions weren't bad. In fact, I worked in NASA on two sides of the house. I worked on the space side, and I worked on the aeronautical side at the Dryden Research Center. Those are two different cultures. It's difficult for a boss at the top to try and mix two cultures like that and make them effective. I think NASA has really three functions right now. It's a space R & D business, it's an aeronautical R & D business, and it's a space operational business with the Shuttle. They're three different cultures. It seems

Dave Scott

to me that NASA would be more effective if you had those three in separate divisions, in separate budgets, separate managements, all reporting to a single boss who is in charge of the space parts of the Department of Commerce, the Department of Transportation, the Department of Energy and so on. Space is becoming such a dominant part of our lives. Looking down the road thirty years from now, hopefully it will be even more so. You need somebody at the Cabinet level who is in charge, who makes decisions and reports directly to the President. This is not meant to create any more bureaucracy, but, the world is expanding into space, and if we don't go, the other people will. Frankly, since we're on the subject, the other part of my soap box speech is that we are rapidly working ourselves into a fourth or fifth-rate space power.

How worried should we be about the Soviet space program, the military aspects of the program?

I'd be pretty worried. Again, in sitting on the outside, it's tough to really get the right perspective sometimes. You'll have to accept my rationale on some of this. If I were running the military, I would say, 'Boy, my communications systems are very important to me. I've got x number of satellites up there, and if the other guy wants to start a war, he can take me out really fast because I know I can take him out fast.' So, I would have what the Advanced Research Projects Agency is trying to do—an array. The Air Force looked at it for a while, but Secretary Aldrich shot it down. It was this array or covey of small satellites, a multiple satellite system. One concept that DARPA and the Air Force came up with about three years ago, was upward of 240 small satellites circling the Earth, providing communications. You can't shoot them all down. It's very hard to shoot 240 of them down. But, in a military sense right now, we are really vulnerable. We rely on satellites for an awful lot of things.

That's right. We rely almost exclusively on satellites for a lot of our military communications, for example, whereas the Soviets still rely heavily on landlines, and "outdated methods"?

Yeah. But, we could solve that problem with these 'light sats' or, as somebody called them, 'cheap sats.' I've looked at them, they're just message relay stations, and they work. In fact, the Shuttle, with our upper-stage, could place thirty small satellites at, let's say, 500 miles up and they'd stay up there for ninety years.

What about too many satellites?

Yeah, there are, but that's controllable. Debris is a big problem right now. There's a lot of concern about debris.

Also, too many satellites?

That can be controlled. Space is pretty big. Take the arc over the United States with domestic communications satellites; they're spaced about 1,500 miles apart. That's pretty comfortable.

Should we be worried that sometime in the future there could be the equivalent of the space Pearl Harbor launched against the United States? Say, twenty to thirty years from now?

That's a tough one. That has to do with an awful lot of variables other than technical and military. On December 7, 1941, we were happily negotiating with the Japanese, right? So from a political point of view, you gotta know what's going on. That's a big job to try to anticipate something like that. That takes a lot of people with a lot of different talents. I don't think that you can say that militarily, we might get caught. You could but the other parts will catch you, too, if you're not careful.

We were talking about your close call on Gemini 8. Can you explain exactly what happened, and what your reactions were at the time?

We were launching to rendezvous and dock with an Agena. The Agenas had had a lot of problems associated with them. In fact, several weeks before we went, one blew up in a test. It was considered a rather squirrelly thing. But, on the other hand, it was so-called man-rated. So we took off and rendezvoused and docked with it. In those days, you didn't have constant communication with Mission Control. You talked to people over various points of the Earth where they had tracking sights, for maybe four to eight minutes. When the orbit track departed the Continental U.S., it was pretty quiet. We were docked with an Agena, which Mission Control thought had a problem. Assuming the Agena was the problem, we went through procedures to turn the Agena off. It turned out it wasn't the Agena after all, it was the Gemini. One of the thrusters on the Gemini was firing intermittently without being commanded, which caused unstable rotation. We really didn't figure it out until we got off the Agena. Then, we realized it was the Gemini and went through the procedures to shut it down. We had to come home, because we burned up about half of our re-entry fuel getting stabilized.

When you undocked from the Agena did either you or Neil Armstrong experience any kind of vertigo at all?

No, we were tumbling pretty fast, but I think we were focused on the problem, and didn't really have time to think about it. Things were moving so fast.

When you got back down and looked at it, did NASA find out exactly what happened, what caused the problem?

Yes. In fact, they changed the design. When they originally designed the thrusters, they designed them to be turned on with a ground. They were always hot, always had power going to them. To get them to fire, to get the fuel valves open you, in effect, grounded it. They suspected that some wire had rubbed somewhere, and it had grounded this thruster intermittently and fired it. So, they reversed the polarity, and subsequently they fixed it so that all thrusters fired only when you supplied power to them.

Before you got into space, you did quite a bit of flying, either jets or on your own. Is it true that you once had to make an emergency landing on a golf course?

Yeah. I was going to graduate school, and we used to fly on Saturdays. They had some T-33's at Hanscom Field in Boston. Everybody going to local graduate schools flew the seven or eight T-Birds. They were pretty run down. A buddy of mine and I were out on a Saturday morning getting our flying time practicing landings at Pease Air Force Base in New Hampshire. And the plane just quit running. About the only place we could go was a golf course.

And were there any golfers on the course at the time?

Oh, yeah, they were all out on a Saturday morning. We had a devil of a time keeping them away from the airplane. We hopped out of the airplane and all the golfers wanted to come up and take a look. You never know whether the thing's going to catch on fire or not and we had to convince them to stay away.

Which of your three space flights did you enjoy the most?

Boy, that's tough. They were all completely different. Each flight was so totally different. If they were all the same, you could pick one. Gemini was the two-man first docking. Apollo 9 was a test flight, a pure test flight, and 15 was an exploration. They were apples, oranges, and peaches.

Was there one spacecraft you favored more than another one?

Spacecraftwise, Apollo certainly had a lot more capability than Gemini did. But, the Gemini in it's day was really pretty good. You have to put it in historical perspective. When you consider Gemini, it was terrific. In fact, we had the first auxiliary tape memory for our computer. We could read in a lot of extra information. Then, you get to Apollo, where we had a much better computer which, by comparison, was not as good as today's cheapest PC.

You were up in space with what we would now consider primitive computers. Children are using computers more sophisticated than what you had, right?

Oh, yeah. Compared to today they were really primitive. But, in those days, they were very capable. Things were just beginning. On Apollo 9, we flew with the first digital autopilot. That was a big deal. I remember the MIT guys came into NASA and said, 'Hey, we're going to build a digital autopilot,' and NASA people said, 'You can't do that, it's not possible.' Now, look what we have.

Some accounts have it that Gemini was pulled together quickly, almost as a last minute proposition. The idea that it would bridge the gap between Mercury and Apollo, until Apollo was ready.

Put together at the last minute? Gosh, the F-86 was built in six to eight months, and it was super. I think it followed pretty logically from Mercury. I don't think it was built to bridge the gap. The Gemini program was really to demonstrate the techniques, methodology, and procedures necessary to go to the moon. You had to demonstrate rendezvous. Nobody had ever done a rendezvous before, and that was mysterious. You had to demonstrate docking, and nobody'd ever done that. We used to worry a lot about electrical discharge between the two spacecraft that had been launched in separate paths. That was a big concern. It turned out not to be, but people worried about it. Then there was EVA, we hadn't done EVA's. So, there were a lot of techniques, procedures, and methods to be developed in Gemini to be able to do the things that Apollo needed to do. It was a nice, logical, intermediary step. Mercury was just a ride around the park. But, that was a big step. The doctors wondered if a human being could live in space. Could you drink in space? That was a big question at the time. They were pretty logical steps.

The Shuttle is quite a big step from the Gemini program. Do you have any desire today to fly aboard that spacecraft?

Oh, I think it'd be fun, but on the other hand, I had mine. I had a good time. And, at some point, you have to hang it up and go do other things. The training is long and hard, and after a while,

I think you get burned out. Simulators, they're terrific things. But, boy after a while—I think the last time somebody counted, I have over 2,000 hours in simulators. They're great machines to learn on. But over and over again, that gets to be long, hard work.

What did you find to be the most aggravating part about being an astronaut?
I've never been asked that question before. How should I put it? It was the show-biz after the flights.

You astronauts had a name for it. You called it going "in the barrel," didn't you?
Well, yeah, in the barrel. But that was more to try to sell the program, and that's a worthy thing to do. But, you know, after the flights, gosh we went seven months straight on the road.

That long?
Yeah. And that gets pretty old. You know, everybody looks at it and they say, 'Gee, it's wonderful to go ride in the parade.' No, it's not wonderful after a while. It's really hard work. A lot of us don't really want to be politicians. I wouldn't want to be a politician, I wouldn't want to go shake hands with everybody in the world. I was a test-pilot. I liked doing that. We had to go perform roles that we really weren't interested in from a personal point of view. We did our duty like good boys; we signed up for the program, and, by golly, we supported the program. It wasn't really aggravating. But it was hard, tedious work.

How did you get into the test pilot business? Is that something you had your mind set on, or did it just sort of come along?
No, I had my mind on it. I started out flying airplanes, flying fighter airplanes. The next logical step for me was to go to test pilot school.

On the Apollo flights, one of the most dramatic moments, at least for the pilot, is the moment of pitch-over when you can actually first get a view of where you're going. Can you describe what the scene was, and your impressions, as you saw it?
You're right. It is a pretty dramatic moment. I was pleased that it looked like it was supposed to look. You don't really know you're going to be at your landing site until you get to see it. It was definitely where we were supposed to be. But, what should I say, the smaller features, the granularity was not exactly what we had expected. We didn't have good radar or good photos of our landing

site because it was so far north. And, as I recall, the best resolution we had was something like 20 meters. So we couldn't see the little holes. There were so many little holes that they obscured the big holes, craters, that we had trained for. The character of the surface was quite different. There was so much more character to the surface than on the simulator. On the other hand, on a macro scale, it was like it was supposed to be. And, what you're really doing at this time is planning your touchdown, and selecting your touchdown point. You're not really gazing at the scenery, you're planning to make sure you get it down when you're supposed to get it down. In our case, we had a heavier LM. We had an extended bell on the engine, a little less margin of fuel, the descent was twice as steep as previous descents. So, it went pretty fast.

So you didn't have time to sight-see.

Not really, no. You're doing a job and your computer is running at full tilt, and the thing to do is to get it down. People had a tendency to level off at 150 feet or so above the surface, and then start back down, which was terribly time-consuming. One of our objectives was to keep it going on the slope, right on in to landing. You have to force yourself to do that. Because your tendency is to level off and take a look before you get right down into it. It takes a lot of concentration. You're not looking around. You pick your landing site and you go.

You landed in a tiny plain surrounded by, if you look at a map, mountains. What kind of navigational and flight problems had to be solved in order for you to be able to make that pinpoint landing in such a place?

There's a guy at NASA named Floyd Bennett who designed our trajectory. We had to come in over the mountains and that's why we had a twenty-five degree descent. That was a tricky navigational problem. We used to say, 'We're glad we didn't see the mountains or we would have pulled our feet up.' We didn't really see them until we were on the ground and looked back, because we came over the top of them. Down to 700 feet, it's automatic. So, you really didn't see that. And, of course, another objective was not to land in the rille. They had demonstrated a pinpoint landing on Apollo 12, and the system worked really well.

We've heard that they picked the easiest landing sites first, and gradually developed more confidence and technique. What were some of the specific problems that you encountered? There's no atmosphere, so you didn't have to worry about air resistance or winds. It just seems like straight Newtonian laws of physics. What other kinds of considerations might the average person not know about?

You're right. It's a linear environment. On the other hand, the dynamics of the lunar module are very unique and very different from anything anybody ever flew. It's a tough thing to fly. It's the toughest thing I ever flew, and I've flown a lot of airplanes. It's a dynamic, three-dimensional system constantly moving. For example, you sit on a thrust vector, that is, the force of the descent engine pushing upward underneath you to slow you down. If you tilt that vector, then your vertical and horizontal components will change. So, even without changing the magnitude of the thrust of the engine, you start moving forward, and if you tilt it forward, you fall down and you fall forward. If you then want to go back to the vertical and if there was an atmosphere, you'd stop, because of drag. But the moon has no atmosphere, therefore you have no drag, so you continue moving forward. If you add power to keep from going down, you will go up. The same situation exists left and right. So, it's like trying to balance on top of a needle. It's a tough thing to fly. That's why they had the lunar landing training vehicle.

Was there anything that compared to flying a lunar module on the Earth? Was it like a helicopter?

The approach is like a helicopter but without any aerodynamics. The handling qualities are completely different. The controls are completely different. We used to practice in helicopters, but, a helicopter's a piece of cake compared to trying to fly the LM Another problem that we had was a limited amount of fuel. If she runs out of gas, she runs out of gas, there was just no margin. So, you have to get it down, you can't screw around. You've only got one chance. It was a demanding task.

It is interesting that you mentioned that landing a helicopter is a piece of cake compared to the LM, because Gene Cernan, a Navy pilot, and maybe prejudiced, said that landing on the moon, compared to landing on an aircraft carrier at night, was piece of cake.

Oh, it could have been. I never landed on a carrier at night, and I understand that's a tough job.

One of your hobbies is photography. We're just curious as to what pictures you're most proud of that you took on the moon?

Oh, I don't know. That's a tough question. Probably all of them. We were fortunate to have a good camera, good training, and good subject matter.

Are there any pictures that you wished you took while you were there that you missed?

We were still clicking away when we left. We got what we really went for. I can tell you one that I like. I was standing back up on a hill looking down at the plain where the lunar module was, something like six kilometers away. We were up high enough that the curvature didn't get us. We could see the LM. I took a 500-millimeter telephoto picture of the LM. When it's blown up to about twenty-four by twenty-four inches, you can just barely see the LM.

We've seen that picture. It's a striking photo.

When you're standing there, it's even more impressive, because behind it you could see a great big crater called Pluton behind the lunar module. And if you know that it's another six kilometers to the crater, and you look at the size of the crater, it must be thirty or fifty lunar modules across in diameter. It's an *enormous* crater. And you could get the perspective of how *small* that lunar module was on that great, big moon, how far away that thing was.

You mentioned after the flight that one of the problems that all of you had was determining distance, because there were no markers with which you were familiar. Can you explain that a little bit?

There's nothing to scale with on the moon. Take trees for example. You know, we scale trees automatically, cars, telephone poles, roads, objects, man-made objects, natural objects on the Earth. You don't have that on the moon. So, you can't tell that you're looking at a large boulder at a great distance or a small rock nearby. If you could get some shadowing in there, if you could see your own shadow, or some other shadow that's related to where you are, or some object related to what you do, that would really help.

Was it disorienting at first?

No. You just have to know about it. You have to make sure you don't chase something. If it's a little bit further down the road, then it's probably a *lot* further down the road.

Can you recall your immediate thoughts when you did your stand-up EVA from the hatch on top of the LM as you looked over the moon and took the initial photographs?

The tremendous amount of different landforms, stratigraphy and character of the surface, how many different things there were out there. There was layering, a few boulders, a lot of craters, a lot of different shapes; a great variety of landforms, just a tremendous variety of landforms, more than I expected.

More than you expected?

Oh, yeah. A great variety up there. You don't get it in the photographs at all.

Was it more than the people on the ground expected also, in choosing the site?

I should have mentioned and talked about that. Choosing landing sites has many different aspects. Site selection was quite a process. On Apollo 15, we had four landing sites before they finally settled on one. The decision process to select the final landing site was a very complex process. A lot of people were involved. A lot of different elements are considered: navigation error, the landing error, the geology and how it relates to other places—all those things. It was a very complicated process. The selection of a landing site has a lot of variables, with different weightings. And it's tough to pick one reason why even one site was selected. But, we went to Hadley because there was a lot of variety, because there were mountains, and there was a rille. Of course, we trained on a simulator, which was really quite good. But, we probably got accustomed to a narrow band of surface feature characteristics when, in fact, there was a real wide band.

When you finally made it out to the surface, you made the statement that 'It's a fundamental truth of man's nature that he must explore, and this was exploration at its greatest.' Was that a spontaneous comment that came to you in the excitement of the moment?

Pretty much. We really enjoyed having an opportunity to go out and do what they called the first extended scientific exploration. It was pretty exciting; three days instead of a day and a half, and we had a Rover. Boy, we were really getting to go do it.

Were you ever amazed that you, Dave Scott, were standing on the moon? Did you ever stop and think, "How did I get here?" What was the process? Did you think, "How lucky I must be"?

You sort of take all of that in stride. I think. It just becomes part of your job. It's tremendous that you get to do it, but you get past that, it just becomes a natural thing to do. Guys would say to me as I headed out to the launch-pad, "Boy, aren't you worried?" I'd say, "No! It's time to go!" You've been thinking this through for a long time. But, it's always exciting to have the real thing.

Speaking of taking things in stride, what was it like to walk on the moon compared to walking on the Earth?
It's very different. In simple terms, it's like walking on a trampoline.

One thing mentioned in one of the articles following the flight was that you and Irwin didn't talk to each other during your rest periods, you didn't share your impressions. You apparently didn't want to disturb each other's thoughts. Was that something you both agreed to do?
Where'd you get that?

That was in a New York Times *article. An impression, I think, by Irwin himself.*
During our rest period we went to sleep because we were tired. Any other time, we were communicating quite a bit. It takes a long time to get suited up, it takes a long time to get out of the suits. You contain the dirt, you pack the rocks, check the rocks, eat and all that sort of stuff. One morning we had an oxygen leak, the next morning we had a water leak. Boy, we were busy in that thing. When we got time to go to bed, we went to bed.

That was it? No small talk?
Not much, We got five or six hours of rest a night. It was hard work. When you finally got in the sack, it was time to go to sleep.

Speaking of Jim Irwin, he said that he believes his irregular heart beats were caused by his time on the lunar surface. Did you experience any problems like that?
The doctors said they saw a few PVC's in my heartbeat, too. But I didn't experience anything. I didn't feel anything. Everybody throws them once in a while, if you're familiar with that. Deke Slayton was the first guy to get caught. Almost everyone, if they're monitored long enough, will throw a couple of PVC's.

And caffeine can induce them and all kinds of things.
Yeah. It depends on the person, too. But, I didn't feel anything.

Jim Irwin attributed his irregular heartbeats directly to his time on the lunar surface. Is that something that can be attributed to the being on the lunar surface?

You'd had to talk to the doctors. I was told that we had a potassium deficiency and that might have made a contribution, but I don't know why the time on the surface would do that, other than that you're working hard. We had a depletion of potassium before we went because we were working hard at the Cape at the time, from what we were told. The best way to get an answer for that is to look at the medical record and talk to the doctors. They looked at that pretty hard.

Did it ever bother you or Jim that, after you had finished with the lunar module Falcon, you had to send her crashing into the lunar surface? Did you believe that she deserved a better fate than that?

Again, that was part of the mission. You don't like to see it go, but that's part of the mission. As a matter of fact, on Apollo 9 we had a lunar module, and when we left it, it was going to be there in Earth orbit for nineteen years. I've often wondered if it ever came down, because it's loaded with all sorts of goodies. You know, once one flew you couldn't go and bring it back.

We understand that you're very much interested in archaeology.

I do like it, that's right.

In that context, what do you think will happen to the Apollo landing sites once people start going back to the moon and establish a permanent presence? What should be done about them?

That's a good question. I've never even given that any thought. Gee, probably make a lunar park. Somebody, someday, will go back, of course. Preservation, certainly, would be a nice thing to do. There's a lot of history there. When people finally get back, they'll look at that old lunar module, and say, 'You mean to tell me those guys came up here in that thing?' (Laughs)

We just though that it would be terrible if, in the future, explorers, colonists, or whoever, went up there and in their curiosity, or worse, ended up despoiling them by tramping over them, taking souvenirs, that sort of thing. They should be preserved somehow.

I think you're absolutely right. That's a good idea. You know, the footprints will be there for another five hundred million years or so. So, yeah, that's a dandy idea.

Your mission was roughly in the middle of the six landing missions. Today, there's kind of a paradox. According to the polls, the American public is very enthusiastic and supportive of the space program. But, at the time of the last lunar landings, interest seemed to be waning. What was the reason for that, in your opinion? And do you think the management was correct in ending the program with Apollo 17?

People got tired of seeing the same thing. That's natural, I believe. And I think, yes, management was justified in terminating it, because you have to terminate it some day. It wasn't just like it was cut off on a moment's notice. There was a certain amount of planning. You have to make a judgment as to when you stop it to get ready to make the next step. That's a complex discussion and a lot of people discussed and debated it at length. In my opinion, the decision was right because we have to move along. There's still a lot to do, but we can probably do it more effectively when we go back the next time.

Was there substance to the notion, then, that it was too risky a proposition to continue and that the chances of losing a crew were too high?

Well, it's risk versus gain. What's too risky? I don't know what too risky is. And how much have we gained? Where do you stop? I think the people who were responsible for the decision had to make it and they made it. In retrospect, I would probably have voted for what they did. You know, six successful lunar landings; we accomplished a lot by learning how to go there, bringing back a certain amount of science. At some point you say, historically, we have to go take another bigger step.

Do you think the next step should have been maybe a more permanent establishment on the moon? Rather than coming back to Earth orbit for a while? Or have we done it the right way?

I think only history will tell. It's hard to say right now.

Well, we're willing to let you tell, too.

The trades have to be made. And that's why I like the Ride Report so much. They did a nice job in making tradeoffs and providing options. You have to balance everything with the budget. It's a tough decision on what you do next, how you do it, the pace, and how you stimulate the public to support it. It's a tough decision. You need some very strong, very dynamic leadership in Washington in order to get the support you need to press on. I would say the next step is going back to the moon and learning how to live on the moon. Really learning how to live there before you try and take the big step to Mars.

What kind of timetable might you be talking about?
Well, I think it depends on the money, and commitment. We did it before in nine years; we can do it again.

Really? That fast?
Sure. Before, we started at zero. President Kennedy said let's do it before the end of the decade. We have a lot of knowledge. Unfortunately we would probably try and re-invent the wheel, which we shouldn't. I had a call from one of the guys at Arthur D. Little some time ago. They're doing a study asking, when we go back to the moon, what do we change? My answer was 'Very little.' Boy, I think the guys who designed that system, everything from the suits to the lunar module, to the Rover, did a marvelous job. We're all set to go back. You have to learn to stay now.

If you were given, let's say, a half an hour on national television to make the most persuasive case you could for a really concentrated effort in space, what would be your arguments?
First, I'd have to go think about that for a long time. I'd have to sit down and see what the receptivity, the trend was today. What do people like? What do they respond to? You know, what are the mores? What are we doing? What are our objectives? What are our problems? Once you do that, then you try to address those, and get people's attention based on what they're interested in, and how we might solve some of the problems. One interesting thing I read, not too long ago, was about the nuclear waste problem, which is becoming very evident these days; one way to get rid of that is to put it off into space. Well, that would cost a lot of money. But would it cost as much money as we're spending now to solve the problem? That's a contemporary question, and to reach a conclusion you'd have to research what the public was interested in and appeal to their interest.

A lot of people like Carl Sagan and others are advocating cooperation with the Soviets in a manned program. What are your thoughts in that regard?

I think it's a great idea if you do it with the right roles and responsibilities. I think Apollo-Soyuz was a good example. That worked out pretty well. Cooperative ventures are the only way we're going to get all of these things done. On the other hand, you have to decide who does what, and how it's done. I don't think you can mix and match. You can't mix and match the hardware other than docking them together. The procedures are different, the culture's different, the way they do things are different from the way we do things. If you separate roles and responsibilities properly, we can work very well together. But, I don't think you can put everybody on an island and have a joint collaborative machine come out of it.

Were there any thoughts after Apollo-Soyuz to continue that sort of cooperative venture, or did it stop there?

I'm sure there was thought. I'm not aware of it. I spent about a year and a half on that. I thought it was great program; it was very well done. I don't know what the government or the Soviets considered after that.

How did you like working with the Soviet cosmonauts and their space people?

I enjoyed it. I did. They're good people. I got to know a number of the cosmonauts quite well, they're very bright guys and dedicated. I don't think much of their system, but ... it's *their* system. But, they're good people, I think they have a strong first team. I don't think they have the depth that we do, in terms of our capabilities and expertise. Yet, they certainly seem to be getting the job done today.

They certainly seem to have more tenacity then we seem to be showing, don't they?

Yep, sure do. The automatic landing of their shuttle, that was pre-e-ety good. That *was* impressive.

Where do you see the Soviet program ten years from now?

If we don't do something pretty quick, I see it as dominant. Absolutely overwhelming. They'll own the sky. And the moon! And they'll be on their way to Mars if they keep going at the same rate.

Are they really any closer in getting to the moon than they were back when we were flying there?

I don't think so. But, I don't know what their plans are. You know, if you'd asked me a year ago whether they were close to flying a shuttle and performing the first flight successfully with an automatic landing within a year, I would have said "Ha, ha!". They're serious, and they have good people. They're sharp.

What would you describe as the biggest difference between the Soviet program and ours? You mentioned that they do things differently than we do. Is there a basic difference between the two programs, a different approach to doing things?

I think we have more man-in-the-loop. We have the people more involved, and if you look at the spacecraft, there's probably a good indication of that. Our spacecraft are designed from the pilot's point of view. We have what we call a functional cockpit. When the pilot wants to do something, he chooses a function that interfaces with everything else in a performance aspect of the spacecraft. The Soviets have a mode control. You push button one and it does this whole thing as a mode. You can have twenty-six buttons and twenty-six modes of operation. We have an infinitely greater number of choices. So, we're more flexible and adaptable and use the pilots more in our system then they do.

Is that just a function of a different philosophical approach, or technical sophistication?

Both. One of the things I have to take my hat off to the Mercury guys for is that they turned a can into something that was flyable. Our spaceships are flyable. Their spaceships, they're flyable, but they really don't have the flexibility that we do. I think that's a difference in philosophy and technology.

Would you enjoy flying on the Soyuz or flying in the Mir space station? Is that something that you might want to experience?

Merely from a curiosity point of view. You know, I'd rather fly our stuff.

How much do you miss the work and the excitement of being an astronaut? Or, are you very comfortable in your lifestyle today?

You have to step out of that at some point. I was satisfied when I left, and I'd had a good time. I knew I couldn't keep doing it forever, and I felt like I left at the right time and got to go do something that was a lot of fun. You just keep moving along. You can never go back and retrace your steps. So I don't have any real desire, because I know I can't. Yeah, I miss it. It was a very dynamic environment. The thing that was probably most gratifying were the people you worked with back then. They were, again, first stringers, the best in the field. That's nice. It's very intellectually rewarding when you work with people like that.

You mentioned the first stringer, second stringer idea. Did the first stringers leave the program because they were just burned out?

I think they looked for new challenges. They're R & D people, they're very dynamic and they like challenges. If it gets to be again and again, the kind of people who like those challenges will go look for something else.

Would it be fair to say that the heady days of Apollo were more of a quest for the employees involved, whereas nowadays the flying of the Space Shuttle has become too much of a business?

That's a big question. You're asking me to say yes or no. Maybe the question is, what's the difference?

Was it, in a way, a romantic time back then?

Sure. Man on the moon by 1970, that's easy for anybody to grasp. The system was just operated differently back then. As an example, our jobs as astronauts were to fly, but also we were engineers. And every spacecraft was different, every mission was different. We lived with the spacecraft, literally lived with the spacecraft from the time it was a shell. We went through all the testing in the factory. You don't do that anymore. These shuttles are flown again and again. So the people are different, they have different jobs. Their job is to go fly several times, the same kind of thing. Sort of the whole idea is a totally different idea. In those days there was a single, focused objective, and it's hard to beat, especially when you're going to have that objective only once.

What nation do you think might put men in space next? Do you think it'd be the People's Republic of China?

With their own program? Well, Hermes is coming along pretty well. They're funding it. So, the European Space Agency, they'll have their program. I think the Chinese will have their program. And you know Japan—watch out!

Is that what you meant by being concerned about the United States becoming a third or fourth-rate space power?

Oh, yeah. We're really falling behind, I think. Especially when the European community becomes a single entity in 1992. That will be the most powerful economic force on the Earth. And they're moving. Of course, the Japanese have money and they're moving.

If we don't pay attention to that, we'll be sitting back and watching them do wonderful things.

Do you see our space station, the one that's supposed to be up in the next decade, bringing back some of our leadership in space?
It won't be enough. It's not a grabber. It doesn't grab people's imagination. There's just nothing there, there's no zip there.

What would be some zip, in your imagination?
Going back to the moon is one. That's the only thing I can think of in the near term. Mars, but that's too far away right now.

What's to be gained by going back there now?
I could speak volumes on that. First, you learn how to live in that kind of hostile environment. Secondly, you can conduct a lot of science, both on the surface, and astronomically. Third, you're establishing an outpost on the frontier. Fourth, you can mine the moon. And if there is indeed, ice in the shadows of the craters in the northern and southern latitudes, you have hydrogen; if you have hydrogen, you also have oxygen. You have all the elements you need to make about anything you want. A whole list of things that will be accomplished by doing that. Read Arthur C. Clarke to get most of them. There're a lot of reasons for taking that next step.

In a philosophical sense, how would you assess the significance of Project Apollo?
I would say it broke the bounds. We went out somewhere and came back. Perhaps Norman Cousins said it best: 'The significance of Apollo was not so much that man set foot on the moon, but that he set his eye on the Earth.'

Chapter 9

JOHN YOUNG
Commander, Apollo 16

Still Flying After All These Years

John Young is the George Blanda of the American space program. Like the resiliant pro football quarterback and kicker who stayed in the game for almost three decades, still taking the field at the age of 48, John Young is still taking to space. Now 58 years old, Young has been an active astronaut since 1962, the longest tenure of any American spaceman. He is probably the most experienced space pilot in the world, having made a record six flights—two of them to the moon. He has flown every type of U.S. spacecraft from Gemini to the Space Shuttle.

In his recent book, *Liftoff,* former astronaut Michael Collins, who flew with Young on Gemini 10, described the drawly Navy Captain as ". . . witty, but rarely allows himself to be perceived as such, especially when outsiders are around. He prefers a cloak woven partially of engineering mumbo jumbo and partially of aw shucks, t'ain't nothin', southern boy platitudes." Collins also noted that Young was "uncomfortable with the invasion of privacy" being an astronaut engendered and preferred shop talk to personal questions. Gus Grissom, the second American in space and Young's partner on the first Gemini flight gave this assessment to *Life Magazine.* "Sometimes John strikes me as a country boy. The way he walks you would be expecting him to be holding on to a couple of plow handles instead of a control stick. But he's sharp. And he often gets impatient with the progress we're making. He also has a fine sense of humor. It's a bit unusual and takes you a while to catch onto, but he knows how to ease the strain."

John Watts Young was born on September 24, 1930 in San Francisco, California. Less than two years later his family moved to Florida, settling in Orlando. As a boy Young liked to draw. He also had an affinity for aviation and spent spare time sketching pictures of airplanes and rockets. He was an honor student in high school where he also played football and ran track. He still runs today to keep in shape.

Young graduated from Orlando High School and went on to the Georgia Institute of Technology to study aeronautical engineering. During one of his summer vacations, he was part of a surveying team that went to Cape Canaveral reportedly to evaluate the site as a possible rocket base. In 1952 he received his degree with highest honors. He wanted to be a Naval Aviator and went into the service shortly after graduation. He served a year on a Navy destroyer then entered flight school where he trained in props, jets, and helicopters. After winning his wings he spent four years as a squadron fighter pilot.

In 1959 Young graduated from the U. S. Navy Test Pilot School and became a project pilot and program manager testing weapons systems at the Naval Air Test Center in Maryland. In the Spring of 1962 he participated in Project High Jump at Point Mugu, California, setting two time-to-climb world records in an F4 Phantom jet. His last Navy duty before becoming an astronaut was as maintenance officer in an all-weather fighter squadron at Miramar, California, an assignment Young describes as "the best job in the Navy."

In September of 1962 Young was named to the Astronaut Corps. He became one of the nine new pilots of the second group chosen to join the Original Seven. The newest astronauts were being slated for Project Gemini, the two-man program set to follow Mercury. Starting his new career, Young modestly claimed he "felt like the greenest rookie in spring training" and "didn't know an orbit from an astronaut."

Young learned his astronauts from his orbits quite well. In fact, the ripening rookie was going to be the first of the new nine to make it into space. In April, 1964, the space agency named Gus Grissom the commander and John Young the copilot of Gemini 3, the first manned test flight of America's second generation spacecraft.

Gemini 3 was a plum. Every test pilot's heart thumps with the competitive ambition of an Olympic athlete, the desire to fly higher, to fly faster, to fly higher faster. To do it best. To do it first. "Extending the envelope," they call it. Grissom and Young were getting the coveted leadoff chance to take the new Gemini out for a few spins and check out its performance.

On the morning of March 23, 1965, Young and Grissom slid into their seats for the three orbit, five hour ride (in a whimsical, if not superstitious gesture, Grissom had christened the spacecraft "Molly Brown" after the "unsinkable" character from the Broadway musical. His first ship, the Mercury capsule "Liberty Bell 7", clanged to the bottom of the ocean after flooding with seawater on its return, and he was determined not to see that happen again.) At 9:24 A.M. the two stage Titan booster ignited and hurled Molly Brown into space.

In addition to proving the spaceworthiness of the new craft and its systems, the flight plan included a pioneering "first" changing orbits. Gemini was designed to actually maneuver through space. The astronauts could "fly" it in and out of different orbits. This was an important advance over the Mercury capsule and contemporary Russian vehicles which, once placed in a particular orbit, were without the means of getting off their beaten paths; they circled on the same track until they fired their retrorockets and dropped out of orbit.

Gemini was outfitted with an array of small liquid fuel jets called thrusters. By orienting the spacecraft and firing the thrusters in a prescribed way, the vehicle would speed up, slow down, or move sideways, causing it to shift into a different flight path. Being able to do this opened the door to orbital rendezvous, the technique of bringing two craft together from different positions as they sailed through space. Perfecting rendezvous was a major objective of the Gemini Program, for it was to be the cornerstone of the Apollo missions: the lunar module would separate from the command module, descend to the moon, then fly back up to rejoin the command ship.

Grissom and Young made three carefully calculated thruster burns during the flight. Each time, Molly Brown obediently responded to the nudging and slipped to a new orbit. Gemini 3 was a technical triuimph for NASA and a personal one for John Young.

Young's next flight was as Commander of Gemini 10. He and his copilot Michael Collins left for orbit July 18, 1966, on a three-day flight. It was a busy three days. Young and Collins rendezvoused and docked with an Agena target vehicle sent onto orbit a couple of hours ahead of them. They fired up the Agena's main engine to boost their orbit to a record high 475 miles. Watching through his half-moon window, Young's eyes bulged as the Agena's business end burst to life. Recalling the scene after the flight Young marveled,

'I never saw anything like that before, sparks and fire and smoke and lights!'

Conserving their own precious fuel, the astronauts lit the Agena's motor twice more to put Gemini 10 in the right position for their second rendezvous, an encounter with the derelict Agena left behind by Gemini 8 the previous March. Gemini 10 closed in, and as Young hove to Collins threw open the hatch and clambered out of the cabin. Connected by a lifeline to the spacescraft, Collins pushed himself from the hatch opening and glided over to the Agena to pluck an experimental package from its side.

Spacewalking is not easy. Astronauts on earlier flights had become exhausted trying to perform even simple tasks. Collins found his weightlessness, the laws of physics, and his pumped up spacesuit devilishly conspiring against his attempts to move efficiently through his planned maneuvers. Back in the cockpit, Young was dazzled by the sight of his partner's floating pas de deux with the gleaming Agena.

Nearly three years passed before John Young entered space again. Six and a half months after Gemini 10, as plans were moving forward to begin flying Apollo, Young's old commander Gus Grissom, Gemini 4 spacewalker Ed White, and first-timer Roger Chaffee perished in a fire that erupted in the Apollo 1 command module during a preflight test at the launch pad. The disaster rocked NASA. Apollo was grounded for nearly two years as the space agency rehabilitated the program. In October, 1968, Apollo 7 completed the recovery with a successful Earth orbit flight of the command-service module. In December, Apollo 8 circled the moon, and in early March, 1969, Apollo 9 flight tested the lunar module. It was decided that one more flight was needed before sending a crew to land.

Apollo 10 was launched to the moon on May 18, 1969. On board were Tom Stafford, Gene Cernan, and John Young. While Young kept station in the command module "Charlie Brown", Stafford and Cernan flew the lunar module "Snoopy" down toward the Sea of Tranquility, skimming only nine miles above the landing site, clearing the way for Apollo 11 to take the final steps in July.

John Young returned to the moon three years later, this time as Commander of Apollo 16. An aggravating series of problems bedeviled the crew and a major glitch in the service module's engine almost wiped out their hopes of landing. Young and his copilot Charlie Duke finally made it down, bringing their lander "Orion" to a touchdown in the lunar highland region of Descartes on April 20, 1972. During their three day visit Congress passed a new space budget and money for the new Space Shuttle.

Project Apollo came to an end in December when Apollo 17 made the last flight to the moon. Young moved onto the Space Shuttle program, and in January 1973 was put in charge of the Space Shuttle branch of the Astronaut Office, an astronaut engineering and operation support team working on Shuttle design and development. A year later he was made Chief of the Astronaut Office altogether, replacing Deke Slayton. Remaining an active astronaut, he retired from the Navy in 1976 with the rank of Captain.

In March, 1978, Young was named spacecraft commander of the maiden flight of the Space Shuttle. The launch of the first orbiter, Columbia, was planned for mid 1979. Development and technical problems ultimately pushed the launch date back to the early part of 1981. At 7 o'clock on the morning of April 12th, twenty years to the day from that surprising flight of Yuri Gagarin, John Young and his copilot Bob Crippen felt Columbia shake her moorings and leap into the sky. Completing their checks and evaluations they brought Columbia back two days later with the first wings and wheels landing of any manned spacecraft. Young flew Columbia again in November of 1983 on a ten day scientific mission making the first use of Spacelab, a mini space station hauled up in the Shuttle's cargo bay.

In 1987 Young stepped down as Chief of the Astronaut Office. He is still on active flight status and also serves as a Special Assistant to the Director of the Johnson Spacecraft Center for Engineering, Operations, and Safety.

Young's many honors for his work and achievements include the Congressional Space Medal of Honor, three NASA Distinguished Service Medals, two Navy Distinguished Service Medals, two Kincheloe awards, the Goddard, Collier, and Harmon Trophies, three Haley Space Flight Awards, the Brackley Trophy from the United Kingdom, the National Geographic Hubbard Medal, in addition to more than fifty other major awards and honorary degrees.

John Young and his wife Suzy live in the Houston area. He has a daughter and a son from a previous marriage

---

John, you were familiar with Cape Canaveral before it became famous as a space center. During a summer vacation from Georgia Tech, you were part of a surveying team working at the Cape. We understand you were looking over the place as a possible rocket launching base?

No. We were just over there surveying.

Oh, then you weren't involved in the search for a launching base?

No.

Do you happen to know how or why NASA eventually settled on the Cape as the launching site?

No, I have no idea. The Cape was picked long before there was a NASA. I mean, whoever was launching rockets in those days did that. I don't know who that was. That was before my time.

Back to Georgia Tech, then. You studied aeronautical engineering and eventually became a test-pilot. Had you planned to become a test-pilot all along? Is that what you always wanted to do, fly airplanes?

Yeah, but I hadn't thought about it, to tell you the truth.

Did you ever ponder the possibility that someday you might be able to fly in space?

I wasn't thinking about it. There was no such thing at the time.

You came into the program in 1962, the year after President Kennedy announced we would land a man on the moon by the end of the decade. Did you have any doubts that the deadline would actually be met?

I didn't think about that. We were trying to make it. I had a lot of doubts about the whole thing.

What concerned you the most? What was the biggest hurdle you saw in being able to get to the moon, land, and make it back?

There were a million problems that's why you had program managers to solve them all. And every one of them was critical.

The lunar module was a big question mark, wasn't it? The Grumman people had a heck of time getting it ready.

They got some people in there that came through. It's a tough problem to design a vehicle like that as light as it was, to do all the things that it could do, that had to operate in space. Charlie Duke was in charge of one of the programs to redo the ascent engine about halfway through the program. But we had two or three cases after the fire where we really had to redo the whole vehicle because it was too heavy to land on the moon and get off. But, those are normal kinds of things. I wasn't really involved in working on the lunar module, though.

John Young

*Not a make-or-break factor, but an interesting one neverthe-
less is eating in space. You worked on space food in the Gemini
program; in fact, you brought attention to it when you smuggled
a corned beef sandwich up in Gemini 3. Do you miss regular
food when you're in space?*

No, it doesn't bother me. When you're doing something like
that, you take what you get. The body's not all that hungry in zero
gravity, anyway. It doesn't need a lot of calories to function in zero
gravity, so naturally the body doesn't think you need it. The food
doesn't really taste appetizing, I think, probably because of that
reason, even after folks worked on it a lot. The food has come a
long way, though. In the Shuttle, we've got a little galley in there
where you can cook and eat things and it does taste pretty good.
It's getting there. It's come a long way, but it still has a long way
to go before it's gonna be just like Mom made.

*We were talking a minute ago about the technical problems
of getting men to the moon. You had quite a few of them crop up
on Apollo 16.*

Oh, about a hundred.

*Well, one of them was when your inertial guidance blanked
out on your way to the moon at the same time you found the
spacecraft to be in a cloud of particles on your way to the moon.
Because of the particles, Ken Mattingly, the command module
pilot, couldn't get a proper star sighting to reset the system. At the
time, did you think that might keep you from making it to the
moon?*

No. They had a read/write that they fixed that up with, a way
of resetting it through the computer with information from the
ground.

*The most difficult glitch that occurred was just before you
were about to start the landing operation a problem developed
in the command module's steering system. Did you tell yourself
then that the landing would probably be cancelled?*

I thought it was a no-go. It was only the secondary steering
system, but you have to have both of them in lunar orbit to do a
landing. If the other one had been out, we would have been no-go.
Those were the mission rules.

*Now, you were the command module pilot on Apollo 10.
Did that experience enable you to help Mattingly at all with that
particular problem on Apollo 16?*

No, not a bit. It took the whole ground control team research-
ing the problem to decide that it was okay.

Was the crew in any position to do anything about it?
No, you can't be putting up with stuff like that. They found
out it was a stable oscillation, so even though you'd oscillate a little
bit, you'd still fly okay.

*It took six hours to work things out, but you were finally
given the go-ahead to land. Do you remember what it looked like
as you flew down into the highlands and onto the Cayley Plain?*
Yeah; it was beautiful. You could see it in 3-D. None of the
pictures show it in three dimensions like the eye can see it. The
eye can see it very easily, down into all the shadows. A camera just
can't record it the way the eye sees it.

*As you took in this spectacular sight did you stop to think,
"Gee, this is even more wonderful than I could have imagined
from the simulations"?*
The simulation was pretty good. We spent a lot of effort to get
the lunar landing models upgraded so they would look very close
to the landing site. In fact, they spent a lot of money on models of
the surface area. Now, they didn't have the differences in color
because people didn't realize what they were. But, they were sure
close in approximations. Then again, you're looking at it through
a television, so it really is not nearly as good.

*Are the colors on the moon real or is the moon basically just
one color, and just appears to have different colors because of
different lighting conditions?*
No, the moon's all different kinds of colors. It's like the Earth,
except for the grass. If you took away all the grass and trees, like
out in the western United States, and do away with the oxidation,
you can have the same kind of colors as on the moon; they vary
from blacks, to whites, to grays, to browns. Some of that's got to
do with sun angles, sure, but in other cases it doesn't. Some of
those features are very distinctive, and you probably need to have
a little geological training to appreciate it. It's a very different place,
and people talk about it being like dirty beach sand. It's not dirty
beach sand. Every *crater* is different, every *rille* is different, every
hill is different. It's like anywhere else; there are places in the
western United States that, in terms of variations in color, look
about the same.

Once outside and working away from the lunar module were you concerned at all about getting lost? On Apollo 14, Shepard and Mitchell at one point couldn't figure out where they were going. Did you have any problems with finding direction?

No, it was real easy. The sun was in the same place all the time. So, you knew where you were. See, the sun doesn't move; well, it moves fifteen degrees a day or something like that, but it doesn't move very far. So, you knew where you were all the time. You knew when you were going north, you knew when you were going south; you had landmarks you'd just aim for, and you'd go right to them.

Ed Mitchell told us that, once on the surface, he and Al Shepard had quite a bit of difficulty finding their way around because it was so hilly and undulating. From reading some of the accounts, you and Charlie Duke had a bit of the same problem. Did that catch you by surprise, too?

I think that's a matter of training, and we didn't appreciate it at the time. We were trying to find craters, like Ed and Al were trying to find Cone Crater. They actually got very close to it, but didn't see it. We did the same thing. We got down to one crater that we were looking for, one of the sinkhole craters on Stone Mountain. When we got back, they said we had been just forty yards away from it. On the surface of the moon, you just look over and see a bunch of really flat places. Then, you walk over to the edge of it and you'll be looking into a crater. If you don't think to do that, you're going to miss it.

Did you have a compass? Can a compass be used on the moon?

We had a compass. The Lunar Rover had an equivalent to a compass on it. There was not enough magnetic field to use a magnetic compass, but the Lunar Rover had a directional system in it that was very accurate. You could drive that way if you wanted to, but you didn't really need to, because you knew where you were going, and you'd just head out in that direction.

You got very dusty walking around on the moon. After your first time out you and Duke got back into the lunar module to clean up and rest for a while. As you were taking your helmet off you were recorded as saying that you got a mouthful of moondust and you said it didn't taste bad. Just what does it taste like?

I have no idea. I can't remember.

Do you recall if you swallowed it? Did you become the first man to eat moondust?

No, I don't think so. That all happened more than sixteen or seventeen years ago. It beats me.

The moon is 250,000 miles away. Did you feel any detachment looking back at the Earth from that far away?

No. Communications were so great, you kept expecting to roll over a rock and see somebody sitting there talking to you. I certainly never felt out of contact with the Earth.

Earlier crews gave demonstrations of one sort or another before they left the surface; Shepard hit a golf ball, Scott did the experiment with the hammer and the feather. Had you planned anything like that?

We had discussed this among ourselves, and of course we didn't have time on ours, I don't think. We were too busy trying to collect data up to the last moment. But if we would have had say, five or six minutes, at the end of the last EVA, and if the crew condition had permitted it, we were gonna show people in real-time using the television just how agile a fellow becomes after twenty or so hours on the moon. We were going to do what we called, in sort of slang terms, "lunar Olympics". We were gonna do things like see how far you could throw a rock, and see how much mobility you have in the full-pressure suit. It would also help the doctors get an idea what metabolic rates might be on human beings if they ever had to do any walking or semi-running missions. Now, we never got around to doing it; it's probably just as well.

Neil Armstrong and Buzz Aldrin commented about separating the lunar module from the command module for the last time. They described it as having a little bit of emotion to it, that "Eagle" had carried them through and they had to leave it behind. Did you feel the same about "Orion"?

It didn't worry *me*. Never thought about it, really. We were just jettisoning the LM. We did it wrong, though.

What happened?

We had mispositioned some switches. It was a communications problem really.

Did that cause a hard separation? Did you get banged around a little bit?

No, no. We just had the switches set wrong. The lunar module was supposed to hit the moon but it didn't.

You are only one of three men to fly to the moon twice. What was your reaction in being there for the second time?

It was like coming back to an old friend. The moon is a very impressive feature. I think we're gonna learn a great deal from the moon that we can put in context of how it applies to our own Earth. And so it was very interesting to go back and see if, in fact, I remembered some of the things; and sure enough, I remembered the ground track and I remembered a lot of the craters. It was a mighty interesting trip; I wouldn't have missed it.

Looking back seventeen years, what is the most vivid impression you have of being on the moon?

I think it was the variety. It's hard to say. It's really something. The Descartes landing site is one of the most dazzlingly beautiful regions on the moon. The view from Stone Mountain has got to rank as being one of the most truly beautiful views that's ever been seen by a human being. It's quite a place. I think we ought to go back as soon as we can, because there's so little we know about it. They say we know more about the moon than we know about the Earth. Well, that's just beans! You know more about a place where you've got five billion people than you can about a place where only twelve have ever been and that's the size of five United States. You just can't know much about a place that way.

John, do you feel that the Apollo program was exploited to the maximum extent that it could have been, or should it have been continued and developed further?

I think all the management was ready to quit when we did. They were really concerned about us losing a vehicle going there. We could have flown three more missions if we had three more Saturn 5's to do it with. But, we probably would have lost somebody. It was a very chancy program. It probably was a good thing to stop when we did. I wish we'd have kept on with the same pace of building spaceships and stuff like that that we were pursuing during that time frame, but we didn't.

Do you have any idea when the United States might send men back to the moon, and do you think we ought to return to the moon?

I think that's the next big program we ought to do. We ought to do it as soon as we can. We ought to do the space station as soon as we can, too. We're not doing either of those, but that's what we ought to do.

Will we get back to the moon by launching from the space station?
You could. That's a way to do it. But you need a lot of capability; you need to have a space station that has storage capability for fuel supplies and things like that, so you can outfit your transportation system to go to the moon, if you want to do it that way. You could do it from heavy-lift direct from Earth like we used to do.

We gave up our heavy-lift capability when we abandoned the Saturn 5. Are we now paying the price for that?
Nobody wanted to build heavy-lift back in those days. Now they're seeing a reason to do it so they're starting back up again.

How long do you think it will take us to get that capability back?
It'll be a while.

When we do go back, whenever that is, do you believe it should be on a full-time basis to colonize and set up a permanent base?
Yes, permanently. To set up a station and end up with people living up there and working up there.

Did the Apollo flights find there were enough raw materials on the moon to support a permanent colony, or would everything have to be brought up from the Earth?
I don't know. You should ask somebody from the Lunar Planetary Institute about that. I think there's enough things like aluminum and titanium, and lots of other minerals that I'm not familiar with that we found, and materials up there to support a base. Now, we don't know if there's water on the moon or not. There are some theories that there might be water on the moon at the poles, and maybe other places. It's hard for me to believe that a place with as much surface area as the moon has doesn't have any water on it at all, but that's what the geophysicists will tell you. It might have water on it. Somebody needs to do a lunar polar orbiter with the proper sensors on it, and go up there and look and see what kind of areas would be the best to land on. Then, we ought to go up there and put up a base. But it's not as easy as that sounds, though.

Do you see that realistically happening anytime within the next twenty-five to thirty-five years?

I see it happening as soon as somebody says we ought to do it, just like President Kennedy did. It's going to take that kind of a thing to do it. It'll take some political decision rather than a technological decision.

More on the President's part than Congress?

Oh yeah, the President would say it, and maybe half the Congress would say we shouldn't. But it wouldn't make any difference whether it was a Democrat or a Republican, actually.

How do you see the space program doing under the Bush administration?

I think it'll do pretty good.

You've been in the space program a long time. You've been through a number of administrations now; did the politicians ever come to you and the other astronauts and ask for suggestions or advice on what to do?

Of course. Everybody you talk to has a different idea of what you ought to do. Some think you ought to go to Mars. I think you ought to go to the moon and do the things you need to so you can get to Mars in a big hurry. Now, Mars is probably the place you ought to end up because it has got a lot of variety and there's obviously water up there. But, you really need a power breakthrough to get to Mars. You don't need to fool around traveling in space; you need to do things in a hurry to get to those places where people can live.

You worked very closely in the development of the Space Shuttle. You were assigned to it almost as soon as it was funded, and have been working on it right along. Did we sacrifice too much to save a few dollars in the development?

We didn't *have* but a few dollars in its development. It wasn't a question of sacrifice; we did everything we could do with the money we had.

Were you surprised at the way the Challenger Shuttle failed?

No.

Michael Collins has commented that he thought if it ever failed it would be in the main engines, because they're so compli-

cated and so state-of-the-art that any major malfunction would be in that area. Solid rockets are by comparison much simpler.

Well, they aren't really that simple. But, there's a lot of other ways you can fail besides the main engines and the solid rockets. A million other things could happen to you. You could run out of electricity if your fuel cells fail. You can run out of water if your cooling systems fail, if you have leaks in your cooling system all kinds of things could happen. You can lose your hydraulics if your auxiliary power units fail, etc., etc.

All manned rockets before the Shuttle used only liquid fuel. Did you have reservations about flying with solid rocket boosters?

Sure. But, I mean, so what? What else could they do? NASA wasn't going to get any money to build fly-back boosters. They didn't *have* any money. You could either build a space shuttle with the solid rocket boosters, or you don't *have* a space shuttle.

There's no way to make those boosters liquid fueled?
Not and reuse them.

As a pilot, how great was your concern that abort capabilities for the Shuttle were very limited during launching?

I'm still concerned. I don't think you've got enough abort capabilities with that vehicle. The rule is you can only lose one of the main engines going onto orbit and abort successfully, and I don't think that's reasonable; it's just not real-world. Sooner or later you're going to lose more than one.

What can be done, then, to improve the abort capabilities of the shuttle?

Not much. We're looking at ways to increase the angle of attack, and I think they ought to have a full-up escape system in it myself, because if you lose more than one of the main engines in the launch phase, then whatever problem happens to you . . .

How might that escape system work?
Just a rocket system getting people out, like ejection seats. You know, light-weight, simple. Although, when you say light-weight and simple you're oxymoroning.

When you flew the first Shuttle mission, you and Bob Crippen had ejection seats. Were you confident with that set-up?
It probably wouldn't have worked the first time, but it might have worked. If it had worked, and we'd had a Challenger accident

on the first one, Crip and I would be here today. Because we'd have gotten out.

What are your impressions of the Soviet space shuttle?
I'm real impressed. I wish them luck.

They're apparently going to test-fly it unmanned. That would be quite an accomplishment, wouldn't it, especially the re-entry and landing. Something like that must be very difficult to do.
I think it's extremely difficult. Maybe they can. You see, I don't know how their shuttle is designed, I don't know what the inside of it looks like. I don't have any idea how they do simple things like align platforms, how they do anything. I don't have a feel for it. I don't know if they use auxiliary power units, or fuel cells, or whatever. I have no idea what's in their shuttle. If it doesn't work during re-entry, I bet we'll almost stop *our* program to see what the heck is the matter with theirs.

The Soviet space shuttle does look suspiciously like ours. Do you think that they somehow got ahold of the U.S. shuttle plans, or that information leaked out of the United States at some point?
I have no idea. But, you know, all that was unclassified at the time. When we were building the space shuttles, there were a bunch of Russians over here looking at everything we were doing. We were working on the American-Russian docking mission, and I've heard tales of people walking around taking pictures of photographs on walls. But you have to do a lot more than that to build a space shuttle. You've got to get into engineering in depth and in detail, and I'm sure they've done all that. You know, even if they *had* the blueprints, just building it is not all that easy. And getting the blueprints, my gosh, it'd be ten carloads—railroad carloads. You just wouldn't do that. But, it does look like ours, I will say that.

One big difference between their shuttle and ours is that theirs has no engines on it. It's carried up solely by their heavy-lift booster and has no power of its own.
That's a big difference, alright. That was the original thought our people in the U.S. program had going in, but they couldn't afford to do it. We carry the engines because we can't afford to throw them away.

There isn't a way to recover engines that are only used to boost it up?

You can think of some sophisticated ways to do that. People have thought about that. But none of those are easy things to do.

What will the next generation of U.S. manned space craft be like?

Unless somebody funds Shuttle II or the National Aerospace Plane, unless somebody really gets serious about that, that's a tough problem. The National Aerospace Plane is a really tough project that we ought to have been working on anyway, but we've just started. People are talking about Shuttle II; that's a big program. People are talking about heavy-lift vehicles; that's another big program. I think the next interplanetary manned vehicle is the space-tug. It ought to be the space-tug, we ought to get that going. That's the one that requires the space station with refueling facilities, refurbishing facilities and all that.

What will the second generation Space Shuttle be like? Will it look different? Will it operate differently?

I don't know if there's going to be a second generation Space Shuttle. Is somebody willing to lay out $20 billion to build one? I don't think so.

There are plans on the drawing board, though, aren't there?

Oh, yeah, everybody's got plans. I mean, Langley can show you all kinds of Shuttle II's. So can the Johnson Space Center. But it's a big project. Unless you get a government that's willing to do that right now, I don't see it happening. And they assume a lot of things about how these new lightweight materials, and new strong materials will work a lot better; it's not clear that we wouldn't gain a lot by just upgrading the shuttle we've got. Make it out of lighter materials, with modern avionics. I don't even say state-of-the-art anymore. I just say *modern* avionics. I think you could increase the payload capability enormously, save a lot of money, and end up with a safer and more reliable machine than we've got. But, where's that big program going to come from? We've already got the space station. That's the biggest program anybody could imagine getting, and it's amazing that they got that.

Do you think we should commit to a similar project like that for Mars or is that too ambitious right now?

I think the Mars landing is tough beyond belief. People like to say what they think they know about how to go to Mars, and they don't even touch the surface of it. When it comes to the technical details, it's tough, And it takes too long. We need power breakthroughs to go to Mars. They're talking about a two-and-a-half year mission to go to Mars and spend forty days up there. I think they ought to have a forty-day trip and spend two-and-a-half years up there. That's my idea of how to go to Mars.

It has been said that the Soviets are on the brink of going. Do you see that coming too?
No, because at the very least it's going to take a launch vehicle they don't have yet to do it.

Are you talking about nuclear power?
Well, I would expect it would be nuclear power, or a plasma drive, or something. But it's not a question of that. It's a question of getting all the consumables hooked on in orbit and heading out. With conventional technology, it'll just take just an awful long time.

Do you think that there's any question about how well a man can hold up for that long out in space?
I sure do. I think you ought to give them some artificial gravity.

The cost of that wouldn't be prohibitive?
I don't think so. I think you can do artificial gravity real easy if you think about it. We had artificial gravity fields in the Gemini program.

That's an interesting point, because as you said, they experimented with it in the Gemini program, but it was dropped.
That's right.

Was that just a question of money and time, too?
Well, it was just an experiment on the last two Gemini missions. George Mueller thought of it. It was a good idea. On one of those missions, either 11 or 12, I forget which one, they spun up, and established a gravity field. That's the way you do it.

How do you mean "spun up"?
They had the Agena at one end of a string, the Gemini on the other end, and then they rotated it. I forget how much of a gravity field they established. It wasn't a heck of a lot, but you could establish more by spinning faster.

Yes, that was Gemini 11, with Pete Conrad and Dick Gordon. While we're on the subject, you flew the mission before that,

Gemini 10, with Michael Collins. He could have used some artificial gravity on his spacewalk.

He did a great job. If I'd just gotten one good picture of him when he was on Gemini 10, why, he would have been so famous he wouldn't have had to do the Air and Space Museum. There he was, out climbing on that other Agena. It was kind of interesting watching him manage that whole thing and do all that work. It would really have blown everyone's mind. That was really something.

Was it fun flying with Collins?

He's the best. He's real good. A great guy. He wrote his latest book, *Liftoff,* all about the space program, you know, but he left out all the best parts.

Really? What do you mean?

Oh, one of these days I'll have to write and finish that off for him. The best book written by an astronaut, though, was "The Quiet Sun" by Ed Gibson.

You were on the first mission of the Gemini program with Gus Grissom. Can you tell us something about him, what he was like? He's become somewhat of a legend in the American space program.

Yeah, I can believe it. He was quiet, a straightshooter, worked hard, and he really contributed to the design of the Gemini vehicle. The displays and controls in that vehicle are a classic way to do it in terms of integration of the crew into the vehicle. It's really an outstanding design.

Were you surprised that he wasn't more vigilant in the Apollo 1 case? He wasn't completely happy with the spacecraft, and there were moments during that last fatal test when he became frustrated and testy about the way things were going. Should he have done something then?

I think Gus was as vigilant as he could have been under the circumstances without getting fired.

That's an interesting way to put it.

That's *exactly* the way to put it. In those days if you complained about what was going on, they would have gotten some *new* astronauts.

We were under the impression that the astronauts had some solid input in that respect. That's not true?

They did after the fire. Before the fire, they didn't have any solid input into the Apollo program. I *guarantee* that.

The cold weather was a big factor in the Challenger accident. Should the crew be in on the decision to proceed with a launch in a case like that?

Oh, they have plenty of people that worry about weather conditions. The crew, when it gets in the vehicle, is in a very poor place to say what the weather is. I mean, they can't see out. The only thing they can do is look straight overhead. So I wouldn't worry about the crew not being consulted. They were consulted on plenty of other things; they had input. Like the day before that happened, Scobee didn't like the way the hatch was operating, and he needed some people in there to come and fix it, and they held the launch just to do that. He did the absolute right thing.

Is it easier now for astronauts to raise their concerns and not have to worry about causing themselves problems with their careers?

I don't think that's ever easy in a big outfit. People worry about that a lot. I'm sure people in the astronaut office worry about it more than anybody because they're the ones who can be taken off the flight crew just like nothing flat.

But they're also the ones who can get killed nothing flat, too?

I guess that's the chance you take.

After the Challenger explosion, you wrote an angry memo to your colleagues in the Astronaut Office, detailing your concerns and opinions about the situation. Did doing that cause you any problems?

I expect it did, but I don't know whether or not it really did. What caused me problems was that somebody released it to the news guys. I write memos all the time, but I don't send them to the newspapers, for cryin' out loud. It's to me trying to get something done, trying to make people worry about something, and you can lose a day on something without a piece of paper. So, you put it on record so it gets done. It's called working papers. I don't see anything wrong with having working papers, but, if you're going to turn them loose to the newspapers, why, you've got to expect trouble.

Besides presidential leadership or public support, what do you think can be done within the agency to revitalize itself?

That could get me fired. There's a lot of shortcomings that we could correct before it starts looking good. Well, I don't want to talk about it. It's terrible.

You must be optimistic, though. After all, you're still hanging in there.

I think maybe one of these days people will come to the same conclusions and do something about it. There're a lot of things the government can do internally to fix a lot of its own problems. When you go to a meeting and there are so many people in that meeting that say why you can't do things, you either have too many people in the meeting or you're the biggest bureaucracy in the world. That's disgraceful. But you can fix that. When you go to a meeting on a real technical issue, and there's a hundred people there and they talk for three days, but there's nobody in this meeting that is qualified to talk about the technical issues, does that worry you? It bothers me and I think it would bother the taxpayers.

John, do you have another flight left in you?

I have two or three more left in me. Whether or not they'll let me do them, I don't know.

You're conmmanding the flight to carry up the space telescope, aren't you?

I was, but now they've got a new commander on that.

You must be disappointed. That would have been an especially good mission.

There are no bad space missions. They're all good.

Has NASA indicated that they're going to let you fly another mission?

Well, I spent twelve hours last week in a simulator.

What keeps you going? Why, after six flights, do you still want to go into space?

It's my line of work. I think we're doing something really important. I think all of us, the whole space program, are doing something really important. It's the key to the future.

John Young

On a personal level, though, is there something about it, something particularly compelling about flying in space that has a hold on you, that makes you want to go back?
It seems like a really interesting thing to do. You always learn something when you do something like that.

What are you looking forward to doing after you retire from the program? What's next in store for you?
I don't think that far ahead.

Do you see yourself someday flying up to the Space Station?
I don't think I'll live that long. [Laughs] They're talking about 1996 before it gets there. I'd be sixty-seven years old, porbably in another line of work.

You're still an active astronaut at 58. Do you think that there is an age cut-off for going into space?
No, there isn't.

Then, the Shuttle would be safe for a senior citizen to fly in if he was in good enough shape?
Sure, they talked about carrying real old people back in the old days. They were talking about taking Walter Cronkite. I don't know how old Walter was but they were talking about carrying older people along if they could pass a physical.

Do the crews of the Apollo missions keep in touch, do you get together?
No, not as a group, but individually, every so often.

Do you think the group should get together once in a while just to keep in touch?
I don't know. It's hard to do, because everybody's scattered all over the country. And some of them are even living in foreign countries.

Have you ever seen the movie "Terms of Endearment"?
No.

Well, one of the characters in it is a retired astronaut who went to the moon. At one point, he says, "You know, the thing that bothers me is that none of us ever got together to compare notes, to talk about what it was like." Do you feel at all like that?
I don't feel too bad about that. Everybody's too busy.

*How would you sum up the enterprise of going to the moon;
what is your idea of the meaning of Project Apollo?*

The *meaning* of it? You go to the moon to do what the
president said. It was to land a man on the moon and return him
safely to Earth within a decade. That's what he said and that's what
we did.

John Young

Chapter 10

CHARLIE DUKE
Lunar Module Pilot, Apollo 16

A New Awakening

"**H**ouston Tranquility Base here. The Eagle has landed."
"Roger, Tranquility. We copy you on the ground. You've got a bunch of guys about to turn blue. We're breathin' again. Thanks a lot."

That memorable exchange took place at 4:17 PM Eastern Daylight Time on July 20, 1969. The first voice was that of Neil Armstrong, announcing to Mission Control and the world that Apollo 11's lunar module "Eagle" had successfully made man's first landing on the surface of the moon. The second voice belonged to Charlie Duke, a 33-year-old Air Force Major who had become an astronaut three years earlier. On that historic day, Charlie Duke was filling the vital post of capsule communicator at Mission Control in Houston. The capsule communicator, or CAPCOM as they call it, is the eyes and ears on the ground for the crew up in space. All the information the crew needs from the ground is relayed to them through the CAPCOM, and vice-versa. Armstrong had personally requested that Duke be Apollo 11's CAPCOM during the critical landing maneuvers. Duke had the same job during the previous "dress rehearsal" mission of Apollo 10. That experience, Armstrong reasoned, made Duke the favorite choice when Apollo 11 was ready to go all the way.

Following the astronauts' progress at his console, Duke had the best seat in the house that day. The final moments of the landing were causing knuckles to go white in the control center. An overloaded computer in the lunar module kept yelling for more breathing room. At the same time, Armstrong saw they were heading straight for a perilous looking pile of boulders, and took more time to scan for a less hostile spot. Fuel was down to less than thirty seconds. Though obviously excited, Duke didn't flinch. The only slip he made the whole time was fumbling the word "Tranquility" as he rogered Armstrong's landing call. Less than three years later, Duke himself would be on the moon.

Charles Moss Duke, Jr. is a tallish, slim, southerner from the Carolinas. He was born in Charlotte, North Carolina on October 3, 1935. He attended Lancaster High School in Lancaster, South Carolina, and then went on to the Admiral Farragut Academy in St. Petersburg, Florida, where he graduated as valedictorian in 1953. He then entered the U.S. Naval Academy at Annapolis, receiving his commission and a Bachelor of Science degree in 1957. After his second naval cruise, Charlie transferred to the Air Force. "I got seasick," he recalled when asked why he opted for the Air Force. He took flight training in Texas and Georgia, and received his wings in 1959. He flew with a fighter interceptor squadron in Germany for three years, then returned to the States to study for an advanced degree at MIT. He received a Masters Degree in Aeronautics and Astronautics in 1964, and headed for the Air Force Test Pilot School at Edwards Air Force Base in California. He completed the program at Edwards in 1964 and stayed on as an instructor.

He had hoped to get a chance to fly in the X-15 rocket plane program, but when he realized the opportunities there were too far down the road, he submitted his application to NASA to become an astronaut. Surprisingly, he discovered it was easier to enter the astronaut ranks than to get to fly the X-15. He received the call from NASA and, in April of 1966, became one of the nineteen new spacemen of NASA's fifth group.

After preliminary training, he settled into the routine, waiting to make it to a flight crew. But, there were many veterans ahead of him, some still waiting themselves to fly; it might be a number of years before he was offered a seat. Occasionally, he wondered if he might not hit fifty by the time of his first flight.

Eventually, he joined the astronaut support crew for Apollo 10. Support crews functioned as administrative assistants to the flight crews, taking care of details so that the flight crews could concentrate on training. But, it was a good opportunity to pay a few dues and get noticed, and it paid off for Charlie Duke. Tom Stafford, commander of Apollo 10, liked his work and asked him to be prime CAPCOM on the mission. He moved on to Apollo 11 in the same roll. Then, when the flight crews were named for Apollo

13, Charlie found himself listed as backup lunar module pilot. This was what he was waiting for. By tradition, since the Mercury days, being on the backup crew for a mission cycled you into a prime crew spot three flights later. Charlie Duke was getting ready to go to the moon.

Apollo 16 left Earth early in the afternoon of April 16, 1972, a month later than originally planned. Mission planners took the extra time to make some modifications to the spacesuits used on the moon, and to do a little mechanical work to the lunar module.

John Young was the commander, Ken Mattingly the command module pilot, and Duke the lunar modular pilot. Mattingly would stay behind in the command ship "Casper" while Young and Duke descended to the surface in "Orion."

Four days later, in orbit around the moon, a tricky mechanical problem with the large engine on the command-service module threatened to cancel the landing. Happily, it was cleared up, and Duke and Young were finally given the go-ahead to take Orion down, six hours late. Their target was the lunar highlands, specifically, an elevated plain called Cayley, an undulating terrace surrounded by hills and mountains located in the region of the crater Descartes, south of the moon's equator. They were being sent there to search for clues and ancient rocks that could explain how volcanic processes might be involved in forming the high ground on the moon. To make the most of it, they brought along a lunar rover and enough supplies to last for three days.

Duke and Young arrived on the Cayley plain at 8:23 PM Eastern Standard Time on the evening of April 20th. They got a night's rest and began their exploration the following morning. During the next seventy-two hours, they made three excursions from the lunar module, making their appointed rounds in the rugged four-wheel drive rover. As in previous missions, they collected rock and soil samples, and set up scientific stations.

With the Rover's TV eye watching, Orion took off into the black moon sky on Sunday evening, April 23rd. Tired and dirty, Duke and Young remained enthusiastic. "What a ride! What a ride!" they crowed. They had been in the moon's uplands for three days, spending almost a third of that time out on the surface. They covered nearly seventeen miles visiting various spots in the landing area, and were bringing back 211 pounds of the moon with them.

They caught up with Mattingly, climbed back into the command module and after spending another day making observations from their perch in orbit, they fired themselves home. On the way back, they opened the hatch and Mattingly crawled out to retrieve some articles from the instrument bay on the side of the service module. Charlie popped his head out and looked around. He was very impressed by the blackness.

Casper splashed down in the Pacific Ocean on April 27th after eleven days in space. It had been almost three years since that tense afternoon in July when, sitting at his console in Mission Control, Charlie Duke had vicariously gone to the moon. Now, he knew what it was really like.

His final flight assignment would be on the backup crew of Apollo XVII. When the Apollo program was over he turned his attention to the Space Shuttle, serving as Deputy Manager for Advanced Planning in the Office of Manager for Operations Integration. He retired from NASA at the end of 1975 and became a businessman. At that time he also left the regular Air Force as a colonel and entered the reserves where he worked closely with the recruiting service. He was promoted to Brigadier General in 1979, and retired from the Air Force in 1986.

He currently runs two companies of his own, is secretary/treasurer of a third, and sits on the board of directors of three others.

His numerous honors and awards include the NASA Distinguished Service Medal, the Johnson Spacecraft Center Certificate of Commendation, The Iven C. Kincheloe Award of the Society of Experimental Test Pilots, the Air Force Distinguished Service Medal with oak leaf cluster, the FAI V.M. Komarov Diploma, the AIAA Haley Astronauts Flight Award, and the Boy Scouts of America Distinguished Eagle Scout Award.

Several years after leaving the space program, Charlie sensed that, despite all the success in his life, something seemed to be missing. He looked for the peace of mind he was after and found it in the message of Christianity. Since then he has been an active Christian Lay Witness. He has formed and is the president of Duke Ministry for Christ. He is also associated with the High Flight ministry of former Apollo astronaut Jim Irwin.

His work in the Christian faith takes him all over the world speaking and testifying to the love and life-changing power of Christ.

Married and the father of two sons, Charlie and his wife Dorothy now live in Texas.

What have you been doing, Charlie, since you left the space program?

I've been involved with various businesses. I started a company called the Orbit Corporation in 1976 and ran that until '78 when I sold it. It was a wholesale beer distributorship; I just didn't like the beer business so I sold out. I did a little consulting in the early days of the Shuttle, and after that I was involved in real estate development until '82, '83, somewhere in there. Since then I've been doing various investments, helping put deals together in oil and gas, minerals and resources, a little waste management deal, things like that. I've been doing a little bit of consulting on the side, and also working for the Air Force with my reserve commitment. That got pretty heavy between '80 and '86, when I retired. I was spending about four months a year at that. Then, in 1978, I had a real encounter with God at a Bible study here locally and committed my life to Christ. I've been doing a lot of Christian laywitnessing around the world, similar to what Jim Irwin does, but he's full-time.

You're not an ordained minister, then.

I'm not a preacher. I don't have a church. I don't have any theological training. I'm not going to Bible School, or Bible College, or a seminary, or anything like that. I'm just a businessman who loves God and tries to radiate Christ's love throughout my business and through my life.

Can you tell us how you arrived at that new point in your life?

It seemed like I was always striving, and I'd arrive at my goals, but there was always something within me that made me strive onward more. It was a "never enough" type thing. And after the moon flight I realized that, gosh, it was going to be six to eight years of mostly inactivity while we got the Shuttle ready, so that was a frustration. So, I left, thinking business would give me the satisfaction I was looking for. But I found, even though I was successful in business, there was something missing there, too. So, I sold the business. And then I went to this Bible study.

I really wasn't searching for God, I thought I was okay. I'd been in church all my life, had been committed to the church, and had been baptized. It's almost like if you're born in America, you're a Christian, you know? That kind of attitude. But at this Bible study I really realized that Jesus is either real or He's not; He's either Lord of all or He's not—make up your mind. In fact, that same question was on the cover of Time Magazine a while ago: "Who is Jesus?" That was going through my mind and my heart. And I just made that commitment that He really was the Son of God, and I committed my life to Him. That was in April of '78.

And I began to read the Bible. The more I read, the more I saw that my life wasn't really in God's order, in God's peace. As I began to bring my life in line with Scripture, more and more the peace of God and the purposes of God were revealed in my life. I look at life in a really different way now; it's the peace. I try to be content in everything I am and where I am. And I'm not *striving* anymore. I could be, but I'm not striving—there's a difference.

Have you found the same sort of thing has happened to other people who have been on a path similar to your own?

Yes, but not necessarily astronauts. There are one or two astronauts that are open enough with their lives to describe what I've experienced. But I know a lot of other businessmen, very successful military men, successful professional men who have had a similar experience to mine. They found that there's something within them that is not satisfied by just things and accomplishments.

Someone once said there's a vacuum that God has placed in all of us that can only be filled with God. Until we find that relationship with Christ we're going to be striving, internally striving, if you will. I've seen that in many, many people around the world. I've had the opportunities to speak with kings, and presidents, and prime ministers, political leaders, and business and professional leaders of the world. They've achieved positions that are very important, but there always seems to be a striving within them. They're looking for answers, so we share what we've experienced.

Was this turn in your life a consequence of your voyage to the moon?

I don't think so. Jim Irwin does. Of course he really experienced God's presence and relates that in his book. It was six years later that I had the awakening; I was on the moon in '72 and was born again if you will, in '78. I came back not really sensing God's presence. It wasn't a spiritual experience for me.

Even so, Charlie, did your flight give you a deeper sense that the Earth, the universe is here for a reason?

It certainly gives you a different perspective of Earth and mankind. I guess I was looking back and I was just, awed with the beauty of the Earth, and awed with that whole experience. Then I came back and I kept realizing that, as someone said, it's Spaceship Earth. From the moon you don't see the U.S. or Mexico or Europe, you just see Earth, and you know we're a lot of different races and cultures and we're all on Spaceship Earth, we're all one. And we've got to learn to love one another so we can solve our problems.

And I really believe that. But for that six years I found that I was saying those words with my lips, but I didn't see any love, and I really felt I didn't even love my own wife. And so things were coming apart at the seams at my home. And it was just sort of empty words. I discovered later on that the Bible says that the heart of man is evil. And when it really gets down to the shorts, it's every man for himself, without God. That's what I was seeing around the world, and so, it was discouraging.

Did you find that a hard thing to reconcile, seeing the Earth and all it's beauty and grandeur from out in space, and also knowing the imperfections of human beings?

Well, it can sort of get you discouraged. It hasn't me; but, you know, I'm sort of an up-beat guy and always have been. I didn't come to God from the depths of depression or the depths of despair or grief. A lot of times people need God through trials and troubles, but I was bucking along a pretty good pace, and really wasn't frustrated at all. But, I did see this, this inconsistency of the beauty of it all, and yet when you got down to the microcosm it was really pretty bad. And I guess it could, it could really depress you and get you down. If you let it.

John Young said something very interesting on the moon. He quoted Descartes when he said 'There is nothing so far removed from us as to be beyond our reach, or so hidden that we cannot discover it.' Does that apply to religion and to Jesus Christ?

Yes, I believe so. In fact it's even simpler than that. There's really no *striving* to meet Jesus. The Bible teaches that God is near and God is evident in his creation. If you just look out around us and really think about it, you can see God in his insurmountable power, in his divine majesty. The scriptures teach us God is near us and all we have to do is reach out and He's there. The simplest person on Earth, without any education, I've found probably finds God easier than the intellectual; because you try to rationalize things away, especially in the Western mind. And that statement is certainly true, God is *not* hidden. He's not some mystery out there that wants to remain a mystery. He wants to be known.

In that sense, is space a good place to go to discover that?

No, no I don't think so. Like I said, I was out in space for eleven days, and I didn't feel close to God. I didn't sense his presence. I was just too busy. Somebody once said 'Stop and smell the roses.' When we just get quiet down here on Earth, I believe we can find God. If we were out in space and got quiet and had time just to reflect, I believe that I would have seen the glory of God because the Bible does teach us that "the heavens declare the glory of God, the skies proclaim the works of His hand." So, the infinite majesty of God is displayed in the heavens. I was just side-tracked with a lot of technical stuff which I was enjoying doing. So I tell everybody you don't *need* to go to the moon to find God. He's in this room, you know, at the Holiday Inn or at the Intercontinental Hotel in Berlin, wherever I'm speaking.

Are you saying He's within us?

Well, He's not within us, but He *can* be within us. There is a New Age teaching that says 'We're all God and God is within us and all we have to do is discover that.' That's not true. I don't believe that.

Looking back on it, do you feel a little disappointed that you didn't have the time to stop a moment and just be reflective about where you were and what it all meant?

No. I look back on it and I wish I had known God before I went. That way I would have appreciated the beauty in a deeper sense, I think. I was actually looking back really quite pleased with everything that we accomplished and did. It was a thrilling experience and I'd do it again if I had the opportunity. And I'd go with a deeper awareness of God and the creation. And that would, I think, be more fulfilling in the long-run.

You mentioned Jim Irwin earlier. You do work in his High Flight foundation, don't you?

Well I'm what you'd call an official director, I guess, because I'm not on the board. But Jim and I are very good friends and we are at meetings occasionally together around the country, and I do work with him in a thing called Project Uplift, which presents motivational, inspirational talks in schools to try and get the kids to apply themselves and to aim high, and to take advantage of opportunities that may come in their lives. So, I worked directly with Jim on that program which is funded through grants from various aerospace companies. And we talk a lot; we're on the phone every once in a while, and our paths cross throughout the country. And we support one another in prayer. We're close friends.

Tell us something about the kind of response that you get when you talk to these kids. Does it give you a sense of optimism about the future?

Charlie Duke

The space program has a bright future. I look at the faces of these kids and see their desires and their aspirations and goals, and most everywhere I speak I'm encouraged by the attitude in the kids, especially junior high kids. They really seem pure, if you will, and many of them have their eyes set on the stars. I have not felt any negative response at all from any of the kids that I've spoken to. When I was working with the Air Force in recruiting I spoke to probably 300,000 kids over a six-year period, and I was really excited about the pride that most of them reflected in the space program and their desire to know more, and to be involved. It was real encouraging, it really was.

One of the interesting things to us is that a lot of these young kids have no idea about what the space program was like back in the Mercury, Gemini and Apollo days; they weren't even born then. What kind of sense do they have about space exploration at that time?

You've asked a good question. In fact I'd usually show them a little movie and the kids were just fascinated with it. You know a high school senior, an 18-year-old, was two-years old when I walked on the moon, and they really don't remember it all. It's sort of like the dark ages. So that's why last year I had the idea of producing a video, so I've done that on Apollo. It's more than a documentary, it's, you know, my experience through my eyes. We used the NASA films for the visuals, but it's my feelings and experiences as I was going through this flight.

I speak at space camps and things like that. And, of course, they're all involved in the Shuttle and they're looking forward to Mars and all. But I think they're learning from history. They're learning from the past and hopefully they will apply those lessons to the future. And I've got a boy that's 21 years old and he's interested in going to Mars one day. Hopefully he'll make it.

Speaking about the future of the program, Charlie, what are your thoughts on it today? Where should we be headed, and how do we get there?

Well, I think that the space station is far enough along so that it should continue. I'm not so close to the program that I could give you a specific technical comment about the design and the implementation of the concept of the space station, but I certainly think it's something that is needed. I was disappointed that we never took advantage of Skylab, and built on it as the Russians seem to be doing with their Mir, but that's hindsight. I thought that was a mistake to just drop it. But that view didn't prevail at NASA and so they went on to the Shuttle, and then on to the Space Station. I think the space station should be built and I think we will see it probably end up as the consortium type; you know, this module from NASA and this module from the European Space Agency, etc. And then from there I think we ought to go back to the moon.

The debate is how to get back to the moon and establish a base. Whether we do it with heavy-left vehicles or whether we do it with those inter-space transfer vehicles that you build and put together out at the space station. I think that debate needs to go on. But I think there's a lot to do there back on the moon. A lot of places haven't been explored, and it will give, certainly, a good experience on existing out in deep space for long durations. And from there, to me, it's only a matter of time until we go to Mars. It could be decided to bypass the moon and go directly to Mars. That would be fine with me. I think either way would be fine. But sooner or later we're gonna get back out into deep space again.

Were you disappointed that there weren't more moon landings, or that Apollo Applications didn't continue beyond Skylab?

Skylab would have been bigger than the Soviet Mir, and would have given us some long-duration spaceflight experience for a cheap price. But we just didn't think about it, really, in that sense.

You mentioned that you left the program when it appeared that it would take six or eight years to get the Shuttle ready. Can you tell us something about your work on the space shuttle. That was a tough program. A lot of compromises had to be made.

Yeah. Well, I left before they had any hardware. I had been working on cockpit configuration, on airlocks, emergency rescue, on-orbit rescue, maneuvering units a little bit, and then I went into shuttle operations. We were looking at budgets for shuttle operations, and back in those days we were coming up with numbers that were staggering; it was gonna be an expensive proposition. And, of course, that was higher than anybody would accept. It was just humongous. So, we had to go back, and go back. And all this time people were fussing and arguing about aerodynamic qualities and flight dynamics and this, that and the other. Would it really work, are the heat-tiles gonna work, and what are the gaps gonna be and would it come apart. And it was just argument upon argument and discussions. I guess I would call it professional discussions, because nobody really argued, but professional differences of opinion. It was a big bow wave of technical problems and a big bow wave of budget problems that I recall. And so schedules ended up slipping a couple of years for the first flight. My impression

Charlie Duke

of the Shuttle back in those days was it was gonna be a big truck, and who wanted to fly a truck around in space. But I was wrong. It turned out to be a beautiful flying machine, the Shuttle itself. It's a thrill to fly apparently, and to operate. I would love to have an opportunity to ride it. It's a great machine.

The Challenger disaster was a great shock. Did it come as a big surprise to you that something like that happened?

Yeah, as a matter of fact it did. I was in Malaysia on a trip. My wife and I were speaking to a Christian organization that has a number of chapters in Malaysia. I didn't know about the accident until 12 hours after the explosion. A newspaper reporter tracked me down over in this little village over there. The question was, "What do you think about the accident?" I said, "What accident, what are you talking about?" "You haven't heard?" "Heard what?" He said, "Well the Shuttle blew up today, killed all seven astronauts." I was stunned, dead silent. Finally I asked him who was on board, and he told me. I did not know Christa McAuliffe or Greg Jarvis, but I had met the other astronauts. Ron McNair and I had been on a program a couple of times together, we were both from South Carolina. So I was just in shock and couldn't believe it.

Was it surprising that nothing as catastrophic as that never occurred during the Apollo program?

Well, no, not really. Of course, we did have the fire early on in Apollo. But we didn't believe that could have happened either. But out of that fire came, certainly, a better spacecraft and a more safely designed system. And I think out of the Challenger disaster that is gonna be true also. I think I would ride Apollo with more security than Shuttle because Apollo had an escape system. It probably would have survived a catastrophic failure like the experience on Challenger, because of our emergency detection system. It was hot-wired, and if there was any trouble in the first three minutes the thing would just fire you off automatically. With the escape tower we had on Apollo we would probably have made it, if everything had worked in sequence. So we had a little bit more security sitting on the pad than I personally would feel in the Shuttle, though I'm not sure the present crews have that same concern.

John Young thought, and NASA management thought that terminating the Apollo series at 17 was probably a wise idea, because it was a very chancy operation flying to the moon, landing and coming back. Sooner or later they would have lost one.

I was just referring to the Shuttle, the launch sequence. Now you're talking about out at the moon, and I didn't have any fear, and I don't think John did either. It was a chancy deal, but we trusted our gear, and we felt like we were trained well enough to overcome any problem except a major catastrophe, which we just basically said, well, that can't happen. But the moon was chancy, yeah. I was surprised they let us land on Apollo 16 actually, with the problems that we had in our command module.

Let's talk about that flight. First of all, it must have been quite an experience making the trip with John Young. Besides being a great pilot, one of the things that strikes you about him is his wry sense of humor. He has a great way of turning a phrase.

If you listen to our voice tapes and watch the video that we sent back, we were chuckling throughout, and laughing at one another. John was, to me, a Will Rogers. He has a dry sense of humor, and his little one-liners just always cracked me up. I remember while we were going around the moon waiting for mission control to decide whether we were going to land or not; we were up there in the LM and we'd been complaining about the orange juice that they'd given us. The potassium they put in it gave us a lot of gas. And John starts talking about 'Man, I got 'em again.' He was having gas and real bad cramps or something. And he started off, and he was just hilarious. We thought we were talking to ourselves, but it turned out his mike button was stuck open, and we were transmitting to mission control. By that time, they listened a little bit, heard all of those four letter words. Six or seven seconds had passed. You can say a lot in six seconds. It was just hilarious.

It had to be reassuring, too, having somebody with his experience on that flight, especially with the problems that you had.

Oh, yeah. John is a real steady guy. I call him "Cool Stone." We worked really well together. Our training in the lunar module, it was just sort of like we were twins joined together. We worked out a scheme and a system, and just really were strengthened by one another. I had a great sense of peace that I was up there with a real competent guy.

The moon presented a lot of different faces to the astronauts who there. It looks different from orbit than it does when you're actually on the surface. Can you give us some idea of the differences that you observed?

Well, from orbit it's rougher. You're looking out on a macrocosm and it's extremely rough looking and foreboding. Especially

Charlie Duke

the back-side. There are craters and mountains and rilles just every-where. And contrasting colors, some just jetblack, and mostly grays, and very bright white areas. It's got this eerie feeling, especially when you're in a low sun angle, and the shadows are real long. You just have this impression that you can never land. The front side is probably a little bit less than that, but even so, it still looks rough from orbit, very inhospitable. Yet, when you get down below a mile where you could see the moon for the first time on descent, we recognized our landing spot and there was no question we had it made, that we were gonna land, and it was gonna be fairly easy to navigate. In fact I looked up right at pitch-over and I saw Lone Star and Gator crater for the first time. I looked up to the North, to a place called North Ray crater, because we had been concerned about the boulder field up there, whether we would be able to navigate through it with the rover, and it was apparent that we were gonna make it. In fact, I commented to John, 'Not too many blocks up there. We've got a free-ride when we get there.' So the closer you get, the more hospitable it becomes, and the more the eerieness and that evil looking terrain disappears, and it becomes a lot more benign.

Speaking of the Rover, Charlie, John Young's always claimed that he set the land speed record on the moon with the Rover.
Year, that's true. We were coming off the side of North Ray crater, and I remember the speedometer went off-scale high, which was about 17 kilometers per hour. We were flying. We hit a bump, on the way down, and it just really felt like were gonna get air-borne. That was plenty fast, I didn't want to go any faster.

Did he ever give you a chance to drive the Rover yourself?
No. I could drive it, I'd practiced a little bit, but we had trained that he would drive and I was the navigator, travel guide, and picture taker, so I had the camera on and the maps in my hands. I'd say think like 'O.K. turn left here,' or 'what's that over there?' You know, stuff like that. And I was talking to mission control. That had worked good in training so that's what we continued.

Did the astronauts have any hand in designing the Rover themselves?
We were supposed to be the first crew to fly the Rover. It turned out they they shifted it up one flight. The J missions, as we called them, originally were gonna start with 16 and go 16, 17, 18. But when they dropped off the last flights they shifted everything up one. And, so John and I, in the early days were responsible for

overseeing the Rover from a crew standpoint, and we did have inputs into the seat operation, switch operations positions, seat belt design, mounting brackets, things that you had to work with and interface with. The crew were primarily involved with how does the thing work from an operational standpoint and can we interface with the systems correctly. For instance, the T-handle, the main control stick, was too small the first time we tried it with our suit gloves on, and we had to go back and make it bigger, things like that. We were close on the development, and on the deployment, too. The thing folded up and was bolted to the outside of the lunar module, and how do you get it off when you get there? So we were involved with a lot of that early testing and kibitzing in the design of the Rover.

You had three working sessions out on the surface. Was that about the limit of a man's endurance under those conditions?

No. Well, that was the limit of the lunar module. I think the crew could go a couple weeks with the proper sleep and rest if you had enough consumables on board. I'm not sure a suit would have lasted that long. Out suits were getting pretty grungy, and we were passing the leak-checks, but you could tell they were getting a little bit looser. But as far as our physical endurance, I was excited and, in fact, we didn't want to come back in each time. We said, 'Aw, come on, give us a few more minutes,' and we'd plead with them. But finally the consumables drove us back in. You were tired when you got back in, but once you got rested up, had a meal, took your suit off and went to sleep, you slept like a baby. And the next day we got up refreshed and ready to go again.

Speaking of sleeping. Did you ever dream when you were on the moon?

I never did.

When the public tuned in the T.V., they saw you and John, kind of bouncing around up there. Can you tell us what was easy, and what was hard about working and exploring on the lunar surface?

The easy part was getting from one spot to another in 1/6 gravity. The hard part was putting the experiments out, especially the ALSEP, the special scientific package we brought. Those were very delicate experiments and required good manual dexterity and balance to set up properly. It was hard work. Working in the suit to collect rocks was hard. The suit was very stiff and very rigid, and it didn't bend too well. So you had to learn how to make it move right. It was a problem working against that suit.

What was the visibility like?
Unlimited. There's no atmosphere up there so you could see forever, without any haze or anything. Everything seemed very sharp and very distinct.

Did your protective visors make it harder to see at all?
No. Sometimes you'd get into the dark shadow and you'd have to pull up your sun visor because you couldn't see very well. It's like having your sunglasses on at night. The lunar visor had these sort of blinders on the side that you could pull down to keep the reflections out and down. I used those a lot. It would destroy some of your peripheral vision, but it was worth it because then it didn't glare inside the helmet.

Was it just too bright to look out through a clear visor?
I thought so. I rarely had just a clear visor, because in the sun it was just brilliant, and you just had to really squint. I just didn't like it. It was hurting my eyes.

A lot of the Apollo astronauts love the 1/6th G environment. They even said it was preferable to both weightlessness and Earth gravity. Did you find that, too?
Yeah, that's true. It was a lot of fun, and easy to work in. Down here you couldn't even pick up your back-pack, but up there you could pick it up with two fingers. You could even pick up the rover—it was only eighty pounds on the moon. So it felt like the things that were difficult or impossible tasks down here were easy to do up on the moon. And you could bounce around and run around, and just have a wonderful time.

Our last question concerns your trip home from the moon. You had to open the hatch so Mattingly could go out and retrieve a piece of equipment from the side of the spacecraft. You commented on the blackness of space, and you later said you had this feeling of insignificance, of one person being in the middle of the universe. Could you elaborate on that a bit?
Well, when you float outside of the spacecraft, you just seem to be surrounded by this blackness, and it was so real and had such a vividness about it that you felt like you could reach out a touch it. Off to the right was the Earth, just a little new moon shape, and over my left shoulder was the moon which was *enormous* in size.

All of a sudden I felt like I wasn't a participant, not a player on the stage, but as if I was in the audience, if you will. It was a panorama I was looking at. Earth to the right, moon back over the left, Ken Mattingly off at the end of his tether, and I didn't have much to do except just float there and enjoy this beautiful sight. It was more like I had paid admission, was just a spectator. And I was just really enjoying that.

Was it a frightening situation?

No, not at all. I felt detached, but it wasn't eerie and it wasn't frightening at all. It was a very pleasant feeling and a very exciting experience to see that panorama unrestricted, outside the spacecraft.

Chapter 11

EUGENE CERNAN
Commander, Apollo 17

Planting the Seeds

G ung Ho! There really is no other way to describe Eugene
Cernan. When you meet him, you are immediately assaulted
and impressed by an energy level that has fueled an extraordinary
career. Gene Cernan's energy level leaves no doubt in your mind
that this man would have risen to the top in any profession he
chose.

His energy level is paradoxically fed and nurtured as he ex-
pends it talking up one of his pet subjects. Usually, it's the space
program, the future of the United States, or any of the many projects
with which he is involved. After you sit and talk with the man,
it becomes quite clear why ABC News picked him as an on-air
consultant. Whatever deficiencies he might have, a lack of confidence, or coolness under pressure are not among them. The man
is sincere. A little background:

Captain Eugene A. Cernan is Chairman of the Board and President of The Cernan Group, Inc., and The Cernan Corporation,
space-related technology and marketing firms. Since its founding
in 1981, The Cernan Group has been involved with the consumer
applications of current technology. Captain Cernan has recently
joined Digital Equipment Corporation as Director, Marketing Development—Government/Aerospace. Additionally, Captain Cernan
acts as a Technical Consultant with the ABC Television network in
support of ABC News and Special Events programming. He appears

with regularity as a news commentator and covers space and related documentary activities.

From 1976 to 1981, Captain Cernan served as the Executive Vice President of International Coral Petroleum, Inc. He was charged with the corporate development of a worldwide supply and marketing strategy. During this period, Captain Cernan continued his education at the Wharton School of Finance and Northwestern University.

After serving twenty years as a Naval Aviator, Captain Cernan retired from the United States Navy in 1976. Thirteen of these years were dedicated to direct involvement with the National Aeronautics and Space Administration (NASA) United States Space Program as an Astronaut. During his years with NASA, Captain Cernan carried out three separate space flights.

Captain Cernan was one of fourteen astronauts selected by NASA in October, 1963. He occupied the pilot seat alongside of command pilot Tom Stafford on the Gemini 9 mission. During this three-day flight which began on June 3, 1966, the spacecraft achieved a circular orbit of 161 statute miles; the crew used three different techniques to effect rendezvous with the previously launched Augmented Target Docking Adaptor; and Cernan, the second American to walk in space, logged two hours and ten minutes outside the spacecraft in extravehicular activities. The flight ended after seventy-two hours and twenty minutes with a perfect re-entry and recovery as Gemini 9 landed within 1-1/2 miles of the prime recovery ship USS WASP and 3/8 of a mile from the predetermined target.

Cernan subsequently served as backup pilot for Gemini 12 and as backup lunar modular pilot for Apollo 7.

On his second space flight, he was lunar module pilot of Apollo 10, May 18–26, 1969, the first comprehensive lunar-orbital qualification and verification flight test of an Apollo lunar module. He was accompanied on the 248,000 nautical sojourn to the moon by Thomas P. Stafford (spacecraft commander) and John W. Young (command module pilot). In accomplishing all of the assigned objectives of this mission, Apollo 10 confirmed that operations performance, stability, and reliability of the command service module and lunar module configuration during trans-lunar coast, lunar orbit insertion, and lunar module separation and descent to within eight nautical miles of the lunar surface. The latter maneuver involved employing all but the final minutes of the technique prescribed for use in an actual lunar landing, and allowed critical evaluations of the lunar module propulsions systems and rendezvous and landing radar devices in subsequent rendezvous and redocking maneuvers. In addition to demonstrating that man could navigate safely and accurately in the moon's gravitational fields, Apollo 10 photographed and mapped tentative landing sites for future missions.

Cernan's next assignment was backup spacecraft commander for Apollo 14.

He made this third space flight as spacecraft commander of Apollo 17—the last scheduled manned mission to the moon for the United States—which commenced at 11:33 PM (CST), December 6, 1972, with the first manned nighttime launch, and concluded on December 19, 1972. With him on the voyage of the command module "America" and the lunar module "Challenger" were Ronald Evans (command module pilot) and Harrison H. (Jack) Schmitt (lunar module pilot). In maneuvering "Challenger" to a landing at Taurus-Littrow, located on the southeast edge of Mare Serenitatis, Cernan and Schmitt activated a base of operation from which they completed three highly successful excursions to the nearby craters and the Taurus mountains, making the moon their home for over three days. This last mission to the moon established several new records for manned space flight that include: longest manned lunar landing flight (301 hours 51 minutes); longest lunar surface extravehicular activities (22 hours 6 minutes); largest lunar sample returned (an estimated 115 kg (249 lbs)); and longest time in lunar orbit (147 hours 48 minutes). While Cernan and Schmitt conducted activities on the lunar surface, Evans remained in lunar orbit aboard the "America," completing assigned work tasks requiring geological observations, handheld photography of specific targets, and the control of cameras and other highly sophisticated scientific equipment carried in the command module SIM-bay. Evans also completed a 1-hour, 6-minute extravehicular activity on the transEarth coast phase of the return flight, successfully retrieving three camera cassettes and completing a personal inspection of the equipment bay area. Apollo 17 ended with a splashdown in the Pacific Ocean approximately 0.4 miles from the target point and 4.3 miles from the prime recovery ship USS Ticonderoga.

Captain Cernan has logged 566 hours and 15 minutes in space—of which more than 73 hours were spent on the surface of the moon and was the last man of Apollo to leave his footprints on the surface of the moon.

In September, 1973, Cernan assumed additional duties as Special Assistant to the Program Manager of the Apollo Spacecraft Program at the Johnson Space Center. In this capacity, he assisted in the planning, development, and evaluation of the joint United States/Soviet Union Apollo-Soyuz mission, and he acted for the program manager as the senior United States negotiator in direct discussions with the USSR on the Apollo-Soyuz Test Project.

Captain Cernan received a Bachelor of Science degree in Electrical Engineering from Purdue University in Lafayette, Indiana, in 1956. He was awarded a Master of Science degree in Aeronautical Engineering in 1963 from the United States Naval Post Graduate School in Monterey, California. Captain Cernan was also awarded Honorary Doctorates of Engineering from Purdue, Drexel, and Gonzaga Universities, and an Honorary Doctorate degree from Western Universities, and an Honorary Doctorate degree from Western State College of Law. His honors include the Navy Distinguished Flying Cross, the Distinguished Service Medal with Star, the NASA Distinguished Service Medal, the FAI International Gold Medal for Space, and the VFW Gold Space Award.

Captain Cernan is an active member of several professional societies. Representative among them are the Society of Experimental Test Pilots, Association of Naval Aviators, Tail Hook Association, American Space Institute, American Institute of Aeronautics and Astronautics, and the American Astronautical Society and Explorers Club. He is a corporate board member of First Interstate Band—Memorial (Houston), Investors Trust, Asamera, Inc., and Up With People, an international educational foundation for young men and women. In addition, he is a Trustee of the Naval Aviation Museum Foundation, Inc., and serves on the President's Committee of Purdue University.

Cernan is married and lives in Houston. He has a daughter from a previous marriage.

Gene, you had a significant part in what is now coming to be known as the "Golden Age" of the American Space Program. When did you first realize that you, yourself, might have a chance to fly in space, even travel to the moon?

Oh, I guess when I was watching Shepard and Glenn and those guys make their attempts to get into space. I was a young Naval Aviator out in California having fun flying airplanes off aircraft carriers. I thought I was too young and too inexperienced and not qualified yet because I did not have enough flight time to get involved in the Space Program. Then, out of the blue, came a telephone call from the Navy that says 'We've been screening people for about six months, and you're one of them that we want to recommend and ask for further evaluation—do you volunteer?' So I said, 'Hell yes!' There was no guarantee that I'd ever fly. Six months later, after an awful lot of interviews and a lot of testing, they knocked down from about four or five hundred people, including civilians, to fourteen of us. It was a very competitive involvement.

Your name was submitted without your knowledge?
I don't think it was submitted at all. I think the Navy just went through the system and pulled people out. I don't know what triggered my name, I have no idea.

What would you say influenced you most in pursuing your career as an aviator and, subsequently, as an astronaut?
I don't know. I was always interested in airplanes. I didn't have one of those storybook childhoods, I never washed planes when I was sixteen to get my pilot's license, or anything like that. The closest I got to that was building model airplanes. I never really flew until I was in college, and then only once or twice. I really didn't start flying until I got my commission and went into flight training. But I always wanted to fly airplanes off aircraft carriers, period. That's what I wanted to do. Aviation was just a challenge to me. I never dreamed of being an astronaut; you have short-range goals, four to five years out there, and you take advantage of the opportunities that come along.

What was so alluring about aircraft carriers?
It's just the greatest, most competitive flying in the world. There isn't anything that compares to it. I still love to fly, and I'll fly anything, whether it's got two turning engines or it's a jet, whatever it is. But, at that time, there was only one thing I wanted to fly, and that was jet airplanes off aircraft carriers because, competitively, there is no better flying or greater challenge to an aviator in the world. I don't care what kind of airplane you're flying, if you've got to come back from a mission and land on a carrier deck somewhere in the middle of the ocean, it makes life a lot more interesting than coming back and coasting to a stop on a ten thousand foot runway. And when you turn the lights out and do it at night, on that pitching deck in the middle of the Pacific Ocean, well . . .

How does it compare to taking a lunar module in for a landing on the moon?
Landing on the moon, compared to landing on a carrier at night, was a piece of cake.

Seriously?

You betcha. You betcha.

Tell us about the landing of Challenger in the Taurus-Littrow Valley on Apollo 17. Was it an emotional experience for you?

Oh, yeah! You're flying in on your back, then you pitch down. All of a sudden you're surrounded by *mountains*. You're at seven thousand feet, already *in* the valley, surrounded by mountains that are higher than the Grand Canyon is deep! I mean, you're *in* there. You planned on it, studied that scene, and you've done it in the simulator a million times. But, all of a sudden you realize, hey we're *really* here! And in our case, we were landing to the west, and the Earth was in the southwestern sky, so it wasn't above us; we could land and see *Earth* at the same time. It's almost like "I don't believe I'm here!". Of course there's also a lot you're doing to make sure you land right. Plus, you want to do it better than it's ever been done before. That's the sort of competitiveness of being a pilot. There's something you've got to prove to yourself, or maybe to other people. It's your ego that drives you on; not *egotism,* but a will that drives you on to go ahead and do something, even if you're scared to death. It's *that* kind of competitive feeling that drives you on. I wanted to land closer than the last guy landed to his prescribed landing site just to prove I could do it.

You were Lunar Module Pilot on Apollo 10, the "dress rehearsal" mission before the first landing was attempted. You actually flew down to 47,000 feet before turning back and climbing up to orbit again. Were the NASA people worried that you and Tom Stafford might decide at that point, well, we're this close, why not bring it all the way down?

We kidded around. But that decision was made six to eight weeks before that, so the descent stage didn't carry a full load of fuel, we didn't have enough fuel to land. Not to keep us from doing it, but it allowed us to do some other things that we needed to do. So we had already bitten the bullet about not going down that last 47,000 feet. But at one time Apollo 10 was going to be the first landing. There was a discussion about whether we should wait until we had the follow-on, lighter LM with more capabilities, or just go ahead and land during Apollo 10. That would have been a great opportunity. But going and not landing, certainly was not disappointing. When I came back, that's when I wanted to go back. I wanted to cover that last 50,000 feet, and I also wanted to command my own crew; that was important to me.

In 1987, on the fifteenth anniversary of your moon landing,
you made the comment that you could describe your voyage as
a religious experience. What did you mean?

No, not a religious experience. I'll leave that to Jim Irwin.
It was spiritual, philosophical—there's a difference. It wasn't the
experience of landing on the moon. It was the experience of
looking back home because, when you look back at the beauty of
our planet, it's overpowering. It has so much purpose. You can
look from pole to pole and across oceans and continents. There
are no strings holding it up. There are no rails that come sliding
through the blackness that surrounds us. It's just too beautiful to
have happened by accident. There has to be some creator of the
small part of the universe that I was privileged to see. It doesn't
make any difference what your religion is, how you address him,
what name you call Him. That's not a religious statement, it's a
spiritual statement. There is a God, a supreme being, that created
this universe because I've seen proof of it, and I can in no other
way comprehend that we came together as we are, and that I
witnessed the beauty and the logic and the purposefulness that I
witnessed without that being the case.

Did you think much about that before the flight?

I got smacked with it during Apollo 10. And going back, on
Apollo 17, I challenged my own feelings. I was one of the few guys
that had to go back there twice to be able to think again about
what I saw the first time. And it just reinforced what I had brought
back with me from Apollo 10.

Out there so far away from home did you have any feelings
or anxieties about being separated from the Earth?

A feeling, yes, but not a detrimental one. Philosophically, there
are two different space programs. One is in Earth orbit. You can
define that from zero to 1,000 or 2,000 or 10,000 miles if you want.
Certainly, zero to 250 miles. You're still going around your own
planet, you are still in your own environment. You are in no way
detached from the gravitational pull of this Earth. You fly, you go
around, you cross coastlines and rivers and cities. You fly through
a sunrise and a sunset every hour and a half.

To go one step further, to the moon for example, you have to
accelerate and you really depart your planet. You leave your planet
and become part of another planet. You are no longer retained by
the gravitational pull of your own planet, but held within the
confines or environment of another. You no longer fly across continents and coastlines and rivers and cities, but you look *back* across

oceans and continents. You can look from the azure blues of the Atlantic across all of North and South America to the deep, dark blues of the Pacific without even turning your head. You don't fly through sunrises and sunsets anymore. You watch them happen in front of your eyes. *That's* being detached. You get the perspective of *really* seeing your planet. In Earth orbit you're traveling a couple of hundred miles above the mountains but you really don't see the Earth as a planet, you never see it all at once. From the moon, you're standing back a quarter million miles and you can watch the world turn on an axis you can't see. There's life going on in front of your very eyes, 250,000 miles away, of which you no longer seem to be a part. That's a different space program entirely. You realize you are detached and have to take steps to free yourself from the attachment of this other world in order to get back home. And there's the chance you'll *never* get back. Do you feel lonely? Does it bother you? No. It's just something you have to think about. And the chances are you don't fully comprehend it all.

Does it change the fundamental way you look at the world, your reactions to the world?

Oh yeah, it must. But you don't come back some kind of "Whoppie!" purist. You come home and still have to face the realities of life—you've got to pay your light bill, your kids skin their knees, there's fighting in the Mideast, and what have you.

Is there an associated sense of self satisfaction, a more peaceful feeling?

It's a more worldly, maybe in a way, a selfish feeling, because you'd like to take everybody in the world up there to look at the Earth the way you saw it. It's not a superior feeling and it's not a feeling that you have all the answers. It's a feeling that we are unique, that mankind is unique, that we do live on a very unique place in this universe. And it also makes you feel and realize how little you understand about existence. About *our* existence. You know, sitting here right now talking about it, going to the moon is a hell of a big deal. But compared to the rest of the universe it's nothing.

Did you return more optimistic, perhaps?

Sure. We're stepping out of the cradle. We're learning something about our past as well as our future. When you get out there and you look at the infinity of space and look at how small our Earth is, there *have* to be other Earths, other civilizations. You look at it theologically and you ask yourself why should you be so egotistic to believe, if you really have a faith in some supreme being who governs the universe, that he should have created only us. It's a very exciting thought. I think it's exciting scientifically, philosophically, and any other way for people young and old to think 'Gee, in the future we may be able to go out and there may be other civilizations we can come in contact with.

You were the last man to step off the lunar surface, and that was sixteen years ago. Are you wistful at all, when you look at the moon now, that we haven't gone back yet, that we might not go back for quite a while?

Not really. Because 100, 200, 300 years from now if you look back at the time it takes between when we first went and when we go back to the moon, even if it's fifty years, it's going to be just a blip in history. So, I'm not bitter because I know it's going to happen. Going back to the moon is not a big deal unless there is a reason to do it. When there's a purpose, maybe for economic reasons, or commercial reasons—which people are looking very closely at right now—we'll go back to the moon.

We're almost at the end of this century; how far out do you think men will have gone by the end of the 21st century?

Oh, we'll be on Mars. Mars is going to be a sister planet. Someday it's going to be like the North American continent was to Europe. People will travel to Mars the way they came to the "New World" from Europe. We will have established ourselves on Mars and might very well go further out into the universe where some of our unmanned probes have been going. We will have an infrastructure in near-space that will be both scientific and commercial. The concept of true space enterprise will have become a reality. And our life here on Earth is going to be drastically influenced by what we are doing in space.

You characterized your mission on Apollo 17 as "The beginning, not the end." Are you satisfied with the way the American space program has progressed since you left the moon?

Let me begin by saying I didn't mean to be prophetic when I said that. I was just getting tired at that point of the press saying, 'How does it feel to be the last? How does it feel now that this is the end?' And I kept saying it isn't the *end.* It's the end of a program, it's the end of an era. But it's really just the beginning—you know, we've done what you've just seen and now we are ready to press on. So, I didn't mean to be prophetic, and indeed I wasn't. Because very little has really happened. I don't think the beginning which

I foresaw has really come about. We had three Skylab missions and Apollo-Soyuz, and then a five or six year hiatus before the Shuttle started flying. And the Shuttle started flying, essentially, as a program of its own; it was a space transportation system with nowhere to go. The real plan should have been to reach out and look on into the future fifteen or twenty years and develop a national goal for this country of which the Shuttle would be just a component. But that never really happened. And here we are today in 1989, with politicians and people who are supposed to know, and the leaders of this country still trying to make a choice of whether we want to stay a world leader in technology. So, yeah, I'm disappointed.

Do you think NASA dropped the ball by not continuing and expanding the moon program, upgrading and developing the Apollo technology further, and so forth?

I think it was a case of economics at that point in time. It was a case of 'How much can we learn before we know enough?' Would one or two more lunar missions be enough, or would thirty or forty more? They thought 'Well, now that we're smarter it may be better not to fly Apollos 18 and 19, and regroup and go back to the moon in the upcoming decade or at the turn of the century.' I think that was a fairly reasonable decision to make at that time.

Are you encouraged by the resumption of the Shuttle flights since the Challenger accident? Are we back on track now?

I'm encouraged because a lot of people worked awfully hard. You know, we're a reactive society, we react to crises. It took a little longer to react to this one than I wanted to. Nonetheless, that period of time will just be blip in history. But we're still a long way from a far-reaching national commitment in terms of a space program. The flight of Discovery was a singular flight. The next few flights were singular flights. We'll add on to the experience and the confidence again in the Shuttle but, you could take the next five, six, seven flights, whatever their missions, and interchange them and it wouldn't affect the series. What I'm saying is they don't really lead to anyplace yet.

If you could become czar of the Space Program, what would you do to get it moving in the right direction?

First off, there are two things I'd do; number one, there's a tremendous amount of support among the American public for space, because they think it's a good thing to do and they know a little about it. What we've go to do is truly inform the American people about the significance of the technological base in this country, and what it's meant to our nation for the last hundred years. It's been a foundation upon which we have developed political leadership in the world. That is eroding now. It's been challenged, and I think we need a national spokesman who people believe to explain to them why the Space Program is important. And not just to get more astronauts in space to take pictures from Earth orbit; it's got a far more basic, fundamental significance than that. The second thing that should be done is that NASA ought to be brought up to a level within government where it can be recognized as a national space council, like we have the National Security Council. At that level they would have direct contact with the President. We need that kind of recognition within our own country.

Let's say all that gets done. Wouldn't a big obstacle still be in the way—money?

You know, we got caught up in the business of cost, and everyone talks about money, but no one really understands what a million dollars is, what a billion dollars is. The cost of space is ridiculously low, and the return on the investment the public makes in space, in terms of the technological foundation it builds for this country, is so great, why, if it were presented to them right, they wouldn't believe it! Less than one penny of every tax dollar you and I contribute goes into the space program. And that's shuttles, the space station, communications satellites, weather satellites, planetary probes—the whole thing. It is relatively insignificant compared to how we're spending a lot of our other money. We can talk about millions, billions of dollars and it sounds very expensive. But it's only one penny out of every tax dollar. What's NASA's budget—eleven, maybe twelve billion dollars? Let's put that in perspective. We spend close to 25 billion dollars not to grow food in this country. So, when someone says to me that we can take the money away from NASA that they're using to put Discovery or put Atlantis in orbit, build a space station, and so on, and spend it instead to build low-cost housing and grow food for the people who are starving to death, it's an anomaly, it's a dichotomy. It's a paradox, because we're turning right around and spending 25 billion dollars *not* to grow food in this country. So how can someone give me the argument that we can use the money spent on space in a better way?

The science writer Ben Bova once said that the American space program was the greatest single investment the United States has made since the Louisiana Purchase.

Absolutely! If you take that one penny of every tax dollar and trace the return on that investment—the return on jobs, on technology, on prestige—I'll tell you, if I owned stock in the Space Program in 1959, investing at the rate of one penny of every dollar I had, I would have made a hell of a deal. Just look at the returns that have come from space: technology that's now in our kitchens, our houses, our automobiles, our hospitals—our whole life across the board. Look at computer technology. How do you think we got into the computer environment that we are today? It's because we decided to go to the moon; the technology didn't exist, so we had to create it. We have to recognize it as an investment in the future of this country. Space is not a luxury. Space is a *necessity*. It's a necessity not only for the technological foundation of this country, it's a necessity for the economic, political, and social well-being of every individual.

You talked about the tremendous amount of support out there among the American people. Just how ambitious an effort will meet with their approval?

A number of surveys have been done and the results show 75 to 80 percent of the people say they strongly support the program. Now, there're a lot of "buts" in that 80 percent; nonetheless they support it and they say let's get on with it. But get on with what? We're talking about a program that looks a generation into the future, that transcends political partisanship and administrations, with a national goal, something that kids in the third and fourth grade can begin to look forward to, and that is reasonably within reach. Let's decide where we're headed and then work on what it's going to take to get there. Maybe it's Mars. If that's the case, we have to start planning and developing now; you don't just immediately build something and go for Mars.

What are the logical steps? You have to work your way backwards. Obviously it's going to take a space transportation system, both manned and unmanned. We're working on that right now. Is it going to take a space station? A lunar base? I don't know at this time, but it's from that kind of preliminary work that you make progress. Look at Mercury, Gemini, and Apollo—three separate entities, but they were really the same space program. They were all leading towards landing a man on the moon. We would not have been able to move into Apollo without the sequence of things that happened in Gemini: we learned to walk in space. Part of that was developing a space suit. We had to learn to spend fourteen days in orbit; we learned how to do that. We had to learn to rendezvous; we learned how to do that. So, we went into Apollo with new

Eugene Cernan

hardware, but with the experience and knowledge that was necessary to proceed with that program. Today, we launch a couple of shuttles and we're right back into the space transportation business—to go where? To do what? We don't have a space station yet. We talk about it but, it's been underfunded, abused and misused.

Congress controls the purse strings, they appropriate the money and can influence policy that way. Are you fearful that projects like the space station will be used as political footballs?

We've got to get some strong leadership in Congress, leadership that recognizes the importance of technology to this country. It's hard for me to understand why there are so many people that, in my estimation, are so naive and who put their own self-interest, in terms of getting reelected, ahead of the interests of the country. That may be a blunt accusation but, in general, I happen to believe it; there are exceptions but, I really believe it's true. We can say we've got a major budget problem, and that's true. We'll continue to have it. But that one penny out of the tax dollar is not going to solve the budget problem. In fact, there are going to be a lot more problems if we don't use more of that tax dollar in the program than is being used now. You know, you can eat your seed corn, but what do you do next year? We're planting the seeds for the future with the Space Program, the seeds of technology.

We pursued a strong space effort in the past in large part because we concerned about losing our edge, particularly with respect to the Soviet Union. But times seem to be changing. Do you believe that America should be the absolute leader in space? And how far do you think we should go in cooperating with the Soviets?

I think cooperation is important, it's significant. People have to bring their resources together; we're a common kind of this Earth. But, I also don't want to abrogate our leadership because, parochially and nationalistically, that leadership means something significant to us, to our way of life, to our well-being. I don't want to have to *ask* someone else for access to space. And I don't want to have to ask someone if we can put a satellite on *their* rocket.

Are you saying we can't, or shouldn't trust the Russians?

It's not a case of trust. I've worked with them very closely. I've learned to trust and distrust them. I have nothing against working with the Soviets; the point I'm making is we won't have to worry about working with the Soviets unless we get on with it because we're only going to be a ten per cent partner because we won't have anything to contribute.

Are we in danger of falling behind the Soviets in space technology?

Let's define technology: is technology sophisticated laboratory capabilities for doing things? We have that, but let's get pragmatic. What good is technology if it's locked inside a building and you don't use it. Absolutely, we're in danger!

Someone once described technology as the ability to get the job done.

What about adding to that the *willingness* to get the job done. The Soviets started with Sputnik; they've expanded and built upon that using some of the same levels of that technology. And they're up in space! They've got a space station, they've got a couple of them. They can go up there unmanned and dock and supply. They've got rescue ships up there and they can live up there for years at a time. They can do things. Not as sophisticated, not as highly specialized as we might do them, but they are and it's working, they are getting their job done. We're *not* there.

Will it eventually take a declaration of the sort President Kennedy made back in 1961 to get us back "there" again?

It's *going* to take some presidential leadership to establish some major goals for this country. And not just political goals. John Kennedy made a strong commitment almost thirty years ago when he said we were going to go to the moon and do the other things, because they were hard, not because they were easy. It was a commitment to the future of this country and the country got behind that commitment and nobody can argue with the results. And it wasn't just bringing some rocks back from the moon; that was a very, very small part of it. You know, Kennedy also said, at the closing of that speech—which is not remembered very much— that we were never going to allow ourselves to flounder in space and not maintain international leadership there. Well, unfortunately, he was wrong because we *are* floundering in space and we are not maintaining international leadership.

What do you say to members of Congress, or those in the private sector who assert that the only way we're going to get to Mars with a manned mission is if we do it with the Soviets on a 50/50 basis?

Well, I don't know that that's the only way, but never say never. It seems to be a reasonably practical way but the Soviets have not necessarily made an offer. They've come and suggested that to us and I don't know that we even responded to them. Maybe that's a good thing to look into because we're not, apparently, willing to commit to anything at this point in time. That's pretty disconcerting.

Do we have anything to fear from the Soviets in space from a military point of view?

We ought to be concerned. They're in space almost on a continuous basis. They're flying over this country over and over and over again in that space station Mir. Yes, they're doing scientific missions, but they don't have two programs. They have *a* program that is basically run by the state and by the military. There are military applications and uses of the Mir, and, by golly, they're making use of it. It's a fact of life. What kind of information and data they are gathering from a military point of view, I don't know. But, certainly, the capability they're building on the ground to get into space cannot be overlooked.

Gene, why did you decide to leave the space program? After your return on Apollo 17 you indicated you would continue on with the shuttle program.

I guess I got dramatic. I thought about going back into the Navy and staying involved that way. I looked at when I'd have the chance to fly again and the Shuttle was obviously going to be four or five years down the line. If I had stayed around I certainly feel I would have flown one of the first couple of flights. But I'm not sure I wanted to go back into the dungeons and do all the engineering and all the things that had to be done for the next five years. I had thirteen years in the space program; I had flown three times, walked in space, went to the moon twice, lived on the moon. I wasn't sure what there was I wanted to do next. To go back into space and go round and round for a couple of days, after you've been to the moon I mean, you don't want to do that. That plus the financial opportunities outside of government service were interesting enough to ease me out.

You're obviously a passionate proponent of the program and bluntly critical of the ways it's being handled. Have you ever thought of entering politics?

That question is asked of me an awful lot and, sure, I've thought of it. But mostly because other people have suggested it. Have I considered it seriously? No. No.

Would you if the right opportunity came along?
Sure, I'd like the responsibility of government service, but I think I would rather work for someone like the President in a position of responsibility where I could get the job done. Going through the whole election process, as great as it is in a democracy, is very expensive. I don't have the kind of money it would take to get into a campaign. And it's gotten almost to be dehumanizing in what a politician goes through to serve his country. I'd rather accept a position of responsibility in someone's administration and do whatever I could through the pipeline. I like responsibility and I'd only want to do something I thought I knew something about and was capable of handling. What we need are people in positions of responsibility who are not overconfident, but confident enough that they can get the job done. You know, surround themselves with other people who fill up their weak points and then, when necessary, be willing to admit they're wrong. In other words, I'm waiting for someone, by God, to say 'Let me tell you, we have done everything possible, but you can never make anything risk free', then be willing to come up front to take the consequences if they're wrong, instead of passing the buck. Von Braun was sort of that way. We need that in the program. We need leadership.

Eugene Cernan

Armstrong

Chapter 12

NEIL ARMSTRONG
Commander, Apollo 11

The First

J acob Zint was an enthusiastic amateur astronomer who lived in the small northwestern Ohio town of Wapakoneta. He would sometimes invite the neighborhood kids into his backyard on a clear night to peek through his telescope for a closeup look at the moon, planets, and stars. One of the youngsters who would come by was a rather shy, studious boy whose curiosity about the sky and flight was as deep as the sky itself. His name was Neil Armstrong. While most of the children would peer into the eyepiece for a quick glimpse of the rings of Saturn or the craters of the moon then step away, young Armstrong would linger there gazing intently. "He would look and look and look," Jacob Zint recollected.

Neil Alden Armstrong was the first child in the family of Stephen and Viola Armstrong, and was born in the house on his grandparent's farm near Wapakoneta on August 5th, 1930. He has a sister named June and a brother named Dean. They were a close-knit family imbued with the respect for diligence and hard work, learning, and an optimism that is particularly characteristic of midwestern mores. Armstrong puts it this way: ". . . it was my observation that the people of that community felt it was important to do a useful job and do it well."

Armstrong's passion for flying seems to have been triggered when, at the age of two, his father brought him to the National Air Races being held in Cleveland. "I must have been a staunch aviation fan before I was even conscious of it," Armstrong concluded. He reports having a "frustrating" recurrent dream as a boy. "I could, by holding my breath, hover over the ground . . . I neither flew nor fell. I just hovered. There was never any end to the dream . . ."

The young Armstrong immersed himself in the lore and science of aeronautics. He obsessively built and flew countless model airplanes, experimenting with different designs and ideas. He even built a wind tunnel in his basement. At fifteen he began taking flying lessons, paying the $9.00 hourly fee with money he earned working at various jobs around town and at the airfield. By the time he was sixteen he had earned his student pilot's license. "He wanted to do something daring and different," a former teacher of Armstrong's noted. "He always had a goal to work on."

In 1947, Armstrong graduated from Blume High School in Wapakoneta where he had excelled in science and mathematics. That fall he entered Purdue University on a Navy ROTC scholarship to study aeronautical engineering. Two years later he was called up by the Navy for active duty and put into flight training at Pensacola, Florida. In 1950 he was ordered to Korea as a combat fighter pilot. He flew 78 missions in Navy Panther Jets from the aircraft carrier *Essex*, winning three air medals. "Apparently I caused a lot of damage to bridges and trains and things, but really, they handed out medals there like gold stars at Sunday School," Armstrong modestly remembers. After the war, Armstrong returned to Purdue to finish his studies, and received his degree in 1955.

Armstrong began his test pilot career as a civilian research pilot working for the National Advisory Committee for Aeronautics (NACA) later reorganized and renamed the National Aeronautics and Space Administration—NASA, first at the Lewis Flight Propulsion Laboratory in Cleveland, then relocating to Edwards Air Force Base in California when a position there opened up. At Edwards he participated in research flights of the X-1, the X-5, various military jets, and the hottest, most sophisticated rocket plane of them all, the X-15. Even before Edwards, Armstrong was sure spaceflight 'was going to become a reality,' he and the other rocket plane pilots and engineers at Edwards in the late '50s were not very impressed, though, with the space capsule concept of the fledgling Project Mercury. They derisively referred to it as "spam in a can"—there was no real "flying" involved as far as they were concerned. "Some of us felt a winged vehicle represented a better approach," Armstrong recalls. "Then, in February, 1962 John Glenn orbited the earth three times in a little less than five hours, and we began to look at things a bit differently." That same year, Armstrong became the first civilian pilot to enter the manned space program when he was selected as one of the nine new astronauts of the second group.

Armstrong made his first space flight on March 16, 1966. Commanding the Gemini 8 mission, he and copilot David Scott were launched into orbit atop a two-stage Titan rocket. They rendezvoused with an Agena target vehicle, and shortly afterward, Armstrong performed the first successful docking, or coupling, of two orbiting spacecraft. Just a half an later, however, the two-joined craft started spinning out of control. Thinking it was a problem on the Agena, Armstrong pulled away but found the culprit was an errant thruster on his own vehicle. He regained control of the craft by using his reentry thruster system but, as a result, was forced to end the mission and come home.

In January of 1969 Armstrong was named Commander of the Apollo 11 mission, the first attempt at a manned landing on the moon. On July 16th, 1969 Armstrong, Buzz Aldrin, and Michael Collins roared into space under the power of a giant Saturn rocket and were put on a heading for the moon. Aboard the spacecraft, Armstrong revealed later, was a small section of the fabric wing material and a piece of propeller from the original Wright brothers airplane.

On Sunday, July 20th, as they circled above the moon, Armstrong and Aldrin entered the lunar module "Eagle", separated from the command module "Columbia" and started their historic descent to the Sea of Tranquility. Armstrong saw that the craft was on its way to a landing in a dangerous looking boulder field, so he kept it hovering until he could pick out a suitable landing spot downrange. The ground controllers were nervously watching the LM's fuel supply dwindle as Armstrong hunted for safety. Finally, at 4:17 pm he settled Eagle down on the surface and reported to mission control: "Houston, Tranquility Base here. The Eagle has landed." He made it with thirty seconds to spare.

A little less than seven hours later, the two astronauts opened the hatch and Armstrong slid out to the ladder. He carefully climbed down the nine steps and at 10:56 pm became the first human being to step onto the moon. "That's one small step for a man, one giant leap for mankind," he proclaimed. Aldrin joined him on the surface shortly after, and they spent the next two hours collecting samples of the rocks and soil around the LM, setting up scientific instruments, and planted the American flag. The following afternoon they fired back into lunar orbit to rendezvous with Michael Collins and start the voyage back to Earth. On July 24th, the three men splashed down in the Pacific Ocean completing the flight, and the goal President Kennedy had set just eight years before.

Armstrong's distinction as the first man to step on the moon brought him enormous, and obvious, fame. He is an intensely private man, though, and prefers a quiet life out of the public's curious and intrusive eye. One of his NASA colleagues points out that Armstrong wants no part of a Lindbergh-like fishbowl.

After Apollo 11 Armstrong was approached with an offer to become president of a major university, but turned it down, apparently concluding he didn't have the right experience for the position. He remained at NASA instead, accepting an appointment as Deputy Associate Administrator for Aeronautics. Then, in 1971, he ended his seventeen years service with the agency to become a professor of aerospace engineering at the University of Cincinnati. He left his university post in 1979 to enter private business as Chairman of CTA, Inc., a computer systems company.

In 1985-86 Armstrong served as a member of the National Commission on Space, and in 1986 was named Vice-Chairman of the Presidential Commission investigating the accident of the Space Shuttle Challenger

Neil Armstrong and his wife Jan live in Ohio. They have two sons.

NOTE: Neil Armstrong was not available for an interview for this book. What follows was compiled from statements he has made over the years which are a matter of public record.

Some people have criticized the Space Program as being a "misplaced item on a list of national priorites." How do you view space exploration as a relative priority compared with the present needs of domestic society and the world community?

Well, of course we all recognize that the world is continually faced with a large number of varying kinds of problems, and that it's our view that all those problems have to be phased simultaneously, it's not possible to neglect any of those areas, and we certainly don't feel that it's our place to neglect space exploration.

At any time during the landing did you think of aborting? Such as when you were getting the "program alarms" because of your overloaded computer system?

Well, I think in simulations we have a large number of failures and we are usually spring loaded to the abort position and this case in the real flight we are spring loaded to the land position. We were certainly going to continue with the descent as long as we could safely do so and as soon as program computer alarms manifest themselves, you realize that you have a possible abort situation to contend with, but our procedure throughout a preparation phase was to always try to keep going as long as we could, so that we could bypass these types of problems.

What was the cause of those "program alarms"?
I suppose we were carrying on a rapid fire conversation with the computer at the point, but we really have to give the credit to the control center in this case. They were the people who really came through and helped us and said continue. Which is what we wanted to hear.

During the last few minutes, before the landing when the "program alarms" were coming on, would you have gone ahead and landed had you not had ground support?
We would have continued the landing so long as the trajectory seemed safe. And a landing is possible under these conditions, although with considerably less confidence than you have when you have the information from the ground and the computer in its normal manner being available to you.

When you were landing "Eagle" on the surface, were you worried about your fuel supply?
Yes, we're concerned about running low on fuel on range extension we did to avoid the boulder field and craters. We used a significant percentage of our fuel margins and we were quite close to our legal limit.

What were your feelings when you realized that your computer controlled landing was taking you right into a boulder field?
Well, first say that I expected that we would probably have to make some local adjustments to find a suitable landing area. I thought it was highly unlikely that we would be so fortunate as to come down in a very smooth area, and we planned on doing that. As it turned out, of course, we did considerably more maneuvering close to the surface than we had planned to do. And the terminal phase was absolutely chopped full of my eyes looking out the window, and Buzz looking at the computer and information inside the cockpit and feeding that to me. That was a full-time job.

Had you planned to take over semi-manual control, or was it your descent toward the west crater that caused you to do that?

The series of control system configurations that were used during the terminal phase were in fact very close to what we would expect to use in the normal case, respective of the landing area that you found yourself in. However, we spent more time in the manual phase than we would have planned in order to find a suitable landing area.

When you finally landed, exactly how much fuel did you have left?

My own instruments would have indicated less than 30 seconds. Probably something like 15 or 20 seconds. I think the analysis made here on the ground indicated something more than that. Probably greater than 30 seconds; 40 or 45. That sounds like a short time, but it really is quite a lot.

When you first stepped on the surface of the moon, did it strike you as though you were stepping on earth, or that it really was another world?

It's a stark and strangely different place, but it looked friendly to me and it proved to be friendly.

Did you plan the words "That's one small step for a man, one giant leap for mankind" before you left the lunar module?

Yes, I did think about it. It was not extemporeous neither was it planned. It evolved during the conduct of the flight and I decided what the words would be while we were on the lunar surface just prior to leaving the LM.

Was the reality of walking on the moon easier than the simulations back on earth?

We had very little trouble. Much less trouble than expected on the surface. It was a pleasant operation. Temperatures weren't high. They were very comfortable. The little EMU, the combination of spacesuit, and back pack that provided or sustained our life on the surface, operated magnificently. We had no cause for concern at any time with the operation of that equipment. The primary difficulty we observed was that there was just far too little time to do the variety of things that we would have liked to have done.

When you finally got a chance to do some work on the surface, how difficult or easy did you find it?

A number of experts had, prior to the flight, predicted that a good bit of difficulty might be encountered by people attempting to work on the surface of the moon due to the variety of strange atmospheric and gravitational characteristics that would be encountered. This didn't prove to be the case and after landing we felt very comfortable in the lunar gravity. It was, in fact, in our view, preferable both to weightlessness and the earth gravity. We had very few problems to go ahead with the surface work immediately. We predicted that we might be ready to leave the LM by 8 o'clock, but those of you who followed on the ground recognize we missed our estimate a good deal. This was due to a number of factors, one we had housekeeping to perform and food packages, flight plans, all the items that we had used in the previous descent to be stowed out of the way prior to depressurizing the lunar module. It took longer to depressurize the lunar module than we had anticipated and it also took longer to get the cooling units in our backpacks operating than we had expected. In substance it took us approximately an hour longer to get ready than we had predicted. When we actually descended the ladder it was found to be very much like the lunar gravity simulations we had performed here on earth.

With the limited amount of time you had on the surface, it must have been extremely difficult for you and Buzz to decide what to investigate?
There were craters that differed widely, that would have been interesting to examine and photograph. We had the problem of the 5-year-old boy in a candy store. There are just too many interesting things to do.

Was there ever a moment on the moon where you were just a little bit spellbound by what was going on?
About 2 hours. (The length of time he spent on the surface.)

Was your schedule so overloaded for the eva that you and Buzz were unable to enjoy the experience?
We plead guilty to enjoying ourselves.

What kind of ride did the lunar module give you during lift-off from the moon?
The ascent was a great pleasure. It was very smooth. We were very pleased to have that engine light up. It gave us a excellent view of our our take off trajectory, and Tranquility Base as we left, and at all times through the ascent, we could pick up land marks that assured us that we were on the proper track. There were no difficulties with the ascent and we enjoyed the ride, more than we could say.

Film of the ascent shows some oscillation. Was it really as smooth as you would have hoped?

The vehicle, due to the changing in our gravity as fuel was used, does a good bit of five degree oscillation throughout the ascent.

Where did the weird sounds including the sirens and whistles come from during the transearth coast?

We were guilty again. We sent the whistle and bells with our little tape recorder which we used to record our comments during the flight in addition to playing music in the lonely hours. We thought we'd share that with the people in the Control Center.

How would you summarize the meaning of Apollo?

I just see it as beginning. Not just this flight, but in this program which has really been a very short piece of human history. An instant in history, the entire program. It a beginning of a new age.

A fitting close to this chapter and this book would be the remarks Neil Armstrong made to a joint session of Congress on Tuesday, September 16, 1969:

"We landed on the Sea of Tranquility, in the cool of the early lunar morning, when the long shadows would aid our perception.

"The sun was only 10° above the horizon. While the earth turned through nearly a full day during our stay, the sun at Tranquility Base rose barely 11°—a small fraction of the month-long lunar day. There was a peculiar sensation of the duality of time—the swift rush of events that characterizes all our lives—and the ponderous parade which marks the aging of the universe.

"Both kinds of time were evident—the first by the routine events of the flight, whose planning and execution were detailed to fractions of a second—the latter by rocks around us, unchanged throughout the history of man—whose 3-billion-year-old secrets made them the treasure we sought.

"The plaque on the Eagle which summarized our hopes bears this message:

"Here men from the planet earth first set foot upon the moon July 1969 A.D.

"We came in peace for all mankind. Those nineteen hundred and sixty-nine years had constituted the majority of the age of Pisces, a 12th of the great year. That is measured by the thousand generations the precession of the earth's axis requires to scribe a giant circle in the heavens.

"In the next 20 centuries, the age of Aquarius of the great year, the age for which our young people have such high hopes, humanity may begin to understand its most baffling mystery—where are we going?

"The earth is, in fact, traveling many thousands of miles per hour in the direction of the constellation Hercules—to some unknown destination in the cosmos. Man must understand his universe in order to understand his destiny.

"Mystery however is a very necessary ingredient in our lives. Mystery creates wonder and wonder is the basis for man's desire to understand. Who knows what mysteries will be solved in our lifetime, and what new riddles will become the challenge of the new generations?

"Science has not mastered prophesy. We predict too much for next year yet far too little for the next 10. Responding to challenge is one of democracy's great strengths. Our successes in space lead us to hope that this strength can be used in the next decade in the solution of many of our planet's problems. Several weeks ago I enjoyed the warmth of reflection on the true meanings of the spirit of Apollo.

"I stood in the highlands of this Nation, near the Continental Divide, introducing to my sons the wonders of nature, and pleasures of looking for deer and for elk.

"In their enthusiasm for the view they frequently stumbled on the rocky trails, but when they looked only to their footing, they did not see the elk. To those of you who have advocated looking high we owe our sincere gratitude, for you have granted us the opportunity to see some of the grandest views of the Creator.

"To those of you who have been our honest critics, we also thank, for you have reminded us that we dare not forget to watch the trail. We carried on Apollo 11 two flags of this Union that had flown over the Capitol, one over the House of Representatives, one over the Senate. It is our privilege to return them now in these Halls which exemplify man's highest purpose—to serve one's fellow man.

"We thank you, on behalf of all the men of Apollo, for giving us the privileges of joining you in serving—for all mankind."

Index